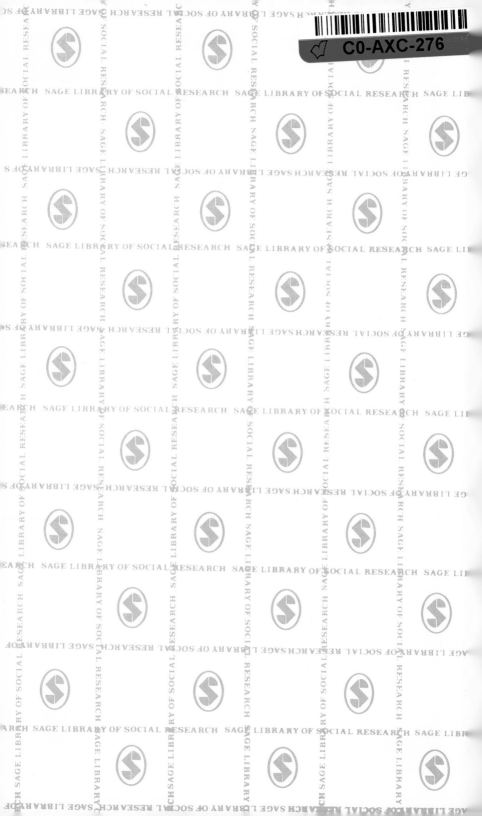

CRIMINAL LAWYERS

Volume 67, Sage Library of Social Research

Sage Library of Social Research

Criminal Lawyers

An Endangered Species

Paul B. Wice

Foreword by FRED COHEN

Volume 67
SAGE LIBRARY OF
SOCIAL RESEARCH

 SAGE PUBLICATIONS   Beverly Hills   London

To My Son Andy

For information address:

SAGE PUBLICATIONS, INC.
275 South Beverly Drive
Beverly Hills, California 90212

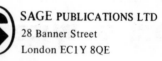

SAGE PUBLICATIONS LTD
28 Banner Street
London EC1Y 8QE

Printed in the United States of America

Library of Congress Cataloging in Publication Data

Wice, Paul B
  Criminal lawyers : an endangered species.

  (Sage library of social research ; v. 67)
  Includes bibliographical references
    1. Lawyers—United States. 2. Criminal law—United
States. I. Title.
KF299.C7W47   345'.73'0023   78-14478
ISBN 0-8039-1097-5
ISBN 0-8039-1098-3 pbk.

FIRST PRINTING

CONTENTS

ACKNOWLEDGMENTS

This research was completed while I was a visiting fellow at the National Institute of Criminal Justice. The financial support and encouragement offered by members of the National Institute as well as the other fellows is greatly appreciated. A most critical element permitting the research project to be completed was the cooperation of the 180 private criminal lawyers interviewed. Whatever success this study may be able to achieve is in large part due to their help. In several of the cities visited, a select few went out of their way to befriend the author and aid him in his endeavor. The following is a list of these lawyers who were extraordinarily helpful and contributed so greatly to the research project: Arthur Lewis and Max Soloman of Los Angeles, Jerry Ladar of San Francisco, Richard Schaefer of Denver, Richard Max Bockol of Philadelphia, and Edward Baldwin of New Orleans.

It must be noted that the views expressed in this study are solely those of the author and in no way represent the National Institute.

FOREWORD

"The profession of advocate," writes Michael Tigar, "in the sense of a regulated group of practitioners [of law] with some formal training, emerged in the late 1200's."* In this book, author Paul Wice tentatively concludes that the private criminal lawyer is a dying breed. Professor Wice studied the practice of criminal law in nine large cities and found the number of criminal lawyers to be one-half to one-third of the figure of twenty-five years ago.

Beset by health problems, economic hardships, professional and social ostracism; unaided by a continuing infusion of new blood, and criticized as to their competence from sources as lofty as Chief Justice Burger and as close as their fellow practitioners, this once romantic breed of lawyers seems to face extinction.

The point, of course, is not that persons accused of crime will go without legal representation but that the private advocate is giving way to the public—or bureaucratic—advocate found in the swelling ranks of defender offices. In every city studied which had a strong public defender system, the private practice of criminal law was found to be impaired and in jeopardy.

This book, however, is not so much a dissertation on how persons accused of crime should be provided with legal counsel. It is a rather personal and impressionistic portrait of those lawyers in nine large cities who are viewed by others and who view themselves as criminal law practitioners, although not necessarily as criminal law specialists.

---

*M. Tigar and M. Levy, *Law and the Rise of Capitalism* (1977): 157.

The author's classification scheme for criminal lawyers relies on the lawyer's style of practice (plea bargainer or trial); time spent in state or federal courts, and the amount of fees received. This model allows one to estimate the lawyer's level of performance but it leaves unresolved the difficult question of quantity. That is, how active in criminal law must a lawyer be before we can safely categorize him as a criminal law practitioner or as a specialist if the latter term includes both a qualitative and quantitative aspect?

Anyone familiar with the practice of criminal law knows that it is virtually unheard of for a private practitioner to handle only criminal cases. Unlike brain surgeons who simply do not deliver babies, criminal lawyers do take on personal injury work and domestic relations cases. Indeed, I know lawyers whose reputation is that of top criminal lawyers but whose income is derived mainly from personal injury work. Parenthetically, one attractive feature of this kind of split is that tort work is a check business while criminal law is a cash business and that has a certain appeal when it comes time to file income tax returns.

I should also note that I know lawyers who hold themselves out as trial specialists but who have yet to go to trial. Thus, I sympathize with Professor Wice's dilemma in trying to construct a classification scheme for the inclusion and exclusion of criminal law practitioners.

The content of the book leaves little doubt in my mind that the author was talking to the right people. That is, the meat of the book is gleaned from extensive interviews with lawyers, and since what is reported comports with my own impressions of the practice of criminal law, it rings true to me.

Methodological problems abound and are inherent in this sort of enterprise. The author concedes, and I agree, that this is not hard social science but more nearly resembles an anthropological study. The lawyers talked and the author listened, recorded, and then created for us this verbal picture of an embattled minority.

The picture which emerges is not likely to stir the hearts and minds of impressionistic first-year law students. Nor is it likely to cause Chief Justice Burger to issue an immediate retraction. We are shown a group of middle-aged, frequently overweight, combative types, who suffer all manner of health problems; who spend more time travelling to court, and waiting once they arrive, than in the library or with the client; who suffer marital instability; who must grub for clients, split fees, and often worry about collecting anything. We see a group of lawyers who are inactive in bar associations and who rarely can organize themselves; a group whose work day is so long that one wonders how they find time to read the newspaper to say nothing of the advance sheets.

As a group, the interviewees preferred representing a guilty client as opposed to one they believed to be innocent. Why? The odds are high that a great percentage of all defendants are going to receive some punishment and the pressure therefore is the greatest with the innocent client.

Success for the criminal lawyer is itself a hazy concept. Outright acquittals or dismissals are not an accurate measure, especially in a jurisdiction where the prosecutor brings only strong cases to the point of trial. Comparative sentences are probably the best measure, yet this does not readily lend itself to hard measurement.

This is a book that I am delighted to see written. It will, no doubt, raise questions about methodology, about generalizations from limited data, about the absence of a control group, and the like.

The author is aware of these issues and spells them out for the reader. Do not approach this book looking for a series of anecdotes about "my best cases"; do not look for an inspirational book with the private practitioner holding back the forces of governmental evil from unwitting defendants; and do not look for the F. Lee Baileys, Henry Rothblatts, or Clarence Darrows. Do look for an effort to convey an accurate picture of the struggle of a dying breed to get cases, get to court on time, and collect a fee. This is law in the pits, and the aroma comes through.

Fred Cohen

Albany, New York
July, 1978

Chapter 1

INTRODUCTION

It is the primary objective of this book to offer the reader an accurate portrait of the profession of the privately retained counsel in criminal cases. This portrait was constructed after a year was spent traveling cross country interviewing members of this beleaguered profession. By its completion, nearly two hundred private defense counsel in nine widely scattered cities (Washington, D.C., Philadelphia, Chicago, Houston, Miami, Los Angeles, San Francisco, New Orleans, and Denver) were interviewed.

In addition to presenting the reader with a demographic identification and description of this national sample of private criminal lawyers, this book also describes their professional folkways both in and out of the courtroom as well as analyzing the importance of local institutions, laws, and policies upon their practice. A final objective of this book is to offer a realistic alternative to the many stereotypes and myths which so often surround and distort the practice of criminal law. Most of these were created by the mass media or through popular literature and usually bear little resemblance to the lives of most of today's criminal lawyers. Based on television shows such as

Perry Mason, Petrocelli, and Owen Marshall, a flattering and uncritical group portrait has emerged. Also contributing to this image are the autobiographies of the legal exploits of some of the profession's superstars. F. Lee Bailey, Melvin Belli, Jake Ehrlich, and Louis Nizer are just a few of these literary lawyers who have dazzled the public with their courtroom triumphs.

It is important to study this group of lawyers and understand their professional activities and personal tensions for a variety of reasons. First, it was discovered that despite the crucial role played by the private criminal lawyer in the criminal justice system, there was little scholarly analysis of his position. Abraham Blumberg in his important study of the Kings County criminal courts presented the following statement on the crucial position of the defense attorney: "It is the lawyer who, in large measure ties together the seemingly disparate elements of police, prosecution, and court organization to help them dispose of a voluminous caseload."[1]

Another justification for conducting research on this topic is related to the unusual status of the profession. Despite the rising crime rate and the parallel increase in possible clientele, the criminal lawyers have become an endangered species whose ranks are shrinking and whose future appears extremely bleak. The reason for this paradoxical situation is primarily the growth of the public defender system, which now provides counsel for approximately two-thirds of all defendants and whose caseload is consistently on the rise. Also, working conditions have generally deteriorated to the point where many discouraged practitioners are looking forward to entering alternative areas of legal practice. To study criminal lawyers today offers one an unusual opportunity to witness the decline of a fascinating and critical element of our legal system as it fights for its survival. The implications for the criminal justice system will be one of our major areas of inquiry.

Review of the Literature

What have previous investigators concluded about the private practice of criminal law? As the relevant literature is reviewed, it is surprising to note the absence of any viable comparative or group study based on a national sample.

Although dealing with another area of the law, the best research on the legal profession has been Erwin Smigel's study, *The Wall Street Lawyer*. His work provided an excellent model for the present analysis despite differences in sample size and location. Smigel's methodology, which combined legal anthropology and sociological investigation, was a useful interdisciplinary approach readily adapted to the study of criminal lawyers.

The only previous study of criminal lawyers utilizing a somewhat scientific approach was Arthur Wood's 1967 treatise entitled *Criminal Lawyers*. It was Sociologist Wood who attempted to draw a comparative picture of criminal lawyers by interviewing 101 lawyers in the following assortment of cities: Jersey City; New York City; Birmingham, Alabama; Brooklyn, New York; New London, Connecticut; and Madison, Wisconsin. No explanation was offered for this odd collection of cities. Wood used a fixed questionnaire, which stressed demographic and social issues, leaving untouched the basic legal issues and practices of the lawyers' professional life. Wood operationally defined a criminal lawyer as one who did at least 10 percent of his practice in this area. A specialist was defined as someone doing at least 70 percent criminal law and a semispecialist as doing 40 percent. Several civil lawyers were included in the sample for the sake of comparison. Wood's use of simple percentages seems questionable given his failure to account for the seriousness of the case. There is a great difference between a lawyer who devotes 10 percent of his caseload to murder and other capital offenses, which may command half his time, as compared with a lawyer whose 10 percent caseload may be dominated by drunk driving and less serious cases requiring very little preparation. Although the book was published in 1967, the data were gathered in 1955. Thus, it has been twenty-two years since any large-scale empirical study of criminal lawyers has been attempted.

Despite the absence of any major treatises on the criminal lawyer, there have been several excellent articles and chapters in books which dealt with broader topics. The three following articles are believed to be among the most interesting and useful studies of the criminal lawyer.

One is Abraham Blumberg's "The Practice of Law as a Confidence Game" (*Law & Society Review*) and the chapter entitled "The Lawyer as Agent-Mediator" in his important work, *Criminal Justice*. The following quote from the first cited article summarizes his analysis of the criminal lawyer:

> The real key to understanding the role of defense counsel in a criminal case is the fixing and collection of fees. It is a problem which influences to a significant degree the criminal court process itself, not just the relationship of the lawyer and his client. . . . The lawyer must then be sure to manipulate the client and stage manage the case so that help and service at best appear to be rendered.

Albert Alschuler's "The Role of the Defense Counsel in Plea Bargaining" (*Yale Law Review*) is another important contribution. This recent article is the most thorough analysis of the criminal lawyer's place in plea bargaining that has ever been written. It is clearly biased against the plea bargaining process and presents a convincing argument based on numerous interviews with highly respected defense attorneys from across the country. Alschuler, currently a law professor at the University of Colorado, has previously examined the role of prosecutors and is completing the final work in the trilogy—the judge and plea bargaining.

Jerome Skolnick's "Social Control in the Adversary System," (*American Bar Foundation*) presents a thought-provoking analysis of the defense attorney's position. Written by one of the nation's preeminent legal sociologists, this article represents a definitive examination of the defense attorney's role from a sociological perspective.

Many of the country's more famous criminal lawyers and several lesser lights with a penchant for literature or the lure of seeing their exploits in print, have taken to writing autobiographical accounts of their professional accomplishments. Their quality ranges from a handful of thoughtful and occasionally perceptive works to a large number of ego-tripping accounts of courtroom victories. The two best (and probably most honest) were written by criminal lawyers of relative obscurity—Jake Evseroff of New York City (Brooklyn) and Joel Moldovsky of Philadelphia.[2] Both books were actually written by journalists (Paul Hoffman and Rose DeWolf respectively), but despite their flaws, the reader does come away with a decent appreciation of the difficulties of practicing criminal law in our urban courts. Most of the legal reminiscences are by the superstars of the profession such as F. Lee Bailey, Jake Ehrlich and Melvin Belli. Beyond the fascinating cases and personal exploits, books of this genre shed little light on the realities of the practice of criminal law for the overwhelming majority of practitioners.

For those readers interested in the more technical aspects of the criminal law profession, the following books were found to be very useful:

(1) Henry Rothblatt and F. Lee Bailey's *The Art of Criminal Advocacy*—an extensive "cookbook" of how to be a successful criminal lawyer, both in and out of the courtroom. Despite its "by the numbers style," its chariness and completeness make it a valuable addition to the general practitioner's library.[3]

(2) Kamisar, LaFave, and Israel's textbook, *Modern Criminal Procedure*, and Paulsen and Kadish's more substantive-oriented treatise on *Criminal Law* are probably the two finest examples of this genre. Both books have a fascinating blend of cases, comments, hypotheses, and secondary materials.[4]

(3) The ABA's Standards for the Defense Function offers an important set of idealized statements about how criminal lawyers *ought to* conduct their practice. It seems to be written by legal elitists who have probably not dirtied themselves very often in the urban criminal courts system, but it is nevertheless an important professional statement.

(4) In the specialized area of ethical problems and moral responsibilities facing the private criminal lawyer, the work by Monroe Freedman is noteworthy. It is a thought-provoking approach to lawyer-client relations and offers a sharp counterperspective to the more traditional analysis offered in the previously cited ABA standards.[5]

(5) One final work which is considered a classic by some criminal lawyers and mocked by others is Francis Wellman's ageless book on the *Art of Cross Examination*, which after seventy years is still considered by many to be the premier book on the subject.[6]

Methodology

GENERAL DESCRIPTION

There are three basic elements which have determined the methodological style of this research project. First is the attempt to make this as objective and scientific an analysis of the legal profession as could reasonably be made. It was hoped that the conclusions, descriptions, and recommendations would be based almost entirely upon empirical evidence.[7] This noble goal soon became just that: a goal towards which the author forthrightly strode, but which realistically he knew he would never reach. In the end it turned out that as in Erwin Smigel's excellent study of Wall Street lawyers, the basis of this work would also range "from well documented evidence where the points seem to be conclusive, to material that is believed to be true but for a variety of reasons is not as well documented, and finally, to speculation based more on insight and intuition than on scientific analyses of collected data."[8] If the current research analysis were to be broken down into each of these categories, it is estimated that 45 percent is strongly documented evidence, 40 percent strong belief based on incomplete evidence, and 15 percent based on insight and intuition.

The degree of objectivity seemed to waiver as the researcher and his large group of subjects began to know each other better. Although initially the author was ambivalent toward his subjects, as he concluded the seemingly endless string of interviews, he became more and more sympathetic to their plight, and possibly the overall objectivity of the project may have suffered. The only defense to be offered is that such a development is typical in this type of situation when rather open-ended and informal personal interviews are being conducted. However, it is optimistically believed that whatever was lost in objectivity by this style of interviewing was more than made up by higher-quality interviews marked by candor, depth, and interest.

The second basic element in the methodology is its unique comparative aspect. Not only were the 180 interviews taken from extremely diverse jurisdictions, but, as will be discussed in the next chapter, great effort was spent on assessing the relative impact of the local variables affecting the practice of criminal law. In other words, the research hopes to answer the question of how the practice of criminal law differs between major cities and offers some explanation and conceptual scheme for why such differences exist and what their impact is.

The third element of the methodology is the interdisciplinary nature of the research. It borrowed from a broad range of academic disciplines in order to comprehensively and intelligently examine the profession of criminal law. Among the various approaches, the anthropological one was often the most useful, especially given the unique nature of the research problem. The closeness between anthropological field work and this project can be sensed from the following quote used by Smigel to describe his methodology in *Wall Street Lawyers*: "When certain patterns become manifest, when certain values were uniformly expressed, when the content of the interviews and observations became similar, a point of diminishing return was felt. When this point was reached, we would move to another section of the agency. Forty people out of 100 employees were interviewed in this way. This procedure is characteristic of anthropological field work."[9]

Like Smigel—as well as Francis and Stone, from whose book on bureaucracy the previous quote originated—the author used personal interviews but selected a flexible set of questions rather than a fixed interview schedule. This allowed for more open-ended responses and permitted the author to go on to new and more complex areas once he had obtained a series of consistent responses on certain preliminary topics. It also allowed the interview to take into account the personal specialization or expertise of each interviewee and tailor the interview accordingly. Finally and most importantly, it may have saved the author's sanity by not forcing him to conduct the identical lengthy interview nearly two hundred times.

Although this method clearly places the research below the rigorous standards of most sociological inquiry, nevertheless, what emerged was a type of sociological journalism, heavily dependent upon the lessons of both sociology of law and sociology of occupations. In the former category the works of Carlin, Ladinsky, and Handler were most useful, while the Caplow and Krause textbooks on occupational sociology greatly contributed to the questionnaire construction and conceptual framework.[10]

Because of the crucial role of the defense attorney as an officer of the court and pivotal member of the criminal justice system, the recent work in political science by Jacob, Neubauer and Cole also made important contributions.[11] Lastly, and most obviously, the field of criminal law itself provided a major source of background data for the research effort.

The major methodological theme which dominates this work, and which must be remembered by the reader, is that this study is primarily an attempt to have the private criminal lawyers themselves explain and critique their professional behavior. For the most part, the author served only as a conduit for the sensitivities, insights, and experiences of these 180 lawyers.

SAMPLING

The sampling stage involved a two-step decisional process: first, which cities were to be selected, and secondly, which lawyers in those cities were to be interviewed. Private criminal lawyers are found primarily in large urban centers. It was also discovered that when a person from a smaller town becomes involved in a serious criminal matter, he will abandon his local general practitioner, and select one of the "big city" criminal lawyers. Many of the lawyers interviewed, especially those in Miami and Denver, spent ·a great deal of time trying cases throughout their respective states.

In choosing our nine cities, primary consideration was given to broad regional representation. It was hoped that the style of criminal law as well as the operation of the criminal justice system would vary sufficiently between these selected cities so that some measure of the impact of local variables would be fruitful. As will be discovered in Chapter 2, such variation did occur and permitted a meaningful comparative analysis of the practice of criminal law in each city. Among the variables found to affect the style of practice were local discovery procedures; degree of politicization of the judiciary and the prosecutor's office; degree of inbreeding of the bar; and several other variables to be discussed in the next chapter.

The second sampling problem, that of choosing the lawyers to be interviewed, was more perplexing. Approximately twenty interviews would be conducted in each city during the ten-day visit. It was estimated that by talking to twenty lawyers in each city, approximately one-third to one-half of each city's criminal law bar would be contacted. Thus, the sample of one hundred eighty criminal lawyers would be chosen from an estimated universe of about five hundred. After completing the interviews, the author believes that the total number of criminal lawyers in the nine cities is approximately four hundred, and consequently nearly 50 percent of the population were interviewed.

Once the parameters of the sample had been established, the next step was the selection of individual practitioners. Because of the crowded schedule of criminal lawyers, and also the necessity for establishing a useful base of lawyers to begin with, an attempt was made to write to ten lawyers in each city who were thought to be criminal practitioners, two weeks before the author would be arriving in the city. The letter explained the purpose of the research project and requested an interview. Nearly two-thirds of the letters mailed out resulted in interviews.

Because of advertising restrictions and the scarcity of criminal specialist programs, it is very difficult to locate a private criminal lawyer. As an aid in this location process, the National Association of Criminal Defense Lawyers gave the author its membership lists while Dean John Ackerman of the National College of Criminal Defense Lawyers and Public Defenders provided his mailing list. In addition, Martindale & Hubbell was perused and the names of lawyers in law firms specializing in criminal law were gathered. In those few firms willing to list a criminal law specialty, it was fairly easy to pick out the criminal law experts. First, most of these "firms" were very small, rarely having more than six members. Secondly, experience as public defenders or district attorneys was an identifying characteristic. Finally, there were the current memberships in the biographical section which listed criminal law sections of local, state, and national bar associations.

An individual appearing on the two membership lists and in Martindale & Hubbell would be chosen in the preliminary sample. Approximately six interviews of the twenty would be arranged in this manner. The quality of this sample as a representative group of criminal lawyers as compared to those located once the researcher was in the city, was generally disappointing. It seems that many lawyers had joined these associations for either intellectual, social, or some unknown reason and did not actually practice very much criminal law. There were many exceptions, but the overall involvement of this preliminary group fell short of expectations.

The names of the majority of lawyers interviewed were obtained during the first two or three days in a city. The first day was usually spent talking to representatives of the public defender's office and the prosecutor's office as well as a judge responsible for the calendar or with long experience in the operation of the local criminal justice system. Each of these officials would be told of the research project and asked to supply a sample of fifteen to twenty lawyers who represented a broad spectrum of the city's private criminal law bar. They were to primarily handle misdemeanors and felonies and should cover a broad range in quality, with equal representation for all types. All of the officials willingly supplied such lists and were highly supportive of the project, offering additional information and advice. Armed with these three lists, the author would then spend the next two days talking to criminal lawyers selected in the preliminary sample. At the conclusion of these five to six interviews, these lawyers would be asked to name ten other criminal lawyers, again representing a broad spectrum, who would be considered worthwhile interviewing.

Therefore, within two to three days, the author would have a large number of lists recommending possible interview subjects. By comparing lists, it was easy to find certain names reappearing numerous times, and these would be the primary source for the completion of the sample. The snowball effect, however, would continue through the week as lawyers would voluntarily recommend someone as an important figure on the local scene who should not be missed. Frequently they would call up these individuals and help set up the interview. On the bases of the variety of sources and the care in searching for multiple recommendations, it is believed that a fair sample of criminal lawyers was interviewed. As a final check, the author would read his sample to the last few interviewees in order to check and see if he in fact was obtaining a sufficiently broad sample, without overrepresenting any category.

It is realized that these sampling techniques fall short of the more rigorous standards recommended in social science methodology, but given the elusive nature of the criminal lawyer, this appeared to be the optimally effective means of sample selection.

INTERVIEWS

Conducting personal interviews with busy members of the legal profession is a difficult task, but fortunately the author had previous experience in related research projects and emerged satisfied at their completion. Earlier interview experiences involved one hundred twenty-five officials concerned with the administration of bail in ten major cities (defense attorneys comprised about one-fourth of this group) and a more recent study interviewing seventy public defenders for a national research project.[12]

One of the most pleasant surprises of the entire research experience was the high degree of receptivity toward the interviews by the large majority of interviewees. Although several lawyers failed to return calls or were impossible to locate, only one lawyer made an outright refusal to be interviewed. Obviously, the interviews varied as to candor and interest, but it was nevertheless reassuring to be able to count on the support of so many.

When one considers that "time is money" to lawyers, it is even more amazing that the large sample was willing to spend between one and three hours being interviewed for a project from which there was clearly no financial return. The criminal lawyers were extremely busy and worked long hours, frequently dividing their daytime work between several scattered courthouses and could only be located in their offices during the early morning hours, after the courts closed in the early evening, or on weekends. The most frequent reason why the author was unable to see subjects was that they were arguing a case out of town or were currently involved in a trial and had to devote every waking moment to courtroom preparation. Despite these drawbacks, nearly three-quarters of the criminal lawyers who were contacted were eventually interviewed. (Reference here is to those criminal lawyers whose names were obtained once the researcher reached the city.)

The problem of attribution and confidentiality was of concern to most of the sample. Since the researcher had not had previous personal contact with the lawyers, they simply had to rely upon his promise that no names would be used in connection with direct quotes. The purpose of the project was ex-

plained to be an attempt to show national patterns and trends
rather than present anecdotal reminiscences or shocking ex-
posés. Attribution, if a quote were to be used, would be only to
a region or city, and never a specific lawyer. It was sensed that
some lawyers were disappointed by this lack of specificity, but
as a general policy, it aided in lowering the anxiety level of the
majority of interviewees.

Smigel pointed out that he sensed that professional ethics
were a bar to candor since lawyers might fear the interviews
would be violating the privileged nature of the attorney-client
relationship. By following a policy of confidentiality and not
discussing pending litigation the problem was minimized.

Certain areas of inquiry were consistently greeted with reluctance or silence by the majority of the interviewees. These
"taboo topics" were usually associated with money problems or
ethical issues, especially those related to suborning perjury. One
could sense the lawyers' realization that there might be some
possible repercussions from their answers, especially when the
interviewer was associated with the federal government.

One-third of the interviewees were totally frank and willing
to answer any question. Another third were courteous and
generally helpful but careful to avoid potentially harmful
topics. The remaining third were skeptical about the project and
cautious during the interview. This last group were most cynical
about social science research, failing to see what good could
ultimately be derived from such an endeavor and also disbe-
lieving the scientific objectivity. The real paradox in interviewing the lawyers was that they were an extremely articulate
group who might potentially offer many enlightening comments, yet their conservative nature and professional paranoia
occasionally made them difficult subjects. In defense of their
paranoia, it might have been warranted given the regularity with
which several criminal lawyers in the sample had been investigated by a federal or state agency or forced to appear before a
grand jury probing one of their former clients. Because of their
mastery of questioning techniques and a high intelligence, it
would have been insulting and foolhardy to try to trick these
lawyers into revealing facets of their professional life which
they desired to keep hidden. The likelihood of failure and the

harm to the continuation of the interview also precluded any attempt at deceptive inquiry.

In order to attempt to ease the personal relationship with the interviewees, the author began dressing like a lawyer (conservative business suits) instead of the relatively informal clothing which he would wear while teaching in college. Smigel was warned, however, that he should not try to look too much like his subjects because as one lawyer said to him: "We don't want you to be too much like ourselves—it takes some of the interest in the meeting away. We can see lawyers any day."[13] The author did notice, however, that most interviewees were much more candid when they assumed that he was a lawyer. (It would be casually mentioned that the author had gone to law school, although it was only for a year. They generally assumed he had graduated and chosen teaching over practice.)

David Reisman also noticed this tendency, and when he wrote his important article entitled, "Toward an Anthropological Science of Law and the Legal Profession," he included the following statement which verifies the necessity for convincing the lawyer that you are similarly endowed:

> Knowledge of the culture of lawyers requires participant observation. And it may turn out that the investigator who has the best chance of picking up this culture in all its nuances will be one who is sufficiently familiar with the counters of legal discourse to share already some of the culture of the lawyers among whom he will move, if he knows some, by the usual journalistic rule, he can pretend he knows more (or sometimes less) and find out still more. He will know where to look, where to probe. He will not be so taken up with imbibing legal phrases and mechanics that he will assign to the lawyers he is observing as much affect in the use of these phrases as is necessary for him in the original learning process.[14]

It is optimistically believed by the author that his year of law school and eight years studying criminal courtrooms would be sufficient participant observation to satisfy Reisman's qualifications.

Among the numerous problems encountered was the tendency of the lawyers to begin interviewing the researcher. It was very easy for both parties to switch roles, especially after the researcher had been bored listening to others speak for a long period of time and welcomed the chance to offer his premature conclusions.

The interviews were recorded on white sheets of paper by means of a developed shorthand style which allowed for fairly complete accounts. An attempt was made to keep notes out of sight of the lawyer (below the desktop, for example) so that he would not feel inhibited. Yellow sheets were avoided because they might resemble legal pads, which are used in taking depositions, and the researcher did not want the lawyer to make this association. Given all of these problems, it is little wonder that the use of a tape recorder was soon discarded as a means of data collection.

As Smigel had warned, the researcher must be carefully attuned to the interviewee's unique quirks, and consequently techniques would have to be adjusted to fit the individual lawyer. Whether the lawyer was old or young, successful or unsuccessful, could have a critical impact upon the style of interview. In dealing with controversial topics, the strategy was either to make your inquiries in as unobtrusive a manner as possible or to display a clear knowledge of the area so that you might bluff the subject into thinking you already had a good idea what the answer was. The main point is for the researcher to realize that he has a strong responsibility to ask penetrating and thoughtful questions which will stimulate and sustain the interest of the interviewee. Given the capabilities of the lawyers, it must be frankly admitted that on several occasions the researcher ran out of gas long before the interviewee was prepared to stop. Trying to sustain the interest of the interviewee is one of the most important gifts of a successful interviewer. Borrowing from Smigel again, the following strategies were used to maintain this goal: (1) scheduling interviews an hour before lunch or dinner; (2) asking provocative questions on sensitive topics guaranteed to evoke a strong response; (3) appealing to the interviewee's ego by flattery and exhibiting a continued interest in his personal achievements; and (4) beginning with easy, nonthreatening questions which would put the interviewee at ease and perhaps lessen his skepticism.

CONCLUSION

This project, in its attempt to capture the essence of the profession of the criminal lawyer, has selected a difficult area of research. As David Reisman wrote twenty-five years ago, "The ethno-centrism of the law makes it a very difficult institution to study on a broad or comparative perspective."[15] By selecting an anthropological approach to this problem, we have even further complicated our task because, as Reisman again reminds us, "an anthropological study must go beyond both the glamorous and the social reform aspects and study the unique structure of the law, the type of people it attracts, their training and the role the law has played in shaping present-day society."[16]

As we move on to the body of this study and address the taxonomic difficulties of dealing with criminal lawyers, let us close this introduction with the words of Gilbert Rosenthal as he addressed the National College of Criminal Defense Lawyers in 1975. This brief excerpt embodies the underlying theme of this study as well as suggesting the necessity for its completion.

> Today they fail to recognize that the criminal defense lawyer may well be an endangered species, there is no closed season in respect to him and frequently it appears that the desire is greater to indict, and if possible convict, an able defense lawyer than a defendant who has achieved some degree of notoriety.[17]

NOTES

1. Abraham Blumberg, *Criminal Justice* (Chicago: Quadrangle, 1967), p. 95.

2. Paul Hoffman, *What the Hell is Justice: The Life and Trials of a Criminal Lawyer* (Chicago: Playboy Press, 1974); Joel Moldovsky and Rose DeWolf, *The Best Defense* (New York: Macmillan, 1975).

3. F. Lee Bailey and Henry B. Rothblatt, *Fundamentals of Criminal Advocacy* (Rochester, N.Y.: Lawyers' Cooperative Publishing Company, 1974).

4. Yale Kamisar, Wayne LaFave, and Jerrold H. Israel, *Modern Criminal Procedure* (St. Paul, Minn.: West Publishing, 1974); and Monroe Paulsen and Sanford Kadish, *Criminal Law and its Procedures* (Boston: Little, Brown, 1962).

5. Monroe Freedman, *Lawyer's Ethics in an Adversary System* (Indianapolis: Bobbs-Merrill, 1975).

6. Francis Wellman, *The Art of Cross Examination* (New York: Collier, 1976).

7. This is in opposition to subjective judgments, historic recantations; or philosophical or legalistic analysis.

8. Erwin Smigel, *The Wall Street Lawyer* (Bloomington: Indiana University Press), p. viii.

9. Ibid, p. 30.

10. Theodore Caplow, *The Sociology of Work* (New York: McGraw-Hill, 1964); and Elliott Krause, *The Sociology of Occupations* (New York: Little, Brown, 1971).

11. Herbert Jacob, *Felony Justice* (New York: Little, Brown, 1977); David Neubauer, *Criminal Justice in Middle America* (Morristown, N.J.: General Learning Press, 1974); and George Cole, *The American System of Criminal Justice* (North Scituate, Mass.: Duxbury Press, 1975).

12. Paul Wice, *Freedom for Sale* (Lexington, Mass.: Lexington Books, 1974); and with Peter Suwak, "Current realities of public defender programs," *Criminal Law Bulletin,* March, 1974.

13. Smigel, op. cit., p. 30.

14. David Reisman, "Toward an anthropological science of law and the legal profession," *American Journal of Sociology*, S7(1942), p. 121.

15. Ibid, p. 122.

16. Ibid.

17. Gilbert Rosenthal, speech before the National College of Criminal Defense Lawyers, in Houston, Texas, summer of 1975.

Chapter 2

DIVERSITY OF THE PROFESSION

There are approximately 400,000 lawyers in the United States, and their professional responsibilities require them to perform a wide variety of tasks. Lawyers find themselves negotiating, drafting, counseling, and litigating on behalf of their clients. Though the last task, litigating, is assumed by the general public to be the most typical and frequent type of work, it is in fact rare for most attorneys to enter a courtroom, let alone try a case before a judge.

The criminal lawyer is the legal specialist who most clearly approximates the public's preconception about a lawyer's professional activities. Despite the public's image of what a lawyer does, there are only an estimated 10,000 to 20,000 lawyers who accept criminal cases "more than occasionally," and a significant number, in the 4,000 range, are employed by public defender organizations.

All of the lawyers interviewed in this study have been identified as privately retained counsel in criminal cases. Their identification as a criminal lawyer was made either by themselves or more often by one of the resource personnel, judges, district attorneys, public defenders, or other criminal lawyers who were consulted in each city. Generally, each interviewee spent a minimum of 15 percent of his time on criminal matters. It was surprising to find how few lawyers identified as "specialists in criminal law" devoted the majority of their efforts to criminal matters. It was important to have a secondary source of identifying references because several criminal lawyers in the sample refused to identify themselves as falling within this speciality, despite a clear recognition by their colleagues and knowledgeable court officials of their active role as criminal lawyers.

It should also be noted that the entire sample of criminal lawyers, with only a handful of exceptions, handled a broad range of felonies and misdemeanors with only a rare petty offense or traffic case. In nearly every city visited, there was a subsection of the criminal law bar who practiced solely in these traffic and petty offense courts. Their cases usually involved drunk driving, public drunkenness, or a wider range of ordinance violations. The law practiced in such cases bears little resemblance to the more serious criminal trials. There are no viable trials, and little legal skill is required in the disposition of these cases. It is best thought of as a bureaucratic proceeding where a brief 5-10 minute appearance before a judge can settle the matter once and for all.

Although this type of practice will be identified and briefly discussed in the next chapter, traffic court lawyers are generally excluded from the major portion of this study for a variety of reasons. First, they do not perform the legal tasks associated with the practice of criminal law and are, in fact, acting as private ombudsmen for the unfortunate citizens dragged before a municipal court on a minor matter. Secondly, they perform their job in an environment isolated from the arena where the misdemeanors and felonies are handled. A third and final reason is that there is a general recognition within the criminal justice community that these municipal court lawyers who inhabit the traffic and petty offense courtrooms are a special breed, clearly distinguished from the criminal defense lawyers handling the more serious matters.

Another characteristic of the criminal lawyers selected in this study is their residence in large urban areas. Smaller cities and towns do not have the amount of crime necessary to permit a lawyer to develop a specialty in criminal law. There are always several general practitioners who are known for their ability to handle criminal matters, but smaller locales are unable to support a criminal law bar. It was also found that a small-city defendant charged with a serious crime would select his lawyer from among the members of the criminal law bar of the nearest large city if he could afford it. All cities in the sample had metropolitan populations exceeding one million.

Classification of the Profession

INTRODUCTION TO THE DILEMMA

One of the general public's most common misconceptions concerning the legal profession is their willingness to lump the entire bar together as a monolithic group. People feel that since all members of this profession have undergone nearly identical educational experiences, lawyers must possess certain common skills which would permit them to solve a wide range of legal problems. The truth is that because the legal questions are so complex and so varied, the contemporary bar is forced into a high degree of specialization, with remarkably little interaction between lawyers of different interests. Thus tax lawyers know nothing of criminal law, and criminal lawyers would have little idea of how to handle business mergers. The criminal lawyer (like the personal injury and divorce lawyer) is primarily a litigator although his skills in negotiating and counseling are also important.

Legal specialization has now developed to the degree that there is even a division of labor within the subfield of criminal law. This raises the question of how to classify the private practice of criminal law. The operational grounds for deriving a taxonomic structure for these lawyers are quite varied and have generated numerous conceptual schemes. The author, secondary sources, as well as the lawyers themselves, have been responsible for contributing to the plethora of schemes about to be discussed. After explaining each of these classificatory concepts, adding brief comments as to the more obvious strengths and weaknesses, this discussion will conclude with a recommended model.

The criminal lawyers interviewed were keenly aware of the divisions within their field of legal specialization, and, as shall be discussed later in this chapter, these differences between criminal lawyers has created such tension as to prevent them from organizing effectively.

POSSIBLE SCHEMES

The most common type of classification system is based on the amount of criminal law practiced as a percentage of the total caseload. This was the approach used by Arthur Wood in his 1967 treatise on criminal lawyers. He operationally defined a criminal lawyer as anyone who had 25 percent of his cases in the criminal field, while a "criminal law specialist" did at least 75 percent of his work in the criminal area. He also offered a term of "semispecialists" for those lawyers handling 25-75 percent.[1] The major drawback to this typology is its failure to acknowledge the varying time and abilities involved in different types of cases. One lawyer may devote 50 percent of his caseload to drunk driving cases, which are handled in a perfunctory and repetitive manner, whereas another lawyer may devote only 10 percent of his caseload to criminal matters, but these may be serious felonies, which often go to trial. The use of percentages of either time or caseload fails to provide needed information about the seriousness of the cases and their methods of disposition.

A second classification scheme creates a dichotomy between those criminal lawyers recognized as willing and able to perform in the courtroom and others identified as "wholesalers," who are skilled in effectively negotiating the best plea bargain available. The former group generally has only a few cases from well-paying clients while the latter group relies upon a fast turnover and volume business. Albert Alschuler's important article on the role of defense counsel in plea bargaining is based upon this conceptual scheme, and it states that, "There are 2 ways for lawyers to achieve financial success. One is to develop over a long period of time a reputation as an outstanding trial lawyer and attract occasionally wealthy people who become enmeshed in the law. A second path is handling a larger volume of cases for less than spectacular fees."[2] Alschuler goes on to comment that he believes that private criminal lawyers can be divided about 50/50 into these two categories. When applied to the 180 criminal lawyers interviewed for this study, this dichotomy offers a realistic differentiation. Its major weakness is its simplicity and its inability to deal with criminal lawyers who can effectively operate both in the courtroom as litigators and outside as negotiators.

A third categorization relates to the type of case handled. Many lawyers saw a fairly sharp difference between those who handled primarily federal cases and those whose cases were mainly in the state courts. This does not mean that many lawyers operated exclusively within either jurisdiction but only that most criminal lawyers had a preference for practicing in either the state or federal arenas. One of the main reasons why a criminal lawyer would begin to find himself spending the majority of his time working in one of these two jurisdictions is related to the type of criminal cases handled. Attorneys dealing with defendants charged with crimes of violence (such as murder, rape, and assault), victimless crimes (such as prostitution, narcotic addiction, sexual offenses) or minor property crimes (burglary and larceny) will most likely find themselves in the state courts. Counsel for defendants arrested for white-collar crimes (tax evasion, consumer fraud, price fixing) or organized crime cases (gambling, interstate auto theft, narcotic dealings) are most commonly going to be in the federal courts. Although there were a few lawyers interviewed who stated a strong preference for practicing in either the state or federal system, most attorneys were motivated in the direction of the arena in which the particular case is usually settled.

Another way of dividing up the criminal bar, utilizing the "type of case" rationale, is to look at the degree of seriousness of the case. This might either be dichotomized or, more realistically, viewed as a continuum, where the seriousness of the case is directly proportional to the amount of possible incarceration and/or fine. One might then examine the types of cases handled by a criminal lawyer and estimate their average seriousness, which would place the lawyer at a specific position relative to the other criminal lawyers. A drawback to this scheme is its failure to account for the large number of criminal lawyers whose clients are arrested for a broad range of crimes and whose average degree of case seriousness obfuscates the reality of their practices, which stretches from one end of the "seriousness continuum" to the other.

One final point in considering the "type of case" schema is that a few lawyers specialize very narrowly in only one type of offense and that these practitioners should be evaluated as a unique group, outside a general conceptual scheme. In every city visited, a handful of lawyers were designated as the "dope lawyers" (defending users as well as traffickers in narcotics), while other common specialties were representing gamblers, pimps, prostitutes, and professional criminals, such as burglars or fences. These lawyers were clearly recognized within the criminal community as having developed an expertise over the years in a narrow area of the criminal law and soon found their practice dominated by defendants with similar problems. The lawyer's reputation is his most important commodity, as we shall discuss in forthcoming chapters, and once his "rep" is associated with success in a particular area, he will continue to be overrun by other defendants involved in the same trouble.

It should be clarified that a large number of lawyers were excluded from our sample because they handle traffic cases, petty offenses punishable by fines or less than thirty-day confinements, or municipal ordinance violations. They are only mentioned because they are specialists in particular types of cases and because they do handle a large volume of business. As a matter of fact, several lawyers commented that drunk driving cases are an extremely lucrative specialty because of their volume, ease of preparation, and relatively high fee. Attorneys can charge $500-$2000 a case because the clients are frequently middle-class citizens with middle incomes who are deadly afraid of losing their driving licenses. With the urban sprawl and inadequate mass transit systems in most cities, many drivers would be virtually demobilized if their licenses were suspended.

A West Coast lawyer whose practice was primarily drunk driving cases estimated his net income from these cases to be $50,000-75,000 a year. He felt that he only had to spend an average of an hour or so per case, which was typically plea bargained down to a lesser offense (such as reckless driving) that would only result in the addition of "points" to the defendant's driving record rather than the greatly feared loss of license. One Denver lawyer, who handles a large number of these cases, pessimistically noted, "you can only win one out of about twenty cases, and this is because of some goof-up in the administration of the tests or by someone in the labs." He also typically tries to negotiate the case down to an offense which will not result in loss of the driver's license.

As noted in Chapter 1, the lawyers in these traffic and petty offense cases rarely try a case and even the infrequent trial resembles an administrative ruling by the judge after a very short period of argument. Thus, few of the criminal lawyer's skills are called into action. Also, the case is often processed in a separate facility away from the criminal courthouse.

A fourth basis of classification is the relative degree of success enjoyed by the criminal lawyer. In empirical and somewhat crass terms, we are referring to his financial success, which seems closely related to the financial capabilities of his clients. Herman Schwartz, a professor of law at SUNY at Buffalo, recognized the importance of this variable as a source of serious division within the profession: "There is a cleavage within the criminal defense bar which is often overlooked but nevertheless real and parallels that everywhere else—a cleavage between lawyers representing the well-to-do and those representing the very poor."[3]

It was commonly pointed out that rating lawyers on the amount of their fees may not have anything to do with their competence, but it does seem logical to assume that there is at least a relationship between the amount of a fee and the lawyer's reputation. A thoughtful West Coast lawyer was even doubtful about this and said he was continually frustrated by the absence of any consistent correlation between the amount of work he put into a case, the success or disposition of the case, and the fee received. He divided his city's criminal lawyers into the following three categories: (1) the top ones, where you get what you pay for and the sky is the limit; (2) the middle range, who give some consideration to what a fair fee is; and (3) the wholesalers, who start at $300-500 for a plea and around $1500-2000 for a trial, which often ends up being a "slow plea."

Two of the more interesting classification schemes are one based on the age or generation gap, and another stressing the geographic location of the lawyer's office. In San Francisco, a city acutely aware of the unusual activities of a rebellious youth cult, one criminal attorney commented that the town was a closed system with the older generation dominating the practice through a series of symbiotic interrelationships. As a younger lawyer, he foresaw a tough struggle ahead. The only feasible route was through an apprenticeship period with either the city's public defender or district attorney, carefully building a base of referral clients and connections prior to moving into private practice.

In cities where the criminal courthouse is located a significant distance from the business center, the location of the lawyer's office is a key factor in classifying him as a successful "downtown lawyer" or merely one of those criminal lawyers hanging around the courthouse. In Washington, D.C., for example, where the courthouse is quite a distance from most of the established law firms, one can easily tell whether a lawyer is a high-class Connecticut Avenue type located in the midst of the business district or a "5th Streeter" whose shabby office is across the street from the criminal courts building in a rundown section of town. Several cities refer to their less prestigious criminal lawyers by citing their address, as for example the "Tulane Avenue bunch" in New Orleans and the "Bryant Streeters" in San Francisco. The obvious weakness of this geographic categorization is that not all of the "downtown lawyers" are either competent or successful, and certainly several good lawyers are found near the criminal courts building, even if it means settling for a second-rate office in a decaying section of town. The convenience of the location and the closer proximity to clients are the common explanations for locating in these low-status neighborhoods.

RECOMMENDED SOLUTION

After a careful review of the literature and the collective wisdom of the lawyers interviewed no classification scheme

emerged clearly superior. One can only rank them in relative
order of utility and then select the best features from each in
order to at least offer the reader some possible guidelines for
future exploration.

Based upon the thoughts of the interviewees, the most useful
classification schemes appeared to be the ones related to style
of practice—plea bargainer (wholesaler) vs. trial attorney—and
to type of practice—federal vs. state—or seriousness of the case.
A close third, and clearly related to the first two, is a taxonomy
based on the lawyer's success.

Upon examination of the first three possibilities, it is apparent that a great deal of overlap exists between them and that
they may be combined to offer a workable, albeit broad,
conceptual scheme, where the left-to-right continuum indicates
increasingly high-quality criminal law performance. (See Figure
2.1.)

The lowest quality category of criminal lawyers would appear
to be dominated by those characterized as wholesalers who
rarely go to trial. They practice almost entirely in the state
courts, and handle less serious cases with less chance of
achieving financial success. At the opposite extreme one finds
lawyers who have no qualms about trying cases and have developed favorable reputations based on their litigating abilities.
These lawyers often seem to take either serious state cases or
primarily federal suits and with very rare exceptions achieve

Figure 2.1: CONCEPTUAL SCHEME

	Plea bargain ——————— Trial	
Low quality	Negative effect ———————————————	Positive effect	High quality
	State ——————— Federal	
Less serious	———————————————	More serious
	Low fees ——————— High fees	
Lack of financial success	———————————————	Financial success

very high financial rewards. This is only a heuristic model and as already noted, many second-rate lawyers may earn large salaries as wholesalers.

Uniqueness of Selected Cities

As indicated earlier in this chapter, the practice of criminal law is a highly diversified profession with a wide range of specialization. We shall now demonstrate that this diversity does not only pertain to the criminal lawyers themselves but also to cities and their respective criminal justice systems. Although the third and final section of this chapter will attempt to group and compare cities on a series of legal, political, social, and institutional variables, this section will stress the unique qualities and factors discovered in each city visited which were of consequence to practicing private criminal law.

WASHINGTON D.C.

Being a federal city, Washington's criminal justice system has many unusual aspects vis-à-vis the other cities visited that are governed by state and local laws. Using the federal rules of criminal procedure was not nearly as significant a factor for Washington lawyers as being forced to have the U.S. Attorney's Office as their courtroom adversary. Relative to other prosecutorial agencies surveyed during this study, the U.S. Attorney's Office was clearly recognized as having superior personnel, funding, and institutional resources.

A second prominent feature of the District's system is the great use of assigned counsel, despite the presence of a well-staffed public defender program. The public defender's office handles approximately 15 percent of the felony/misdemeanor caseload, and most indigents are assigned counsel (40 percent of total caseload). Because the assigned counsel system is federally funded, the $20-30 an hour lawyer's fees make it a much more popular source of cases than in any other city visited. Many lawyers, especially the old-timers who inhabit the courthouse and the inexperienced ones recently graduated from law school, depend upon these assigned cases for their livelihood and can usually make between $15,000 and $25,000 annually. These lawyers are referred to as C.J.A.'s because the federal Criminal Justice Act appropriates the funds necessary to operate the program. It is administered by the public defender's office who has a full-time staff in charge of making assignments. The judges oversee these assignments and have the final say as to how much money an attorney may receive based on his submitted voucher of time and expense.

PHILADELPHIA

The most noticeable aspect of the Philadelphia criminal bar was its extremely inbred nature. Of the twenty-three lawyers interviewed, twenty-two were locally raised and educated. The significance of this fact will be discussed later. Another unusual local condition was the use of the "slow plea" rather than the traditional form of plea bargaining where a lenient sentence is exchanged for a guilty plea. A special waiver panel of judges will conduct a rather perfunctory trial, barely resembling an adversary proceeding, but at least the defendant has preserved his right to appeal by maintaining a not guilty position.

The district attorney's office and the Court of Common Pleas were equal to those in Chicago in the extreme politization of both institutions. What exacerbated matters even more in Philadelphia was a feud between the city's major newspaper, *The Inquirer*, and the District Attorney, Emmet Fitzpatrick. All lawyers interviewed were cognizant of the sidewards glances that both the district attorney's office and most judges threw towards *The Inquirer*, but were less certain of the impact of such media awareness upon their performance. Somewhat related to the politicized district attorney's office was the department's rather restrictive discovery procedures, which placed most defense attorneys at a severe disadvantage.

LOS ANGELES

Most of the Los Angeles criminal lawyers pointed to their criminal court's extreme regionalization as its most exasperating and unique feature. This decentralization has divided the criminal caseload into numerous widely separated court districts, ranging all of the way from Long Beach to Van Nuys. As a result, the lawyers are faced with the unenviable task of spending a great part of their day traversing the city's infamous expressways. This regionalization has also caused the criminal bar to be scattered all over the vast city. Such geographic dispersal has greatly contributed to the disorganized condition of the criminal bar and discouraged many lawyers from developing a criminal law specialty.

On the more positive side, Los Angeles has one of the most reputable and efficient court systems in the country. Nearly all the lawyers interviewed in the city stated their respect and appreciation for the high quality of the criminal courts. The city also boasts one of the premier public defender agencies in the nation. This is great for indigent defendants, but has been the death knell for the private criminal lawyer, as nearly 80 percent of the defendants utilize the county's public defender services.

SAN FRANCISCO

The San Francisco criminal bar reflects the city's civilized airs and toleration of alternative lifestyles. Several of the lawyers clearly represented anti-establishment political and social ideologies. It was very refreshing to sense the outrage of many of these attorneys and realize that the much maligned and generally decaying adversarial system was alive and kicking in the criminal courthouse on Bryant Street. The dress, speech, and demeanor of these criminal lawyers placed them in sharp contrast to much of the legal profession as well as criminal lawyers in the other cities visited.

The author was also greatly impressed by the high quality of the San Francisco bar. The city seems to attract some of the leading criminal lawyers from San Diego, Washington, D.C., Philadelphia, New York, and a variety of other distant locales. The city does have a unique charm and sophistication rarely matched in the world, so it is little wonder that it has attracted so much legal talent from so far away. As a result of this widespread appeal, the competition among the city's criminal attorneys is intense and has probably been the major factor leading to the fragmented condition of the private defense bar.

NEW ORLEANS

The state of Louisiana has been a great aid to the private defense bar by imposing the severest penalties of any jurisdiction surveyed. The result of these archaic and punitive statutes is to make defendants panic, causing many to invest their life savings in hiring the best counsel available. (The public defender's office is still a fledgling operation with a small, overworked staff which has not yet fully captured the public's confidence.)

Like in Chicago and San Francisco, the New Orleans criminal courthouse is located in a run-down section of town several miles from the city's business center. The criminal lawyers who have established their offices at Tulane and Broad Streets surrounding the courthouse have generally been categorized as "second-class" criminal lawyers in distinction to their more wealthy and establishment-related brothers having offices near the business district. As in Washington, D.C. and San Francisco, a tension exists between the two groups, which has subverted any organizational endeavors to establish a unified criminal bar.

The city resembles Philadelphia in its extremely politicized district attorney's office as well as in its restrictive discovery proceedings. In contrast to Philadelphia and most other cities, however, the New Orleans district attorney's office operates the most efficient and competent screening department of any city visited. Nearly half of the police felony arrests are dropped, and once the office has decided to file charges, there is a strong likelihood of conviction.

MIAMI

The most noteworthy fact about the practice of criminal law in Miami relates to the type of cases handled. The region has a booming federal practice due to its position as one of the major centers for narcotics traffic in the country. It has also been portrayed as an ideal location for all types of con artists who can ply their trade on unsuspecting senior citizens and tourists. The fraud and serious narcotics cases have provided an abundant and oft-times lucrative criminal law practice.

The city of Miami was originally included in the sample because of its sizable Cuban population, of which many are middle-class professionals, such as doctors and lawyers. Despite the numerous Cubans arrested for crimes in Miami, Cuban lawyers are rarely hired. One lawyer explained this situation by pointing out that the Cubans, like most other criminal defendants, realize that you need a lawyer with inside connections, and since the Jewish lawyers are thought to have those connections, Cubans avoid using their countrymen.

Miami was the only city studied where criminal lawyers complained about abuses of a referral system. Several civil attorneys would refer cases to criminal lawyers and demand the traditional one-third fee even though the bar association's ethical code states that such a fee be paid only if the referring lawyer contributes in some way to the actual preparation of the case. Since most criminal lawyers depend upon civil lawyers for many of their best clients, they must swallow their pride and kick back the money. Refusal to pay the fee would mean loss of referrals, which would then be directed to another criminal lawyer more desperately in need of cases.

CHICAGO

This city has the most unusual feature of two court systems—one for the 'rich and one for the poor. Although critics of the American criminal justice system have long argued that such conditions exist on a de facto basis in this country, Chicago has gone a step further to bless it with de jure status. The city has two criminal court facilities—one is located in the downtown business district commonly referred to as the Loop, while the other is located in a dilapidated section on the Southwest side at 26th and California. The new courthouse in the Loop is adjacent to the corridor of high rise office buildings which house most of the city's lawyers, while the older Cook County Criminal Court Building is near the jail, and the only lawyers in close proximity are public defenders and state attorneys (prosecutors), who have no choice because their offices are in the courthouse. To save private attorneys from driving out to the slums, all cases tried at 26th and California involve indigent defendants using public defenders. All cases in the Loop courthouse are handled by privately retained counsel.

Chicago has long been known as a highly political city, and it is little wonder that its courts have also had a rather tarnished reputation. They seem to be on a par with Philadelphia in terms of the degree to which political considerations impinge upon the operation of the city's criminal justice system.

HOUSTON

This is the only city in the survey which does *not* possess a public defender system. This is a statewide predicament, although local lawyers fear that such a program is imminent. The only impediment currently thwarting such an incursion is the frugality of the state and the occasionally effective lobbying efforts of the Texas private criminal bar. This leads to the second unique feature found in Houston which is its highly organized criminal lawyers' association, particularly at the county and state levels. The city is also the headquarters for two national associations of criminal lawyers. The Bates College of Law houses the National College of Criminal Defense Lawyers, which is primarily an educational association presenting some of the best professional seminars in the country. The other organization is the National Association of Criminal Defense Lawyers--currently the only viable national organization for private defense attorneys.

The city has long been famed for its defense bar headed by the illustrious Percy Foreman and his current protégé, Richard "Racehorse" Haynes, who was recently featured on a national television show as the country's top criminal lawyer. Despite rather mediocre academic credentials, the criminal bar, as observed in courtroom trials, are an exciting and highly competent group. Like the San Francisco group, one truly has the feeling that the adversary system is still alive in Houston, with the defense usually in the driver's seat.

DENVER

The Denver private criminal lawyers approach their practice in a very business-like manner, lacking the flair found in a number of their San Francisco and Houston counterparts. Their criminal practices are viewed as a business which is often abandoned for more lucrative civil practices in real estate, domestic relations, and personal injury.

As in Los Angeles, the Denver lawyers are debilitated by the logistical problem of having their practice frequently extend over the whole state and often the entire Rocky Mountain region. With Denver being the only major city in a six-state area, any person arrested for a serious crime in this enormous area would look toward Denver as the source of his defense counsel.

Variables Affecting Quality and Style of Practice

We shall now examine the legal, institutional, political, and social variables which appear to affect the quality and style of the practice of private criminal law. Within each of these categories, three to four subvariables will be defined and examined. It is best to view each of these variables as a continuum on which each of the cities may be placed relative to each other. Since many of the concepts do not lend themselves to clearly quantifiable terms, the parameters for each variable will be set by the two cities which merit placement at either of the extreme ends of the continuum (relative, of course, to the rest of the cities visited).

The first variable to be examined, the amount of discovery generally provided to defense counsel, establishes a continuum whose parameters stretch from Miami and Los Angeles, where the district attorney is required to turn over practically everything, to New Orleans at the opposite end, where defense counsel receive the barest of information. The federal rules of discovery, which apply to lawyers in Washington, D.C., fall about midpoint between these poles. In addition to the mere ranking of cities upon these selected continuums, this section will also evaluate the significance of a city's placement at a particular point. In other words, referring to our earlier example, one would like to have some idea of what practical significance it is to the lawyer in Los Angeles, that he has open discovery, while the lawyer in New Orleans is plagued by a closed system shutting him off from nearly all of the prosecutor's information.

Before beginning the analysis, a few significant methodological ground rules and caveats need to be emphasized. First, the reader must be reminded of the temporal nature of the evaluations of each city's position on the various conceptual scales. This information was compiled from September 1976 through May 1977 and therefore it is quite possible that legal procedures or institutional variables might have changed since that period. For example, with the election of a new District Attorney in Philadelphia in recent months, that city's discovery procedures as well as the quality of the office may have shifted significantly. The attempt to provide a relative ranking of each city for the numerous variables is made for illustrative purposes and is not intended to denote a fixed position.

The second methodological feature is that these rankings are based primarily upon the subjective evaluations of the criminal lawyers interviewed. Especially when considering such difficult issues as the relative competence of the institutional variables (i.e. prosecutors, public defenders, and probation officers) one is forced to rely upon the personal opinions of the sample of attorneys.

LEGAL PROCEDURES

As Max Weber sagely instructed sociologists, the rules are rarely neutral and this clearly applies to legal procedures as well. Three legal procedures were discovered which varied significantly from city to city, and which also seemed to be of importance to the quality and style of defense that the private bar could provide. They related to (1) the amount of discovery; (2) the importance of the preliminary hearing; and (3) the role of the defense attorney during the voir dire.

Amount of Discovery: Discovery is the procedure by which the opposing sides in a legal dispute learn the essential elements of their opponent's case. In civil law, there is usually open discovery so that at a pretrial conference both sides will be able to assess the relative strengths and weaknesses of their respective arguments. In criminal law there is significant variation from state to state and sometimes, on an informal basis, from community to community, as to how open the discovery procedures are in allowing the defense to examine the strength of the state's case. In reform-minded jurisdictions, the defense also has an obligation not to keep certain things from the prosecution. Thus, the Perry Mason style of defense, in which a last-second witness or piece of evidence miraculously appears before the judge just prior to the conclusion of the trial, is a fictional account of criminal procedure designed to build suspense at the cost of distorting reality.

Whether a court system utilizes open or closed discovery is of crucial importance to the defense attorney. It can greatly affect the lawyer's relationship with his client. In an open system, the lawyer can go straight to the prosecutor's files and obtain an official set of the facts of the case, which usually amount to the essentials of the state's case against the defendant. By learning the facts of the prosecutor's case, the defense attorney need not face the difficult task of trying to force his client to voluntarily disclose this information. Nearly all lawyers interviewed felt that clients' veracity is questionable and in need of thorough verification. This forces the attorney to devote extra hours, frequently wasted, verifying a client's version of the facts, which also puts a strain on their relationship—especially when the attorney is forced to confront the defendant with his prevarications.

A lack of adequate discovery may also impede an early or at least an intelligent plea negotiation, which may eventually result in a jury trial and severe sentence or a premature settlement of the case without an aggressive defense. In the cities which tended toward closed discovery, there was often a failure to plea bargain, and a large number went to trial, frequently without a jury. Philadelphia is probably the best example of a city whose district attorney has taken a hard stance toward giving information to the defense attorney, and where, as a result, an extremely large percentage of cases go to trial—albeit nonjury trials, which are frequently described as "slow pleas." At the other extreme, Los Angeles and Denver with very open discovery policies, probably try only one-third of the percentage of cases tried in Philadelphia. They are also able to initiate their plea bargaining at an earlier time and are therefore blessed with a significantly smaller backlog than is found in most cities with closed discovery.

Importance of Preliminary Hearing: Another legal procedure which varied significantly and appeared to have diverse ramifications was the importance of the preliminary hearings. Their importance stretched from a very short perfunctory hearing, which was frequently waived, to a long and serious proceedings, serving as a discovery tool, during which the prosecution was forced to demonstrate the existence of probable cause.

A preliminary hearing is usually held seven-ten days after arrest. The judge quickly reviews the facts of the case to decide if the defendant should be bound over for possible indictment to the higher court which would ultimately try the case. Since most judges look to the indictment issued in the higher court as the most important determination of probable cause, they will commonly transfer the case upwards with little critical examination.

A few cities, such as Los Angeles and Denver, viewed the preliminary hearing as a significant proceeding and would spend a long time, if necessary, inquiring into the probable cause issue. These cities hoped to use this proceeding as a demarcation point for cases which should either be eliminated entirely from the docket or reduced to a less serious charge and kept in the lower court. In these cities, defense attorneys were forced to prepare for preliminary hearings if they wanted to take advantage of the opportunity to have the case either dismissed or recharged to a lesser offense. Occasionally, the courts also permitted the defense counsel to use the hearing as a type of discovery proceeding which would clarify the strengths of the state's case. Despite the extra work, lawyers in cities with meaningful preliminary hearings (Los Angeles, San Francisco, and Denver) were most appreciative of the opportunities offered.

In the majority of cities, the preliminary hearing was not a very important proceeding—the key charging or screening decisions coming either before (New Orleans) or after (Philadelphia). Most lawyers in the cities without meaningful preliminary hearings were envious of the few locales where it was an important stage. Meaningful hearings seemed to be closely related to the general willingness of a court system to open up its discovery proceedings and allow the defense a viable opportunity to probe and examine the strength of the prosecution's case. As one might imagine, the cities which tried to utilize preliminary hearings to their fullest capacity were able to have defense counsel initiate plea bargaining at a very early stage. They also made for better lawyer/client relationships because it was easier for the lawyer to establish the facts of a case. Defense lawyers interviewed in cities where the preliminary hearing was not being used to its full potential were frustrated and disillusioned by the charade and nonproductivity of the proceeding.

Role During the Voir Dire: The selection of the jurors during the voir dire is of crucial importance to the criminal lawyer and will be discussed in great detail in Chapter 7. Despite its cruciality in *all* jurisdictions, there was a great deal of variation as to the significance of the role of the defense attorney during this process. For fear of lengthening jury trials due to what was described by several lawyers as unreasonably drawn-out voir dires, the federal courts have taken the lead in minimizing the defense attorney's role. In these courts, the judge questions the jurors, and even though the attorneys can submit to the judge a list of preferred questions, they were not permitted to engage in any direct conversation with the jurors.

This was a difficult variable to chart because several cities have allowed the individual judges to make the decision as to how broad or narrow a role he was willing to permit the attorney in jury questioning. Thus, there may have been as much variation within a city's judiciary as between the overall policies of entire jurisdictions. With this caveat, nevertheless, Washington, D.C. and New Orleans seem to have been least willing to permit the attorneys much questioning leeway, while Denver and San Francisco were most willing to allow lawyers to question jurors directly.

As expected, jury trials in cities which permitted the lawyer an expanded role during the voir dire did experience longer trials than did jurisdictions which exercised a restrictive view. Whether the amount of difference in the length of trials is sufficient to warrant an incursion into the defense attorney's role is an issue too complex to be adequately dealt with here. It was clear, however, that virtually every lawyer interviewed wanted an opportunity to *directly* question the jurors. They strongly believed that the more they could find out about them, the greater the opportunity to interact with them, the better

Figure 2.2: LEGAL PROCEDURES

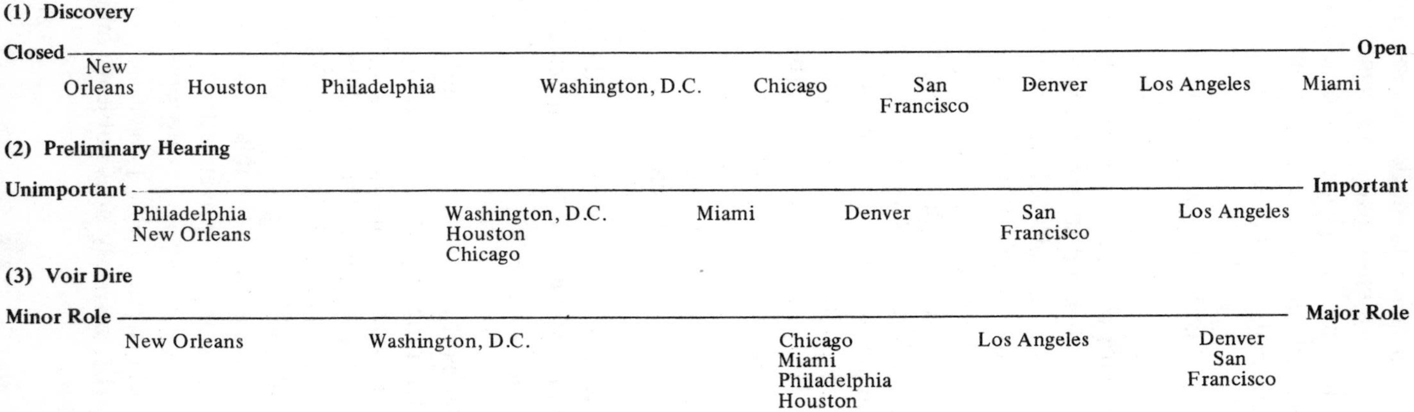

(1) Discovery

Closed ———————————————————————————————————— Open

| New Orleans | Houston | Philadelphia | Washington, D.C. | Chicago | San Francisco | Denver | Los Angeles | Miami |

(2) Preliminary Hearing

Unimportant ———————————————————————————————— Important

| Philadelphia New Orleans | Washington, D.C. Houston Chicago | Miami | Denver | San Francisco | Los Angeles |

(3) Voir Dire

Minor Role ——————————————————————————————— Major Role

| New Orleans | Washington, D.C. | Chicago Miami Philadelphia Houston | Los Angeles | Denver San Francisco |

chance they would have to devise a reasonable strategy for
rejecting jurors that would convict the client.

Figure 2.2 illustrates the placement of all cities on the three
legal issues selected for discussion. It is interesting to note the
consistent location of cities on the different continuums.

INSTITUTIONAL VARIABLES

Beyond its formal legal procedures and rules, the criminal
justice system must also be viewed as an institution composed
of a number of actors and subgroups whose performance may
greatly influence the stability of the entire system. Therefore,
when one wishes to examine the behavior of the private criminal lawyer, the analysis must also focus upon the other groups
or organizations who are also inextricably involved in the
administration of justice. Examples of these organizations are
the public defender's program, the prosecutor's office, and the
probation department. The strengths and weaknesses of these
actors are of key importance to the private defense counsel.
Two additional issues to be examined are the degree of regionalization of the court system and the geographic distance between the criminal courthouse and the major business district
where the city's elite attorneys are located.

Size and Quality of the Public Defender Program: Of all the
variables discussed within this section, the size and quality of
the local public defender program appears to have the most
direct impact on the private defense bar. In strictly economic
terms, the private criminal lawyers are in competition with the
public defender's office. The larger and more respected the local
public defender program, the greater the percentage of cases
they will be handling, leaving the remainder to the private bar.
Such cities as Los Angeles, Denver, Miami, and Philadelphia
have not only large public defender staffs but programs of high
quality. Defendants sense that they can receive virtually the
same quality defense at the public defender's office as they
would get from the type of private attorney in their price range.
The four cities listed above who do possess high-quality programs receive between 70-80 percent of the criminal court
caseload, and that certainly does not leave much for the private
criminal attorney.

A few cities may have large public defender staffs but do not have the reputation within the community. San Francisco is an example of a jurisdiction with a fairly large staff, which has failed to win the public's support. Such programs have continued to be viewed as political offices which have maintained a number of second-rate lawyers who have paid their political dues and are rewarded with a "soft job." At the far end of the spectrum are those cities whose public defender programs are understaffed (New Orleans), underworked (Washington, D.C.), or nonexistent (Houston).

Competence of Prosecutor's Office: The practices and capabilities of the prosecutor's office are also of major interest to the criminal lawyer, who, naturally, is most concerned with the competence of his opponent. This competence may be based upon the quality of individual prosecutors, the investigative resources available to their office, or simply their close working relationship with the judiciary. The prosecutor's office can determine policies in such key areas as discovery, plea bargaining, and sentencing. Most lawyers, as well as the majority of students of the administration of justice, regard the prosecutor's office as the most powerful organization within the criminal justice system, exceeding even the judiciary.[4]

The most respected prosecutorial staff was found in Washington, D.C., where the U.S. Attorneys are given that responsibility. Not only do these U.S. Attorneys have excellent investigative resources, and an absence of the budget problems plaguing most municipal prosecutors, but their high pay and solid reputation allows them to select staff members from hundreds of qualified applicants from all over the country. The defense attorneys in the district know that once the U.S. Attorney has decided to go to trial, he will have a real fight on his hands. The Los Angeles and recently the San Francisco district attorney's offices are right behind Washington in terms of competence, leadership, and reputation.

One of the primary reasons for a prosecutor's office failing to achieve a high degree of competence relates to the quality of leadership and the resulting *esprit de corps* of the office. In both Philadelphia and New Orleans one finds prosecutor's offices plagued by internal strife and low morale. The blame for this condition was generally placed on the district attorney—

Figure 2.3: INSTITUTIONAL VARIABLES

Quality of Public Defender

Lowest —— Highest

| Houston | Washington, D.C. | New Orleans | Chicago | San Francisco | Philadelphia | Los Angeles | Miami | Denver |

Quality of Prosecutor

Lowest —— Highest

| Philadelphia | New Orleans | Chicago | Houston | Denver | San Francisco | Miami | Los Angeles | Washington, D.C. |

(Progressivism)
Professionalism of Probation Department

Lowest —— Highest

| Houston | New Orleans | Miami | Chicago | Denver | Philadelphia | San Francisco | Los Angeles | Washington, D.C. |

Harry Connock in New Orleans and F. Emette Fitzpatrick in Philadelphia. Assistant prosecutors complained of a lack of responsibility and loss of freedom as the main reasons for the low morale and high turnover of personnel. Private criminal lawyers in these cities felt very confident about going to trial, particularly if they knew they were going to be facing an inexperienced prosecutor.

Competence and Professionalism of Probation Department: In cities where the judge relies on a presentence report written by the probation department, defense attorneys are very much interested in working with probation officers.[5] The most professional probation departments, Washington, D.C., Los Angeles, and San Francisco, permit and sometimes encourage the defense attorneys to contribute to the presentence report or at least check it ahead of time for erroneous information.

In cities where the presentence report is not so significant a factor in influencing the judge's sentencing decision, probation departments are less likely to be professional. Criminal lawyers would therefore disregard them and try to write their own reports or prepare careful statements of mitigating factors for the presentence hearing. This was found to be the case in Miami and, to a lesser degree, New Orleans.

A third variation was found in probation departments that were desperately overworked or prosecution-oriented in their reports. Criminal lawyers in such communities were, again, forced either to write up their own reports stressing the defendant's good character or else try to discredit the probation report at the presentence hearing by disclosing errors and prejudicial and unfounded statements. The probation departments in Chicago and Houston fell into this category.

GEOGRAPHIC VARIABLES

Degree of Court Regionalization: A few of the cities studied have decentralized court systems in which criminal cases are tried in a number of regional courts dispersed throughout the city. Although Los Angeles is the extreme example, San Francisco and Chicago have also begun to move in this direction. The Los Angeles experience needs to be carefully examined because other cities are experimenting or at least contemplating similar regional courthouses.

In Los Angeles the decentralization has totally destroyed the chance for the development of an organized, or at least cohesive, private criminal law bar. Because criminal cases are scattered throughout the extensive Los Angeles County, the legal community is equally scattered. Without one central criminal courthouse, no "5th Streeters" or "Bryant Streeters" could develop.

A second hardship on the legal community besides the loss of fraternity is the complicated logistical problem of making prompt court appearances. It is entirely possible that criminal lawyers with three to four court appearances a day in scattered court districts would be driving over 1000 miles a week. One Los Angeles lawyer confided that the hardest thing he had to do each day was to figure out how to solve these logistical problems. He must estimate which judges were most likely to grant him a tardy appearance, in addition to engineering the optimal routes to the various courthouses. This lawyer also explained that the city's criminal lawyers drive such grandiose cars because they spend so much time on the road.

Isolation of Criminal Courts: Several cities in this project have chosen, for a variety of reasons, to establish their criminal court complex in an isolated section of town, a significant distance from the central business district where most of the legal community is traditionally located. The major impact of having the criminal courts isolated from the mainstream of the business community of the more desirable downtown area is to cause the development of a dichotomized legal community. The dichotomy is not only between criminal and civil lawyers, but also between those criminal lawyers who are forced to handle a large volume of state cases and the more prestigious ones who handle federal cases and only the most serious felons or middle-class, white-collar criminals. The practical effect of these cleavages within the legal community has been to strangle any attempts at organizing the private criminal lawyers, and without organization, the criminal law lobby will be a feckless and virtually silent voice within the criminal justice system and the state and federal legislatures. The cleavages have also handi-

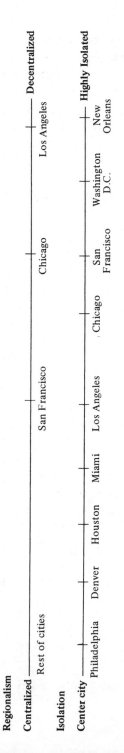

Figure 2.4: GEOGRAPHIC VARIABLES

capped criminal lawyers vis-à-vis the rest of the legal profession, especially within their formal organizations.

Cities whose criminal courts have been isolated in run-down sections of town are San Francisco (with its Bryant Street Bar), Washington, D.C. (with its 5th Street Bar), and New Orleans (with its Tulane and Broad Bar).

Figure 2.4 briefly summarizes the two geographic variables as they affect the various cities in the survey.

POLITICAL FACTORS

The judicial branch of government in this country has been idealized as an apolitical institution whose goal of equal justice under the law must be achieved without outside interference. Realistic observers of the courts have concluded, however, that politics still exert an influence upon judicial behavior.[6] The amount of this political influence varies from jurisdiction to jurisdiction and manifests itself in a variety of forms. Some of the more common ones involved the selection of judges, favors for interest groups, campaign contributions, and a diverse body of unethical practices by lobbying groups and concerned individuals.

Degree of Politization of Prosecutor's Office: In arriving at an estimate of the degree of politization of a city's criminal justice system, the researcher must examine both the prosecutor and the judge. Prosecutors appear to fall within two categories—either the career type who is devoting his life to fighting crime in his city and is disinterested in political advancement, or the political activist who is using the prosecutor's office as a stepping stone to higher political achievements. In the sample of cities visited, the prosecutors in Philadelphia, Chicago, and New Orleans clearly fell into the role of political activists while those in Miami, Los Angeles, and Washington were career activists. Because of their rather short tenure in office, it is difficult to categorize the prosecutors in San Francisco and Houston.

The prosecutorial role of either careerist or politician has important ramifications for the private criminal lawyers. In political offices, the prosecutors are less likely to be experienced since elections are continuously sweeping large numbers of prosecutors in and out of office. This is an aid to the defense attorney considering trial against an assistant district attorney who has little trial experience. On the other hand, in the cities visited, the political prosecutors kept a very tight rein on their assistants, and this lack of independence was found to greatly restrict their plea bargaining capabilities. They would have to receive approval from superiors at every stage of the negotiation, a frustrating process which inevitably led to many trials that initially possessed bargaining possibilities. Assistant prosecutors within careerist offices were usually granted significantly more decision-making independence. This was probably related to the longer experience which most of them possessed compared with short-term assistants in the politicized offices.

Degree of Politization of Judiciary: The degree of judicial politization did not fall neatly into two groups like the prosecutors. Instead, judicial political activity is best viewed as falling on some point on a continuum. There seemed to be no relationship between the selection process (elected vs. appointed) and the degree of politization. The general political nature of the community and whether it tolerated judicial politics were important but very difficult to operationalize in even quasiscientific terms. There appeared to be a breakdown into the older cities with the remnants of a traditional political machine, such as Philadelphia, Chicago, and New Orleans, as contrasted with newer reform cities whose progressive spirit undercut the development of such a "machine" system. The judicial systems of Los Angeles, Denver, and Washington, D.C. seemed to fall into this second category, while Miami, San Francisco, and Houston waivered somewhere between these two extremes. This categorization is very similar to the approach used by Martin Levin in his study of the Pittsburgh (traditional) and Minneapolis (reform) criminal court systems.

If one were to attempt to compare the nine cities as to the amount of corruption within each city's judiciary, it is believed that the relative rankings would be consistent with the politization continuum, with the most politicized systems also being the most corrupt. The controversial topic of corruption will be dealt with in greater detail in Chapter 5 and is only introduced at this point because it relates to the relative ranking of criminal

justice systems analyzed in this study. Judicial corruption is
defined in this project as a general tendency for members of the
city's judiciary to be influenced by outside factors of questionable propriety. Chicago and Philadelphia impressed the author
not only with their jaded history of judicial corruption but with
the continued presence of questionable outside influences. Los
Angeles and Washington appeared at the opposite end of the
spectrum, with honest and relatively apolitical judiciaries.

What effect did the degree of corruption and politization of
his city's criminal judges have upon the private criminal lawyer?
The overwhelming number of lawyers interviewed wished to
practice in an apolitical and honest court system. Life was easier
when one could limit oneself to the merits of the case without
being forced to consider extraneous factors such as the political
climate or the judge's willingness to accept off-the-bench
"favors." Besides the ethical qualms evolving from such an
environment was the inevitable strain of yet another form of
competition among private lawyers as they each attempted to
gain the favor or attention of the judge. Additionally, the
possible illegality of these actions might eventually lead to
disbarment of conviction of the attorney.

Newspaper Influence: In most cities the media pay scant
attention to the criminal courts unless a trial of great notoriety
is taking place. This has mixed effects. Unfortunately, the
media relinquish an opportunity to educate the public as to the
realities of the court system. By opening up the behavior of the
judges and others in the criminal justice system to public
scrutiny, their level of performance might be better evaluated,
otherwise the warped images presented by television shows will
continue to serve as the public's source of knowledge. Also on
the negative side, the newspapers who actively cover the criminal courts seem intent upon chastizing lenient judges, whose
attempts at fair and impartial justice shock the conservative and
prosecution-oriented editorial staffs who control most of our
nation's major newspapers. The result of such newspaper coverage has been to have the judiciary constantly looking over its
shoulder trying to render decisions which will not be upsetting
to the media or the general public. Again, as one ranks the
newspaper involvement in criminal justice matters in the nine

cities, the picture resembles the one for politization and corruption. The Philadelphia *Inquirer* and the Chicago *Tribune* head the list at one extreme, while the Washington *Post*, the Los Angeles *Times*, and the Miami *Herald* are found at the other.

The criminal lawyers, as expected, preferred to not have the media publicize cases because of their consistent proprosecution bias. Several lawyers felt that their clients' cases were seriously damaged by newspaper articles depicting the sordidness of the supposed offenses as well as intimidating the judges into taking strong proprosecution positions.

A few lawyers enjoyed having their name and picture in the media for both egotistical and pragmatic reasons—pragmatic in the sense of strengthening their reputation within the community. The outcome of the case was irrelevant since most readers soon forget which side was victorious. On balance, however, most lawyers were upset by newspaper publicity and felt that it made a difficult defense impossible.

SOCIAL FACTORS

Thus far all the variables which have been assessed for their possible influence on the quality and style of criminal law have been directly associated with the internal operations of the criminal justice system. The final group of factors are designated as social because they are all external to criminal justice system and its principal actors. They relate primarily to the broader range of societal pressures and influences which seem to have a bearing on the private practice of criminal law.

Degree of Inbred Nature of the Bar: Jerome Carlin's study of solo practitioners depicted a group of locally raised and educated lawyers.[7] Since many criminal lawyers are solo practitioners or operate out of three-four person associations, the author was interested in seeing if Carlin's observations of Chicago lawyers was also accurate for the geographically dispersed group of cities surveyed in this project. Although many lawyers practiced criminal law in the city where they were raised, visible differences did emerge between the cities. Philadelphia was the most inbred city in the sample with twenty-two out of twenty-three criminal lawyers interviewed being both locally raised and educated (undergraduate and law school). In Chicago and New Orleans the proportion of local recruits was nearly 75 percent and in Houston and Denver approximately 60 percent. At the opposite end of the scale, Washington, D.C., followed by Miami and San Francisco had the smallest percentage of home-grown legal talent. In Washington, D.C., and San Francisco, one found almost a national bar as lawyers flocked to these cities from all over the country.

The effect of the degree to which criminal lawyers originate in the local area is difficult to assess. One possible result of a highly inbred legal community might be an increased fraternization as well as greater opportunities for developing local criminal law organizations. This was found to be true in both Philadelphia and Houston, which seemed to have both the best organized and most socially affable collection of criminal lawyers in the sample. Each group of criminal lawyers had its favorite "watering hole," and by 7:00 these establishments would be brimming over with attorneys exchanging anecdotes and bragging about their latest courtroom victory. In San Francisco, Washington, and Miami criminal lawyers rarely saw each other professionally, and because of the absence of any established center of conviviality, they were also socially isolated from their colleagues.

Degree of Competitiveness: Given the strains of economic competition among the urban criminal lawyers, any additional impetus to this struggle is certainly undesirable. Nevertheless, the attractiveness of certain cities as places to live and practice law has served to exacerbate the omnipresent competitive pressures. The result of practicing criminal law in one of these popular locales is to generally exclude all but the most capable and make it nearly impossible for beginning criminal lawyers to survive. San Francisco and Washington, D.C. appeared to be the most desirable cities for criminal lawyers. The lawyers came from every region of the country, usually bringing along an impressive vita including prestigious academic credentials. This was found to be especially true among the younger lawyers, although it was surprising to find so many middle-aged attorneys from Philadelphia, San Diego, and New York coming to San Francisco in mid-career. The cultural and scenic attractiveness of the city were given as the main reasons for the move.

Miami also seemed to attract lawyers from the northeast at all stages of legal careers, probably because of the attractiveness of the area—particularly its climate.

What about the criminal lawyers in cities such as Philadelphia and Chicago that do not possess geographical attractiveness? Since competition for criminal cases is keen everywhere, the decrease in competition was nearly imperceptible. Beyond this, however, the criminal lawyers seemed to be much more congenial socially and had generally closer ties professionally with one another.

Ethnic Homogeneity of Clientele: An interesting variable which appears to influence both jury selection and client relationships is the ethnic homogeneity vs. heterogeneity of the local community. Washington, D.C., with a population nearly three-fourths black, was by far the most homogeneous city studied, while San Francisco and Chicago presented a wide array of ethnic groups ranging from American Indians to Chicanos and Southerners. Most of the remaining cities were approximations of Chicago and San Francisco.

With a widely divergent group of jurors, the criminal lawyer must make many difficult judgments about what the implications of a defendant's or juror's ethnic background will be. This must also be analyzed keeping in mind the several cross-pressures such as economic condition, religion, and job which may diminish or increase the significance of the ethnic background. It simply is another complicating factor for the criminal lawyer who already has his job cut out for him.

The criminal lawyer also finds his job complicated by having ethnic clients with language problems. Thus, in Los Angeles, San Francisco, and Houston, where many of the arrested are Mexican-Americans, the criminal lawyer must devise some way to surmount this language barrier. Some have hired translators or associates who speak Spanish, while the most desperate have returned to school themselves. Most of the Cubans in Miami seemed to be of a slightly higher social class and either spoke English themselves or had a member of their family present who did.

In conclusion, the lasting impression is one of great diversity between the cities visited and of the significance of local institutions and practices to the private defense attorney.

NOTES

1. Arthur Wood, *Criminal Lawyers* (New Haven, Conn.: Yale University Press, 1967).

2. Albert W. Alschuler, "The defense attorney's role in plea bargaining," *Yale Law Journal*, May 1975, p. 1179.

3. Herman Schwartz, "Trial lawyer and the future," *Trial*, 7:2, July/August, 1971.

4. See Abraham Blumberg's *Criminal Justice* or George Cole's *The American System of Criminal Justice* as leading and respected advocates of this position.

5. Example of where the probation department appears unimportant is in Houston where Texas law permits jury to sentence defendant in certain circumstances.

6. Best recent example of this idea is Martin Levin's *Urban Politics and Urban Justice* (Chicago: University of Chicago Press, 1976).

7. Jerome Carlin, *Lawyers on their Own* (New Brunswick, N.J.: Rutgers University Press, 1962).

Chapter 3

WHO THEY ARE: A GROUP PORTRAIT

Before examining how criminal lawyers ply their trade, it is important first to view them as human beings and determine what kinds of people have chosen to become private criminal lawyers and what paths they have followed to reach this position. We believe that at least partial answers to these questions can be provided. Additional topics covered in this chapter include attempts at defining and classifying the major personality types within the sample of criminal lawyers, their professional activities, and their perception of their occupational status.

Personal Background Data

AGE

The most notable characteristic of this sample of criminal lawyers is the absence of the very young and the fairly old. Nearly seventy percent of the sample are between the ages of thirty and fifty, with the median age for the entire group being forty-two. The reason for the late start as criminal lawyer is probably that so many served a three-four year apprenticeship at the district attorney's office or some other public agency. Law students, who usually graduate in their midtwenties, will take a public job for a few years, often to establish future contacts for their private practice. Only 1 percent of the sample was under thirty. Once in their thirties, however, many of the lawyers left their first job and began to practice criminal law as 35 percent of the sample were between thirty and forty. Two other factors contributing to the absence of very youthful criminal lawyers are, first, that many tried other professions before practicing and, secondly, that many of the sample came from humble economic origins and had to work several years to save money for law school, and when they finally went, it was frequently in an evening program that dragged on for several years beyond the prescribed three-year full-time program.

At the opposite end of the age spectrum, only 29 percent of the sample were over fifty. Broken down into ten-year periods, 19 percent were in their fifties, 7.3 percent in their sixties, and 2.9 percent in their seventies. The major reason for the small percentage of "senior" criminal lawyers given by a large number of lawyers interviewed was that the profession simply "burns out" its talent by late middle age. The rigors of an active criminal practice, especially for those who are constantly in the courtroom, is physically debilitating. The occupational hazards of heart conditions, ulcers, and a variety of stomach problems were frequently noted among the casualties of criminal practice. Other manifestations of the pressures of the job included mental breakdowns, serious drinking problems—leading in turn, to other physical problems—and marital troubles.

Many of the lawyers in the mid-to-late forties acknowledged the imminent appearance of these physical, mental, and social breakdowns and were already in the process of leaving the practice of criminal law. Their plans were usually for a gradual departure till they would only handle one or two criminal cases of their own choosing. As an alternative form of practice they usually entered some type of civil trial field, such as divorce, personal injury, or general business. Not a single lawyer planned to move into a large corporate law firm or even knew of any other former criminal lawyer who had made this move.

The 10 percent of the sample of criminal lawyers who were over sixty offered a range of interesting answers as to their ability to survive. Most of them began to be more selective in their criminal cases. The older criminal lawyers, as a group, were fairly successful and could continue in practice on a reduced caseload because they were not under serious economic pressures to handle a large number of criminal cases. The group of older lawyers were usually irascible and feisty attorneys whose strong constitutions had endured years of courtroom battles. Being of strong body and will, they knew the limits of their endurance and with the blessings of financial security, could keep their caseload within reasonable proportions.

RACE

Despite recent improvements, the black and brown minorities were still underrepresented in the sample of cities surveyed. The entire sample of lawyers interviewed was 87 percent white, 11 percent black, and 2 percent Chicano. Although the black percentage was nearly equal to the percentage of blacks in the national population, it was far behind the average black population of the cities visited (32 percent nonwhite) and even further behind the racial composition of the lawyers' clientele, which was estimated at over 60 percent nonwhite. The Chicanos were even more underrepresented with their meager 2 percent slice of the sample in sharp contrast to their national population figures and their percentages in the cities studied.

Washington, D.C., with a black majority of approximately 70 percent of its population, had by far the greatest percentage of black lawyers interviewed (35 percent). Miami and San Francisco were most typical with about 10 percent black criminal lawyers, which underrepresented their black populations by a three-to-one ratio. These low percentages were blamed on many years of discrimination and a rather recent development in which younger black lawyers turn to politics or lucrative civil practices rather than the less prestigious criminal law practice. Young black lawyers with a social conscience were much more likely to be found in the public defender's office, which offered regular paychecks, no discrimination, and social respectability. Older blacks were very resentful of their treatment by white judges in the "old days" but generally believed that race was not a major factor in the criminal courtroom, with a few exceptions. Each city had its designated group of bigots on the bench who evoked the ire of white as well as black lawyers. Fortunately this problem seemed to be on the decline and the racial question simply not important in case disposition. A few black lawyers even went so far as to candidly admit that they thought that their race was an aid in front of liberal or moderate judges, who would lean over backwards not to demonstrate any type of behavior which could be viewed as racist.

The black lawyers all had a largely black clientele, although they thought that they represented an average of about 10 percent whites. Most black lawyers were anxious to have white clients because as one Miami black lawyer explained, "when the jury looks up and sees that white man with a black lawyer, they start to think that that lawyer must really be tops if the whites are going to him." The black lawyers were uncertain as to the reaction of blacks on juries to their appearance in the courtroom. Most felt there was some racial pride but overall, it did not seem to be of decisive import, especially when lawyer and client were of the same race.

There was some apparent tension between black and white lawyers on the question of competence. Several white lawyers in each city made comments about the poor quality of legal defense offered by the black lawyers who were recently admitted to the bar. The essence of their criticism was that many blacks had been preferentially admitted into law schools through a lowering of standards and that this policy had now spread to the state bar exam which was also charged with being unfairly graded in favor of blacks so that as many as possible could begin practice. Since none of the interviewed offered any proof of either of these forms of affirmative discrimination, it is impossible to place much faith in their truthfulness. What was significant, however, was the large number of white criminal lawyers who believed this and were willing to discuss this dubious judgment with the interviewer. It is ironic that only five to ten years ago most states were being sued by angry blacks charging that the bar exams were discriminating against them and that they usually had their cases argued by white attorneys.

The Southern black criminal lawyers have, paradoxically, made the greatest gains in recent years, yet still badly under-represent the percentage of blacks in the community. Miami and New Orleans are the two cities in the sample where this problem was most acute. The absence of black law schools has traditionally handicapped blacks seeking law degrees in Florida and Louisiana and now that most racial barriers are down for admission, the meteoric rise in the numbers of students competing for the few law school positions in each state continues to frustrate the black applicant.

Turning to the Chicanos, one finds an even greater problem with a handful of criminal lawyers and a mounting number of potential clients. Even in cities with large Mexican-American populations, such as Los Angeles and Houston, only a handful of Chicano lawyers are available. The same is also true of the Cubans in Miami, who are an especially interesting group because so many of them came to the United States with Cuban law degrees and attempted to continue their practice. The bar exam and its language problem were difficult hurdles for most to overcome, but of the several who did, almost no one chose the field of criminal law. Cubans who were arrested also did not seem anxious to hire their countrymen.

All minorities appear to have concluded that their racial and ethnic counterparts are not adequate defense counsel in criminal matters and prefer a white man. Black, Chicano, and Cuban lawyers, as well as a few whites, offered the same explanation: Recent minorities (Chicanos, Cubans, etc.) have learned from the more court-wise blacks that you need a lawyer who has connections with the primary movers of the criminal justice system—the judges and prosecutors. Because this legal elite is overwhelmingly white and may be counted to be on the best social and professional terms with other whites, it is only common sense to hire a lawyer whose racial and, just to be sure, ethnic background matches the current crop of judicial officers. Thus, in Miami, with a judiciary and a prosecutor's office staffed by many Jews, the blacks have taught the Cubans that Jewish lawyers must be used in criminal cases if one wishes to have an attorney who has a chance of working within the system. Whether or not such ethnic congruence leads to favoritism is unproven and irrelevant because this is what most of the minority defendants believe.

SEX

Only 2 percent of the sample of criminal lawyers were women. The author made a conscious effort to include women in his sample but several of those contacted were too busy to be interviewed. Even with the study's methodological short-comings, it is hard to imagine more than 3 to 4 percent of our nation's private criminal lawyers being women. This is surprising given the rapid influx of women into the legal profession, and, in fact, the number of female prosecutors and public defenders is getting quite substantial in several jurisdictions. Nevertheless, few women practice private criminal law, and it has been that way for a long time.

The major explanation given by the male criminal lawyers for the absence of female counterparts usually centered around the sleazy clientele, possible physical risks, and women's lack of the necessary combative nature in the courtroom. The latter reason was the most common. It was thought that women were best at some nonlitigation type of civil cases, where their minds could be put to good use; once before a judge, a woman's self-confidence and intelligence would quickly evaporate. The success of such prominent women attorneys as Gladys Root Towle and Adela St. John Rodgers in the criminal courtroom should have dispelled such chauvinist traditions, yet to most male criminal lawyers, these few female success stories are merely exceptions which prove the rule of male legal supremacy. It will be interesting to see what the next decade holds for the rise of female criminal lawyers as their recently inflated numbers begin to offer viable competition for males in all areas of legal competence.

ETHNICITY AND RELIGION

The myth of the criminal lawyer as a member of an ethnic and religious minority seems to have validity as far as the sample surveyed in this project is concerned. Approximately 50 percent of the lawyers interviewed were Jewish, followed by 30 percent Catholics, and 20 percent Protestants. This is a rather shocking reversal of the distribution of the national population with nearly three-fourths being Protestant while less than 5 percent are Jewish.[1] The breakdown into religious and ethnic groups is illustrated in Table 3.1. In order to avoid controversy, the Jews are listed as both an ethnic and a religious group. The Irish, WASPS and Italians visibly dominate the remaining groups, with 18, 18, and 12 percent of the sample coming from each respective nationality.

The most obvious question is, why are so many Jews practicing criminal law? The answer, supplied primarily by the Jewish lawyers themselves, concerned the history of anti-Semitism in the larger civil law firms. Shut out from these elite practices, Jewish lawyers were forced into solo practices or small firms which handled those kinds of cases not taken by the major firms—personal injury, divorce, small business problems, and, of course, criminal. Even though anti-Semitism has abated in hiring practices for most firms, the knowledge of its recent existence continues to drive many younger Jewish attorneys away from the blue stocking firms, where their admittance might be perceived as a form of tokenism.

On a different level, one thoughtful attorney stated that because historically Jews perceive themselves as a mistreated minority, they can more readily identify with and desire to defend other minorities who are possibly mistreated by the majoritarian state. Moving beyond these questionable explanations, one may add one final contributory factor—the urban location of most Jews. Because criminal law is practiced pri-

Table 3.1: **Religious and Ethnic Identification* (in percentages)**

Religious:		
	Jewish	49.7
	Catholic	31.0
	Protestant	19.5
Ethnic:		
	Jewish	49.7
	Irish	18.0
	WASP	17.0
	Italian	13.0
	Northern European	4.1
	African	10.0
	Eastern European	1.4
	Mexican	2.0

*The total percentage is over 100. This is due to some lawyers having dual ethnic origins.

marily in cities, it is demographically logical to expect to find a large percentage of Jewish lawyers practicing criminal law. Also, as Jews entered into criminal practice, they became a haven for later entrants. Because the practice of criminal law is so dependent upon reputation and contacts, these more recent Jewish lawyers naturally turned to their older coreligionists as sources of possible clients and permanent employment.

In cities with fairly large ethnic populations, such as San Francisco, Chicago, and Philadelphia, the non-Jewish criminal lawyers were either of Irish or Italian background. In Philadelphia, for example, all twenty-three lawyers belonged to one of these three groups—Jewish, Italian, or Irish.

The next largest group were the White Anglo-Saxon Protestants with 16 percent of the sample and their ethnic neighbors from Northern Europe (Germany, Holland, and Scandinavia), who comprised only 4.5 percent. These two groups, which demographically dominate the nation, were a rarity in the practice of criminal law with the exception of Southern cities that had no noticeable ethnic population. Thus, a third of the lawyers in New Orleans, and three-quarters of the lawyers in Houston were of either WASP or Northern European ethnic origin. Miami, despite its Southern location, was dominated by Jewish lawyers, who had followed a migratory pattern down from New York.

Of what import is the fact that so many criminal lawyers belong to ethnic minorities? One might reasonably conjecture that these criminal lawyers have some sense of the plight of their black and brown clientele. It is even possible that due to their experience of oppression, minority criminal lawyers are most willing to confront the prosecution and judiciary. Many lawyers spoke emotionally of their concern for symbolically standing between the possible oppression by the state and the constitutional rights of the individual. Despite the platitudinous nature of such feelings, they were emotionally expressed by a large percentage of the sample, in a very convincing way.

PARENT'S OCCUPATION

When Carlin analyzed Chicago's solo practitioners, he discovered that most came from rather humble origins.[2] In specific terms, most of their parents were lower middle-class shop-keepers or laborers without much of an education. In this study there was a wider diversity of occupations among the parents of criminal lawyers than Carlin found. However, if one considers the general economic rise of ethnic groups in the twenty years since his book was written, the present findings may be more consistent with the earlier research.

Table 3.2 has divided the parents' occupations into three major groups with important subdivisions within each. The top economic group is professional and upper-class and includes the subcategories of lawyers, bankers, architects, and corporation executives. Twenty-three percent of the sample had parents in these professional occupations. There were only 9 percent of the sample whose parents had been lawyers, and only about one-third of these were known as criminal specialists. It was surprising to hear from a large number of the interviewees that they strongly opposed their children becoming criminal lawyers. Most gave the profession's economic hardships and debilitating effect on family life as their prime reasons for this stand.

The second occupational category is defined as middle-class and includes small business owners, skilled craftsmen, lower-level managers, and salesmen. This category attracted the parents of 63 percent of the sample with small businessmen (27 percent) and low-level managers (20 percent) accounting for the

Table 3.2: **Parents' Occupation (in percentages)**

Professional:		
	Lawyer	9.4
	Banker	1.2
	Corporate executive	3.9
	Professional miscellaneous	9.4
Middle Class:		
	Salesman	15.3
	Low-level bureaucrat	15.3
	Craftsman	1.4
	Low-level management	4.7
	Small business	27.0
Lower Middle:		
	Farmer	4.7
	Laborer	8.2

large majority. The final category is defined as working-class, which is somewhere between the middle and lower socioeconomic status. Only 13 percent of the sample came from these lower backgrounds, and their parents were either farmers (4.7 percent) or laborers (8.2 percent).

WHERE RAISED

As one might expect, most of the criminal lawyers were raised in the city in which they now practiced (57.3 percent). This is in sharp contrast to national census figures, which have most of our nation shifting locale every five years,[3] but these lawyers realized the importance of deep community roots, especially as an aid in obtaining clients. Philadelphia, as previously noted, is the most inbred city with twenty-two out of twenty-three lawyers interviewed being raised in the "City of Brotherly Love." Chicago is almost as inbred, with 90 percent of the lawyers raised locally and the few outsiders coming from within the region.

At the opposite end of the continuum, Washington, D.C., San Francisco, and Miami attracted a large percentage of outsiders from other regions of the country although Washington did have a large percentage from other mid-Atlantic communities. Only about one quarter of the criminal lawyers in Washington and San Francisco were local, with San Francisco's bar having migrated from the farthest reaches of the country. The cultural and scenic attractiveness of San Francisco and the political and governmental happenings of Washington were the reasons given by most lawyers for the appeal of these cities.

Miami is an interesting and unusual case in that 65 percent of its lawyers did come from another region—the New York metropolitan area. What developed were two sharply contrasting groups of lawyers—the Jewish émigrés from New York and the WASP types who had been long-time residents of the area. Denver and Los Angeles also attracted many outside lawyers (approximately 40 percent in each city), but they came from widespread areas. The national sample, as illustrated in Table 3.3, had 57 percent locally raised, with an additional 6.5 percent from the same state and 5 percent from the same region. This left nearly a third of the criminal lawyers who had come from outside the region. This

Table 3.3: Where the Lawyers Were Raised (in percentages)

	Local	State	Region	Outside Region
Houston	22	33	27	18
Washington, D.C.	27	–	33	40
Denver	62	–	–	38
Philadelphia	96	–	–	4
San Francisco	31	6	–	63
New Orleans	58	17	9	17
Miami	36	–	–	64
Los Angeles	55	–	–	45
Chicago	92	–	–	8
National Average	57.3	6.5	5	31

mobility appears to contradict nationally what Carlin found in Chicago, albeit our Chicago findings were in agreement. The implications of the degree of inbred nature of the criminal law bar as a variable affecting the style and quality of local practice are discussed in Chapter 2.

EDUCATION

The quality of undergraduate and legal education was divided into four categories. The highest rated were the top twenty schools according to the American Council on Education and include the Ivy League and most prestigious institutions in the Midwest and Far West. Twenty percent of the sample attended these prestigious schools as undergraduates, and the percentage of those who graduated from this highest stratum of law schools was twenty-five. The next category were quality schools believed to have national reputation. This group, totaling approximately fifty, included the major state universities as well as private schools, such as Tulane, Vanderbilt, and Duke. Approximately a third attended these schools as undergraduates, but only 26 percent went to them for law school. The third category, adequate schools with regional and state reputation, had the highest percentage of undergraduates, 36 percent. At the bottom of the four groups were the lower-quality schools, recognized only within the local area. These were frequently evening or part-time programs specifically gearing the student toward passing the bar exam. Attendance at this lowest rung

Table 3.4: Quality of Education (in percentages)

	Undergraduate	Law School
Highest national reputation (top 20)	20.0	25.4
Quality school with national reputation	32.5	33.0
Adequate school with regional or state reputation	36.3	26.9
Lower-quality school, only locally recognized	16.0	14.6

should not condemn the graduate to poverty since our present Chief Justice of the U.S. Supreme Court graduated from just such an institution in St. Paul. Only 16 percent of the sample graduated from these lower-quality schools as undergraduates, and a slightly lower percentage (14.6 percent) matriculated there for law school. Given the Carlin study, one is surprised not to find a larger percentage attending these relatively inferior institutions. Table 3.4 summarizes the statistical breakdown.

The percentages within the four categories were fairly consistent for most cities with the exception of Washington, D.C. and San Francisco. Probably due to the competitive nature of law jobs in these two cities, one found criminal lawyers with exceptional academic credentials, especially among the youngest attorneys. Nearly half of the lawyers in these cities attended a law school of the highest caliber. The absence of high-quality schools in the South may have skewed the results for Houston and New Orleans, but if one concentrates on the next two divisions, there seemed little variation.

The most common assumption of laymen would be to correlate the academic credentials with success in the practice of criminal law, success being defined either by reputation or financial standing. Although such an analysis lacks rigorous methodological precision, the 180 interviewees seemed to challenge this hypothesis, finding virtually no relationship whatsoever between education and legal success. This lack of relationship is primarily due to the importance of certain techniques and abilities in the practice of criminal law which are not in the law school curriculum. As Jack Evseroff, a famous New York criminal lawyer, explained, "I would have to say that about 75 percent of this practice of criminal law is attributable to experience in the practice of criminal law. Only 25 percent is attributable to cold hard research with respect to legal concepts. You learn by doing. You learn how to try a case by trying a case."[4]

The abilities which most criminal lawyers viewed as keys to courtroom success were being able to think quickly on one's feet, instant and accurate personality analysis, and ability to develop lawyer-client relationships leading to trust and cooperation. These are skills developed in life and unrelated to the philosophic and legalistic topics stressed in the law school curriculum. The lawyers interviewed were not antiintellectual but simply looked beyond academic credentials in order to judge their fellow criminal lawyers.

Personality

It is often a serious error to generalize about the wide range of psychological behavior patterns observed during this study, but a rather clear modal personality type did emerge which possessed certain basic characteristics shared by a large majority of criminal lawyers. This personality type was dominated by an extremely strong ego which was usually combined with an aggressive or combative nature. Additionally, the typical lawyer was often a contradictory blend of cynicism and idealism, although usually dominated by the former.

The egotism and competitive nature are essential personality ingredients for the successful criminal lawyer. To be able to stand in front of a usually antagonistic judge and an outwardly hostile prosecutor, with a critical audience of jurors, fellow lawyers, reporters, and courthouse hangers-on, is a staggering responsibility which would seem to make a strong ego a vocational imperative.

It was interesting to note the early development of these personality traits in the lawyers interviewed as they discussed some of their prelegal experiences. Many of the lawyers were former athletes, and several, despite growing paunches, still attempted to remain active in athletic competition. One West Coast lawyer was an active rugby player on the top amateur team in the nation, while another wrestled regularly in the police department gym. Several were successful athletes, either

winning national collegiate honors or, as one exceptional individual, being an all-pro linebacker. A larger number were boxers
of both amateur and professional rank during their youth, and
their spirit never seemed to lose its pugnacity.

Turning to the extroverted and egotistical characteristics, one
often thinks of actors as being most frequently endowed with
these traits, and again it was noteworthy to find so many of the
private criminal lawyers to have been former thespians. (A few
were still actively engaged in amateur dramatics, and it appeared
that even more would enjoy an opportunity to act but did not
have the time.) The ability to act and deceive the audience as to
one's true feelings is a critical ability for the private criminal
lawyer. Not only must he convince the jury of the strength of
his legal arguments, he must also himself appear to be convinced
of his client's innocence. This is especially important since
many jurors during the course of a trial begin to judge the
defendant by his lawyer's performance. Since many of the
lawyer's clients are guilty of some crime, if not the specific one
charged, it is imperative that this deception take place.

Despite the identification of this recognizable modal personality type, the lawyers were still a fascinating collection of
unusual individuals. In order to try and capture some of this
variation, we will present six divergent personality types which
were present in all cities.

The dedicated newcomer: In nearly every city there were
always two to three dedicated newcomers, who were characterized by enormous energy, modest egos, high intellectual
abilities, and disappointing financial assets. Washington, D.C.
had the largest collection of this type, primarily because of the
presence of an assigned counsel system which would throw out
a few cases to everyone. These young lawyers, often coming
from the top law schools in the nation, soon became a bitter
group. Their economic situation, their shoddy treatment by the
court, and their generally low status, were constant sources of
discontent within the legal community. At least half of them
realistically estimated they could not continue in the practice of
criminal law for more than another twelve-eighteen months.
They will be a grave loss.

Strictly a business: Several of the lawyers who had been in
the criminal practice for a few years developed cynicism to the

degree that they only viewed their firm as a business and could not be concerned with broader social issues impinging upon the criminal justice system or with their clientele's social matrix. Such criminal lawyers were frequently "wholesalers" who dealt on a volume basis and negotiated the large majority of their cases. They were only concerned with an efficient business operation in which the satisfied client was only one of many concerns. This did not mean they were not good lawyers, nor unable to try a case, or even disdained by their clients. It was merely a posture which connoted a business specialization in which the client's psychic needs and the lawyer's humanitarian ideals were not to be found.

Flamboyant and colorful: A few of the criminal lawyers interviewed were the flamboyant and colorful stylists that the public so often associates with the successful defense attorney. Although the superstars of the profession—men such as Percy Forman and F. Lee Bailey—were not interviewed, each city had a handful of lawyers whose lifestyles were faithful to this stereotype. One West Coast lawyer whose practice was dominated by pimps and prostitutes, operated out of a penthouse office on the Sunset Strip. His staff were beautiful young ladies of starlet quality who were housed in palatial offices including a rooftop swimming pool surrounded by life-size Greco-Roman statues. The waiting room and the lawyer's private office were like art galleries with a dozen original paintings from the French Romantic period lining the walls. The lawyer himself, a former vaudevillian, was impeccably attired and gestured with hands heavily laden with diamond and gem-studded rings.

Although this Hollywood attorney may have been an extreme example of a particular style, many lawyers displayed a moderately scaled-down version. These lawyers rationalized their flamboyant lifestyle in terms of a business necessity. They argued that potential clients are impressed by flashy behavior and view it as an indication of a successful practice. It is hard to balance such a rationalization with the pleasure which most of these lawyers seemed to take from their behavior pattern. One wonders if they would still be flamboyant and colorful regardless of the anticipated reaction of their clientele. It did seem true, however, that not only were clients snowed by this colorful style but that it was also remarkably effective in winning the affection of the jurors, especially when faced with a stodgy, hard-nosed adversary from the prosecutor's office.

The elder statesman or the "lawyer's lawyer": Another recurring personality type discovered in each city was the small group of elder statesmen of the profession. These classy criminal lawyers were not merely aged, but rather had won the respect of their colleagues as the lawyer who lawyers would go to if they had a criminal problem. It was amazing to see the unanimity of opinion regarding their choice as to the handful of lawyers who were repeatedly selected by the entire sample in each city. These lawyers often find their practice filled with cases involving the defense of their fellow lawyers.

As a group they possessed the highest academic credentials. They tended to primarily practice federal criminal law, and their few state cases involved fairly complex white-collar crimes. They obviously were thought of as excellent trial attorneys, but their lofty professional reputation also allowed them to be effective negotiators when necessary. Their offices were frequently the most impressive in terms of tasteful decor and prestigious location.

The irascible old-timer: One of the most enjoyable experiences of this research was having the opportunity to meet some of the irascible and feisty old-timers who had survived the rigors of the practice and lived through periods of remarkable legal, social, and political change. Although they were a small percentage of the sample (only 10 percent were over sixty), they usually provided the most entertaining and memorable interviews. Because the practice of criminal law is characterized by a Darwinian-like economic struggle, it appears probable that the few lawyers who had been able to survive and endure thirty-forty years of practice had to be not only physically tough but very competent. Since most crime is committed by the young and the aging offender is either in prison or has run out of energy, it was unlikely that aging criminal lawyers could rely upon the support of a group of clients who are from the same age group. Instead they had used their reputation in the community to pick up the children, grandchildren, nieces, and nephews of their previous clients. Also since most of these senior criminal lawyers had already made the bulk of their money during their heyday twenty years ago, they appeared to continue in practice out of love for the profession rather than economic necessity.

These older lawyers offered a great perspective for viewing the current generation of criminal lawyers. It was through these interviews that one could best appreciate the magnitude of recent changes in criminal law, such as the rise of the public defender system and the due process revolution developing out of the *Miranda* decision. Many of these lawyers still seemed to live with one foot in the past. They were frequently located in old buildings where they had initially set up practice decades earlier. Many even had their original secretaries, whose arthritic fingers had long since deprived them of earlier typing skill, but whose presence seemed a gentle reminder of past glories and a stable buttress in an unpredictable and changing world. The interview often served as an opportunity for reminiscing about these earlier triumphs, and after a short period, the inevitable scrapbooks would be pulled out as the author was pleasantly escorted down memory lane.

The brain: Just as there are certain brilliant doctors whose deficient bedside manner deprives them of complete professional acclaim, so in the legal profession are there lawyers whose mental acuity is sharply contrasted with their inability to maintain harmonious client relationships. In offering this comparison, one should note that the doctor's pleasing personality is less crucial to his success and professional stature because medicine is such a result-oriented vocation and because patients are more willing to tolerate character defects if they can be helped. The criminal lawyer is in a slightly different position because his personality is more directly tied to his courtroom performance. His ability to draw the jury to his side is quintessential, and lawyers whose behavior alienates jurors will soon have a difficult time finding clients.

These intellectually gifted criminal lawyers were highly respected by their fellow practitioners and frequently utilized by others as sources of information and advice. Their practices involved complex cases which were commonly won or lost on pretrial motions and maneuvers. In fact, their legal acumen was usually limited to the fine art of pretrial motions rather than to strategy during the actual trial. If a case of theirs was not won at the pretrial stage, they would often bring in another lawyer whose personality was more suited to courtroom performance— possibly one of the colorful and flamboyant types described earlier.

These six personality types are ideal, and in reality many lawyers would have characteristics garnered from a number of these categories. It is estimated that only two or three lawyers in each city were clearly recognizable as falling into one of the personality types, although they usually were the most memorable ones interviewed.

After examining the personalities of criminal lawyers, several important questions may be raised, although, as we shall soon learn, they are without answers at this time. First, how does the criminal lawyers' personality profile compare with that of other lawyers with civil law specialties, such as corporate, tax, personal injury, or divorce law? With no control group of civil attorneys, this research unfortunately is unable to offer any empirical evidence on this question. Arthur Wood's study of criminal lawyers did utilize several civil lawyers as a type of control group, but his fixed questionnaire failed to raise the type of issues that would have shed any light on this question.[5] Frequently, the lawyers interviewed in this sample, described most civil attorneys (especially those working in large firms) as a rather bloodless group, who appeared to be fronting for corporate enterprises and had very little personality of their own. This perception, however, appears to be of questionable validity.

The second question which seems to logically develop from our findings is whether the criminal law attracts individuals of a certain personality type or molds them once they have entered the practice. This type of "chicken or egg" conundrum is nearly impossible to solve, and common sense seems to indicate that there is truth in both possibilities. Thus, lawyers with strong egos and competitive drives are naturally attracted to trial practice, of which criminal law is the most dramatic. Once in criminal law, however, one's ego and aggressiveness must be either raised to a higher level or unnaturally sustained over a long period of time if courtroom success and professional recognition are to follow.

THE HAZARDS OF THE PRACTICE

The necessity of displaying a certain personality while facing the enervating rigors of courtroom battles and the anxiety of economic survival have resulted in many criminal lawyers suffering from a variety of physical and mental breakdowns. These manifestations are not to be blamed entirely upon the profession, but it certainly exacerbates whatever conditions are present, even serving as the catalytic device necessary to trigger the problem. It was shocking to discover the number of heart conditions, stomach disorders, and hypertension among the sample. Many lawyers commented that they viewed these illnesses as occupational hazards. One Eastern lawyer said that, "The strains of the profession overwhelm one's physical capabilities and make breakdowns inevitable for all except those endowed with either remarkable constitutions or the common sense to slow down or switch professions."

The frequency of lawyers with body styles ranging from husky to obese was also noteworthy, and this condition can be viewed as eventually contributing to some of the physical illnesses just mentioned. A Philadelphia lawyer offered a plausible explanation for the recurrence of weight problems, stating that trial lawyers are so psyched out on the day of a trial, that they are usually unable to eat, and by evening, they become starved and gorge themselves. Because of the tension, they also eat much too rapidly to allow for proper digestion. Their long hours and exhausting activities mean the absence of the necessary physical exercise to counterbalance the erratic eating pattern, and further compound the problem.

Two additional social and physical problems appeared to emerge from the pressures of criminal law practice: alcoholism and marital problems. It is impossible to approximate the number of alcoholics within the private practice of criminal law, but each city produced three-four who were willing to admit that they had serious drinking problems and several others who came close to such admissions. Again, this was spoken of by all lawyers as an occupational hazard. The problem was also heightened by the seemingly natural gregariousness of most criminal lawyers and the presence of favorite bars and taverns conve-

niently located. Several cities had specific drinking establishments where the criminal bar was an omnipresent constituency
after the courthouse was closed.

The high divorce rate among criminal lawyers was regrettable
but not unexpected. Over 40 percent of the sample had been
divorced at least once while another large group described a
family life that was virtually nonexistent. The main reason given
for this social breakdown was the long hours demanded by the
practice which robbed even the well-intentioned of the opportunity to maintain a reasonable family life. The previously
noted strong egos also led to selfish behaviors on the part of
many who spurned family life for the more glamorous pursuit
of wine, women, and song. Some also saw this romantic life as a
reward for working so hard during the day; something they
owed to themselves.

As we shall see in the next chapter, most private criminal
lawyers are loners and their practices are solo or take place
within a small firm of less than four partners or associates. Their
personalities would also seem to make this an inevitable style of
practice. Many admitted that they were in criminal law so that
they could remain free and independent. They disdained the
bureaucratic life of large corporate firms, despite the acknowledged financial rewards.

Entrance Patterns into the Criminal Law

As Arthur Wood found in his study of criminal lawyers, most
entered criminal practice later than was the case with the rest of
the legal profession. Thirty-five percent of his sample began
criminal work between twenty-five and thirty-five, and nearly
half had previous full-time work before specializing in criminal
law.[6] During the past twenty-five years since Wood collected his
data, the age of beginning criminal lawyers has continually risen
as has the percentage of those who had first tried some other
type of work before developing a criminal specialty. With only
one out of the 180 lawyers interviewed in this study being
under the age of thirty, it is estimated that at least 75 percent
of the sample were between twenty-five and thirty-five when
they began their specialization. It was also discovered that
between 80 and 85 percent of this sample had held a full-time

job in an unrelated area prior to practicing private criminal law and that approximately a third of these had had two separate noncriminal positions before becoming criminal lawyers. When the lawyers were asked why they chose criminal law, most had a difficult time answering. Although many had had an interest in the subject, it was rare to find an attorney who had carefully plotted his legal career so that he would eventually enter a criminal practice.

Of the 34 percent who had held at least two jobs prior to specializing, most had seemed to move in one of three directions—either from a government job to the prosecutor's office (8 percent), from the prosecutor's office to a small firm (15 percent), or from the prosecutor's office to a government position (3 percent). All this moving around appears to indicate that most criminal lawyers had not been clearly motivated in any one direction after law school graduation. However, once they had begun specializing in criminal law, most of the sample interviewed had remained in the area for a national average of approximately twelve years. The figures presented in Table 3.5 are for the combined types of jobs held prior to subsequent specialization.

Only approximately 15 percent of the sample had continued in the first position they obtained following graduation from law school. The figure may even be a few percentage points lower since several of those initially practicing on a solo basis have since joined small firms and altered their interest in criminal matters. The most obvious trend indicated in Table 3.5 is

Table 3.5: Previous Work Experience* (in percentages)

Prosecutor (federal and state)	38.0
Public defender (federal and state)	12.0
Civil servant (federal and state)	10.0
Legal services (civil)	2.0
Clerk	2.0
Miscellaneous nonlegal business positions	13.2
Civil law firm	4.0
Different criminal firm	14.1
Same criminal firm	8.8
Solo practice	8.0

*The total is more than 100 because many of the lawyers had held two or more earlier positions.

that a great many criminal lawyers (38 percent of our sample) started out on the prosecutorial side (either federal or local). It is even more intriguing when one realizes that only 12 percent of this national group came from public defender offices which would be at least ideologically congruent with their subsequent work. The explanations offered by the lawyers for this seemingly paradoxical development were very convincing. Many lawyers started out before public defender offices began operations and so if they desired an apprenticeship before beginning their own private practice, they had no alternative exception to gain experience and make contacts within the district attorney's office. Most lawyers believed that the prosecutor's office was more prestigious than the public defender's. Working as a prosecutor was also believed to be more conducive toward establishing good relationships with judges and policemen—two groups that would be important sources of clients once a move was made into private practice.

The ideological switch from prosecution to defense seemed to present no dilemma. Sèveral of the lawyers believed that being a prosecutor had made them better defense attorneys because they had a good idea of how their adversary would customarily handle a case. One Eastern lawyer added the comment, echoed by several other exprosecutors, that he became strongly motivated because he remembered some of the tricks and unethical behavior commonly engaged in by certain unscrupulous prosecutors. As an exprosecutor, he believed he could successfully blunt such overzealous work by the district attorney to convict a defendant who was not going to receive his full constitutional due process guarantees.

It was surprising to find so few former public defenders moving into the private sector. Those who truly enjoyed their role of defender of the indigent in criminal cases usually stayed with the public defender's office because of the financial security it offered. They knew of the extreme difficulty facing the beginning private criminal lawyer and most were unwilling to relinquish a decent and regular salary for the uncertainties of a private practice. For most, however, after two to three years in the public defender's office they were ready to leave the defense bar, public or private. They were frustrated by their inability to win more than a handful of cases. They also were upset by the scornful attitude of most defendants, who were irritated at having to use public defenders. These disappointing lawyer-client relationships contributed greatly to their disillusionment with the defense bar. It was generally thought that more former public defenders moved into becoming prosecutors than into private practice as defense counsel. Again, this was most likely due to the greater pay and prestige of prosecutor's offices, in addition to being a beginning step in political careers in several cities.

It was interesting to note the wide variety of job backgrounds from which the criminal lawyers emerged. Among the more unusual were disc jockey, professional football player, auto racer, and union organizer. The more typical jobs were in large insurance firms or business corporations while a few had been associated with labor unions in a variety of capacities. Many of these criminal lawyers had been anxious to leave their nonlegal jobs at the first opportunity. Many also stated that they had not been very successful financially in these business ventures and had gone into criminal law because it seemed to offer the chance for the quickest monetary success.

Most of the sample of criminal lawyers who had been working as civil attorneys left these practices because of boredom or frustration. The frustration was a product of the bureaucratic nature of most large law firms who handle the majority of a community's civil law problems. They sensed a loss of independence and freedom, which they thought could be recaptured in a criminal practice, despite the diminished status and monetary remuneration.

As Table 3.5 illustrates, there was quite a bit of movement by criminal lawyers from small firms to solo practice or from one small firm to another. (All of these firms were between three and eight people and handled primarily criminal cases or at least the individual involved did most of the firm's criminal work.) Over 14 percent of the sample made this type of horizontal move from one type of criminal law practice to another. One of the more interesting aspects of this mobility pattern was observed among the older criminal lawyers who had traditionally served an apprenticeship period with a famous old-timer. He would then pass along a few minor cases (which his status would not permit him to take) and then observe how the newcomer handled himself. If the newcomer passed the test, he would be entrusted with more serious cases and also would periodically receive advice and suggestions from his mentor. As a result of this apprenticeship, a young lawyer had usually had an easy entrée into a successful criminal law career. This commendable system has vanished in most cities, although many of the lawyers interviewed in Philadelphia were the last vestiges of the tutelage of such respected lawyers as Brem Levy or Tom McBride.

Very few criminal lawyers were able to utilize nepotism to aid their career. Of all 180 lawyers interviewed, only two went into criminal law practices run by their family. The reason given for this absence of generational movement was that the reputation of a criminal lawyer is the only thing he really has to offer a potential client, and, unfortunately, an individual's reputation cannot be transmitted genetically or willed to succeeding generations. Also, most criminal lawyers realize the difficulties and dismal future of their practice and actively discourage their progeny from following a similar path.

A final comment on entrance patterns into the practice of criminal law is based on statements made by the majority of individuals interviewed, which did much to downplay the romance and attraction of this profession. The large majority of the sample stated that the primary reason they entered the practice of criminal law was economic necessity. This might have meant that the only jobs available after law school were those in small firms that were willing to pass along the poor-paying, frustrating criminal law cases. Many of the Jewish and Italian lawyers interviewed, who had been systematically excluded from the large, elitist civil firms, had few options available. Many simply had to take the plunge and hang out a shingle for themselves until, after several months of near starvation, they discovered the one or two cases that would come along and provide their first victory.

Professional Activities

Most of the criminal lawyers were not very interested in partaking of the plethora of professional activities organized by various local, state, and national bar associations. This is not a recent phenomenon, as Wood's 1955 study indicated the same attitude toward these legal organizations. He found that only 14 percent of his criminal lawyers were members of the ABA while 30 percent of the entire legal profession held memberships. Additionally, only 19 percent counted themselves as active members of any professional organization.[7]

Nearly half of the present sample belonged to some type of association, but no more than 10 percent of those interviewed described themselves as being active participants in the organizations' affairs. The degree of vitality among criminal law groups varied greatly between the cities visited. Houston had by far the most vigorous group of lawyers and associations at both the local, state, and national levels. The local Harris County Criminal Lawyers' Association was an active group trying to stave off the emergence of a public defender system by organizing a more effective assigned counsel program. At least half of the criminal lawyers interviewed in Houston were regular members of the county association with 25 percent actively participating. At the opposite end of the participatory spectrum was Los Angeles, whose regionalized court system had not only spread the criminal law offices throughout the mammoth county, but contributed to the moribund state of the local professional associations. Only two of the twenty lawyers interviewed in Los Angeles were active in professional organizations at any level.

This lack of professional activity was usually explained by very heavy schedules which left little or no time for participation in organizations. Also, because many criminal lawyers preferred work in small firms or solo practices, and operated as loners, they were uninterested in this type of social activity. The criminal lawyers also rationalized their lack of professional spirit by pointing to the increasing domination of the entire legal profession by the major corporate firms, which meant that participation of private criminal lawyers was neither desired nor expected.

Although there are a large number of state bar associations with sections specializing in criminal law, most of these groups are rather feckless and failed to earn the support of most of the criminal lawyers interviewed. The Texas state association of criminal lawyers seemed to be the only exception, but even this organization seemed on the verge of collapse. There are cur-

rently only two national organizations which are interested in
the unique problems of private criminal lawyers, and both are
administratively based in Houston, Texas. One is the National
Association of Criminal Defense Lawyers, which is a fairly new
organization with a few thousand members. According to its
original founder and still its most devoted member, Tony Friloux of Houston, it is striving to raise the membership significantly in the next decade and believes that it can be a viable
voice for the profession. After talking to several members of the
NACDL, the author was much less optimistic about its future
potential. Many of its members seemed to have joined out of
intellectual curiosity or some type of professional reflex. In
either case, a large part of its membership does not regularly
practice criminal law, and conversely, a great many of the
nation's most active criminal lawyers have ignored the association. The other group is the National College of Criminal
Defense Attorneys, which is headquartered at Bates College of
Law of the University of Houston. Its purpose is educational
rather than social or political. It conducts the finest seminars in
the country for all levels of expertise and is widely respected for
the superior quality of its faculty and innovative teaching techniques. It also publishes a highly respected criminal law journal.

Most of the organizational activity among criminal lawyers
appears to be at the local level, and even though the activity at
this level is probably the most successful and vigorous relative
to state and national associations, it is still frustrated by lack of
support and few tangible achievements. Most lawyers also commented that they were just too busy to allocate additional time
for these activities (see p. 100).

As noted in the previous section on personality, most of the
criminal lawyers appeared driven by strong egos and often
preferred to work alone or with a loosely knit group of a few
associates who respected each other's privacy. Such individual-
istic professionals whose temperament and interests discourage
group efforts are poor candidates for joining and actively participating in professional activities at any level. The few who did
attempt to try their hand in these groups typically had a brief
and unrewarding experience. They were easily frustrated when
their own plans were stalled or criticized. They proved to be

unwilling to engage in the give and take necessary to perpetuate such activities. Most cities had a list of defunct associations which had attempted to organize the local criminal lawyers, but with a dismal record of failure, ineptitude and a discouragingly short life span.

Contributing to the negative image of the professional groups was the belief of several lawyers that these associations were being misused by their leadership as a means of generating business for themselves or some other equally self-serving purpose. There may have been a tinge of truth to these charges in a few cities, but generally they seemed to be unjustified rationalizations for inactivity.

The lawyers also pointed to the transitory nature of these groups as another manifestation of their defective condition. The groups only became resuscitated when a specific problem presented itself to the criminal law community, and once it was resolved, the association fell apart. The current Houston criminal lawyers association, which is so vigorously joining together to stave off a public defender program by improving the quality of the maladministered assigned counsel system, is an excellent example of this phenomenon.

One final obstacle to the development of a viable professional association of criminal lawyers is a dichotomy within the profession which appears to draw the potential members apart. In most cities there were two classes of criminal lawyers—the wealthy and successful group that primarily handled federal cases or very serious state matters, and the struggling group which would take almost anything they could get. The tension and lack of sympathy between these factions have created a cleavage which would destroy almost all attempts at producing a unified criminal lawyers' association designed to represent and benefit the entire profession.

Several of the lawyers interviewed were greatly upset by their inability to organize their colleagues into a professional group. They stated a need for such associations in order to counter the well-organized and powerful district attorney's offices as well as presenting a united front to the rest of the bar. A few lawyers even went so far as to believe that an organized criminal bar would reduce the abuses and prejudicial treatment of criminal lawyers by criminal court judges.[8]

A feasible remedy offered by a small number of lawyers was to forget about the creation of separate criminal bar organizations because lack of status and poor image would continue to undermine the efforts of such groups. What was needed, these lawyers maintained, was to join efforts under the alliance of Trial Lawyers Associations, which includes many powerful civil trial attorneys with great national reputations. The group has had a remarkable record as an effective lobbyist at both the state and federal levels. By joining with this organization, the criminal lawyers would be able to discard their own negative image and join with a respected group whose prestige and success had already been established.

Perceptions of Occupational Status

In addition to the long hours and financial insecurities, one of the most upsetting things to criminal lawyers about their professional careers was their perceived lack of status within the legal profession. Paul Hoffman offered the following comments on the problem of why there was a reluctance to enter the practice of criminal law:

> Reasons for this reluctance are not hard to find. Most lawyers consider criminal practice "grubby." Other branches of law offer more money, more regular hours, and surely a more congenial clientele. Far better to be ensconced in a skyscraper office pushing papers across a desk than to confer with clients through the bars of a jail cell. Far better to practice in a civil court among men of substance than in a criminal courtroom crowded with the dregs of society. Far better to have a corporation on a regular retainer than to have to badger clients for fees. And U.S. Steel never issues a midnight summons calling its counsel to some police precinct house. . . . So the criminal bar has become a netherworld of the legal profession.[9]

The criminal lawyers seem either unable or unwilling to correct the negative image described above. As already noted, the criminal lawyers are sharply divided among themselves and appear incapable of mounting a cohesive attack to construct a more favorable image both in the legal profession and in the general public. The private criminal lawyers further contribute to the low status by actively cultivating an image which presents them as a shadowy group with inside connections. The criminal lawyers enjoy being viewed in this perspective since they realize that it has a great appeal to their clientele, who often believe that they need a lawyer who can successfully "deal on the inside." It is also important for criminal lawyers to appear to be legal magicians who will do *anything* that is required to win a case, regardless of its dubious morality. Although this aggressive posture may be enticing to future clients, it certainly fails to convey an image which would win the admiration of fellow practitioners.

The private criminal lawyer obviously suffers from guilt by association. The public reflexively links the client with his attorney and fails to appreciate the professional and constitutional responsibility which the latter must exercise. The public seems to reason that if a lawyer chooses to defend a guilty man, then the lawyer must himself also be tainted with some guilt. Adding to the problem is the geographic isolation of the criminal courts and the lawyers' offices. Away from the mainstream of commercial activities, the criminal justice system and its many actors become a substratum of the local political scene. They only seem to gain recognition in the form of public exposes of notorious crimes while the day-to-day business of private criminal law continues outside the gaze of public scrutiny.

The private criminal lawyers are well aware of their sagging prestige but believe in a number of positive professional attributes that allow them to think favorably about their careers. They regard themselves as result-oriented practitioners who have the good fortune to receive almost immediate gratification. As one Philadelphia lawyer commented, "I love the idea of having a clean desk at the end of each day." In contrast to other attorneys whose cases may linger for years, the criminal lawyer has a high turnover business. The excitement and unpredictable nature of the criminal practice also serve as an inducement. In summary, the criminal lawyer enjoys describing his activities as "working with people, not just money" in an environment of freedom and independence rather than the stifling bureaucratic organization of most larger law firms.

The previous paragraph illustrates the tensions between the criminal and civil bar. This antagonism, especially from the criminal lawyer's perspective, was felt by nearly all interviewees. The tension between civil and criminal lawyers has been an ongoing phenomenon for many years. As Joel Auerbach chronicled in his excellent history of the American Bar, the problems started near the end of the nineteenth century as the legal elite sensed an economic threat from outside groups and began to effectively organize against them.[10]

The social class tension described in Auerbach's Marxian interpretation of bar politics, may be validly applied to the criminal/civil split. The demographic backgrounds of most of the older lawyers in the sample—Jewish, Italian, Irish, and first generation college graduates from working class roots and night law schools—had clearly excluded most of them from entrance into the elite civil firms which dominated the legal profession. In addition to past discrimination, the criminal lawyers also felt that they were more clearly symbolic of the true lawyer—one who doesn't sit around board rooms rubbing shoulders with corporate clients but actually engages in the pristine act of lawyering, i.e., litigating cases.

As the specter of white-collar crime has sneaked into corporate headquarters, in this post-Watergate era of heightened morality and stricter policing, an interesting new competitive tension has intensified the civil/criminal cleavage. Although civil firms have traditionally been more than willing to refer criminal matters involving their clients to a select group of criminal lawyers, they have recently begun to retain more of these cases within their firms. Whether this change of heart has been due to a fear of losing these clients on a permanent basis to criminal lawyers (this was the explanation offered by most criminal lawyers) or saw it as a rational economic decision, it has again heightened the dislike between both groups as they compete, for the first time, for the same clients. One interesting development related to this change of attitude is that several large civil firms are now hiring criminal law specialists for the first time to service clients who find themselves with a criminal problem. These criminal law specialists are usually former experts in federal criminal law or some white-collar crime, such as tax fraud or embezzlement. Only a select few firms have made this move, although most of the criminal lawyers are aware of its occurrence and are nervously awaiting its future impact upon their practices.

Most of the criminal lawyers interviewed were antagonistic toward civil firms and were sensitive to their own lack of status within these prestigious firms and the bar associations they control. Nevertheless, the criminal lawyers were much more concerned with their image within the general public rather than within the profession. The private criminal lawyers have effectively constructed a series of myths and rationalizations concerning the merits of their profession. It is particularly important that the general public continue to see them as the only remaining obstacle between the freedom of the individual and the possible oppression by the state. Once the public forgets this and sees no difference between the quality of defense offered by the public and private criminal lawyer, their profession will have taken a critical step toward extinction. Thus, in contrast to their rather cavalier disregard for the attitude of the civil lawyers, the criminal lawyers are most interested in maintaining a high level of public appreciation and respect. Unfortunately, they have not had the time or organizational ability to generate any clearcut public support. It will be interesting to see if the continued pressure of economic survival can unite them in an intelligent and successful campaign to raise their status among the public.

NOTES

1. Bureau of the Census, *Statistical Abstract of the United States* (Washington, D.C.: Government Printing Office, 1974).

2. Jerome Carlin, *Lawyers on Their Own* (New Brunswick, N.J.: Rutgers University Press, 1962).

3. *Statistical Abstract of the United States,* op. cit.

4. Paul Hoffman, *What the Hell is Justice: The Life and Trials of a Criminal Lawyer* (Chicago: Playboy Press, 1974).

5. Arthur Wood, *Criminal Lawyers* (New Haven, Conn.: Yale University Press, 1967).

6. Ibid., p. 39.

7. Ibid., p. 129.

8. I believe any realistic evaluation of the judicial misconduct would probably find it uninfluenced by the bar's organizational success.

9. Hoffman, op. cit. p. 23.

10. Jerold S. Auerbach, *Unequal Justice* (New York: Oxford University Press, 1976).

Chapter 4

MAKING A LIVING

General Comments on the Practice of Criminal Law

As with most legal specialists, the private criminal lawyer rarely spent all of his time and energy on one area of specialization. As Table 4.1 indicates, only 21 percent of the lawyers interviewed devoted more than 95 percent of their time solely to criminal cases. Nearly a third actually spent less than half of their time on criminal matters. The typical respondent practiced criminal law approximately 60 percent of his time. As we shall see in Table 4.4, most of the criminal lawyers turned to general business litigation or concentrated upon personal injury and domestic relation cases as an alternative to their criminal prac-

Table 4.1: **Percentage of Criminal Cases Handled**

Less than 10%	4.3%
11-25	15.9
26-50	8.0
51-65	21.0
66-80	18.0
81-95	12.0
over 95	21.0

tice. These lawyers were also quick to add that they found these civil cases much more lucrative although not nearly so interesting or challenging.

The specialization process was found to continue even beyond the subfield of criminal law as many narrowed their practice to specific areas of criminal law, such as drunk driving or gambling. Table 4.2 presents the various specialties of the lawyers interviewed. A specialization was operationally defined as any area of the criminal law which comprised at least one-half of the lawyer's criminal caseload. The areas of specialization were unavoidably vague due to the definitional variations between cities as to what crimes are felonies, misdemeanors, and petty offenses.

Nearly half of the criminal lawyers did not claim any specialization and handled a broad cross-section of all types of criminal matters. These lawyers, as a group, appeared to be defending a disproportionate number of misdemeanants. Their reluctance to classify themselves as specializing in these less serious cases was probably caused by their wish to present themselves to the interviewer in the best light. Also, because most lawyers believe that the top lawyers handle the most serious cases, few were willing to admit having a practice dominated by these lesser categories of crime. Nearly every lawyer in this group insisted on relating the details of his most recent murder case as if defending a murder suspect was an honored experience within the profession.

The two largest areas of specialization were serious felonies (15.9 percent) and federal white-collar crimes (17.8 percent).

Table 4.2: Criminal Caseload Specialization (in percentages)

Serious felonies	15.9
Federal white-collar	17.8
Middle-class crimes	4.9
Drug cases	4.1
Serious misdemeanors	3.2
Misdemeanors and petty offenses	2.3
Constitutional issues (e.g., first amendment, pornography)	1.6
Gambling	2.3
Drunk driving	1.6
Sex and prostitution	.08
All types (no specialization)	46.9

These lawyers were probably the most successful criminal lawyers in their respective cities, in terms of both professional recognition and monetary gain. The areas of specialization fragmented after these two major categories. In each city, the study located an occasional specialist in substantive areas of the criminal law, such as drug cases (4.1 percent), gambling (4.1 percent), constitutional issues (1.6 percent), drunk driving (1.6 percent), and sex-related crimes (1 percent).

Another method of classifying criminal lawyers is on the basis of their type of practice. Table 4.3 confirms the fact that most criminal lawyers are either solo practitioners or practice in association or partnership with a handful of other lawyers. Nearly a third of the sample practiced entirely by themselves, while only 12 percent worked together, in association or partnership, with more than five other lawyers. The difference between association and partnership is fairly significant. To be in association with other lawyers means to share space and facilities, such as secretaries and a law library, while there is no sharing in earnings. The group of associates simply pay a joint rent for all of these shared conveniences. A partnership, however, means that profits are joint and that decisions are usually made in a collegial or hierarchical fashion.

The criminal lawyers surveyed seemed to favor the partnership style of operation but with so few partners that there was really only a semantic difference between the categories. Very few lawyers (3 percent) practiced in normal-sized law firms, and the Edward Bennett Williams firm in Washington, D.C. was the only large (over twenty members) criminal law firm discovered in any of the cities visited. The two lawyers interviewed from this prestigious firm felt very positive about practicing criminal

Table 4.3 Type of Practice (in percentages)

Solo practice	30.0
1-4 associates	18.9
over 5 associates	2.0
1-2 partners	15.5
3-4 partners	23.7
5-10 partners	6.6
over 11 in firm	3.0

law in this unusual environment. They did not seem to suffer from the loss of freedom and bureaucratic stranglehold that most criminal lawyers imagined to be inherent defects of such a practice. They admitted that they rarely had an opportunity to pick and choose cases because of their junior status, but they strongly believed this to be outweighed by the interesting nature of nearly all the cases which were attracted to a firm such as theirs with its national reputation. In addition, they thought it was most rational to "practice criminal law the best way the best lawyers are practicing it and this is the style of our law firm." With so many highly qualified colleagues within the firm, they felt secure in knowing that they could always receive help on a tough case. They also took pride in the impressive research and investigative resources available to them. In summary, they believed they had the best of both possible worlds and were able to take many complex and fascinating cases that they could never have handled as a solo practitioner. It is puzzling that the field is dominated by solo practitioners and minute law firms despite the obvious advantages of bigness discussed by these two lawyers.

When questioned about why so many of their colleagues were in solo practice, most of the criminal lawyers answered that it was a blend of preference and practicality. One astute Philadelphia lawyer commented that he found a partnership in criminal law to be neither successful nor workable. This was repeated by many other lawyers in various cities, who pointed to a number of additional factors: (1) criminal clients want only you and you cannot palm them off on an associate; (2) your stock and trade is courtroom performance, and only you as an individual can provide this; (3) to be a good trial lawyer you must be a prima donna, and several prima donnas in one office will usually be unable to work together; and (4) there are economic hardships because you will be unable to associate on cases with others and will be knocking yourself out of many multiple defendant cases which cannot be handled within the same firm due to the obvious conflict of interest problems created.

A West Coast lawyer stated his preference for the solo practice on more personal bases, but one could sense that his attitude was typical of most criminal lawyers. He selected solo practice because (1) he was a born skeptic and did not trust

Table 4.4: Civil Law Speciality (in percentages)

Personal injury	26.7
Domestic relations	23.3
General litigation	11.1
General business	13.3
Labor law	7.7
Real estate	6.6
Miscellaneous	9.9
Tax	1.1
Workmen's compensation	1.1
Discrimination	3.3
Probate	2.2
Restraint of trade	1.1
Postal law	1.1

other people; (2) there were only a few possible partners, and they had the same misgivings about him as he had about the rest of the profession; and finally (3) he sensed a need to have his fingers in everything and suffered from an incapacity to delegate authority.

As most criminal lawyers did not spend all of their time practicing criminal law (see Table 4.1), what type of civil practices did they usually choose? As expected, Table 4.4 shows that most criminal lawyers engaged in a civil law specialty in which they could best capitalize on their abilities as litigators. Thus, personal injury (26.4 percent) and domestic relations (23.3 percent) were the most popular civil law specialties for half of the sample. Others were less specific but also showed a preference for litigation, classified in the most general terms. Labor law (7.7 percent) and real estate law (6.6 percent) were the next most popular specialties followed by a wide range of miscellaneous interests from postal law to restraint of trade, all usually reflecting some earlier academic or experiential interest.

The reasons given for selecting civil law specialties—in addition to the ones already mentioned—were that they seemed lucrative and well-suited for a future switch from criminal to civil law, which so many of the lawyers appeared to be contemplating. There was no relationship between type of criminal specialization and civil law interest.

One of the most discouraging aspects of the practice of criminal law for most of the interviewees was the length and intensity of the workday. The average criminal lawyer would work a six-day week with twelve-hour days. A typical day would begin at 8 A.M. as the lawyer tried to take care of personal business and prepare for whatever court appearances were required. Since court usually begins at 10 o'clock, this would leave the lawyer only two hours in which to straighten out his affairs. The lawyer was rarely able to return to his office until the late afternoon (4:30-5:30 P.M.) when the court was adjourned. The early evening (5-8 P.M.) would be reserved for seeing clients and for preparing the next day's cases. Most lawyers would work at least half a day on Saturday seeing clients and researching cases, while several would come into the office on Sunday mornings if extra work was needed on a complex case. Many of the younger criminal lawyers appeared to be the most driven and would put in the longest hours. A young Los Angeles attorney, who had recently left the financial security of the district attorney's office, gave the following self-analysis:

> The scariest thing for a young lawyer is leaving the security of living off the public teat. It is a cold business out here—I used to have some free time as a district attorney, but since I entered private practice I've worked seven days a week and fourteen hours a day for the first six months, but now I feel I can make it and have overcome that subconscious fear of failure, so I've been cutting back a little. I just realized it wasn't that important after I knocked 'em dead the first year. I just won't work that hard anymore.

The primary exception to the workdays described was lawyers in cities with extensive assigned counsel programs, which caused slight adjustments schedules. A lawyer in Washington, D.C., whose caseload was dominated by assigned cases, gave an example of such a modification: "My average day has me in the court in the morning to pick up a case and do some discovery, maybe a few status hearings and then maybe a trial in the afternoon or work on pleas. Catch 22 is with scheduling more than one case per day but knowing you won't get paid for waiting for that one case."

Another experienced Washington criminal lawyer was also agitated about a system which forced him to be in court early each day to sign up for the available assigned cases: "What you cannot do is take one or two cases because they can tie you up as much as twenty to thirty so you really cannot just do a limited practice. The only way to survive is to handle a large number of cases." (The unusual Washington assigned counsel system and its significant influence on the city's criminal bar will be discussed in greater detail in Chapter 8.)

The decentralized criminal court system of Los Angeles presents the city's private criminal bar with a perplexing logistical problem each day (see pp. 39-40). One Los Angeles attorney confided that he had two associates who did nothing but aid him in the management of his calendar. These assistants would call the various courts the preceding day before an appearance to try to determine when each judge would take the bench and possibly be ready to hear the particular matter. Occasionally, they would have to make a harried trip to one of the courts in order to conduct a holding action until the attorney could appear in person.

The problems of travelling great distances seemed to be increasing for criminal lawyers as the economic competition became more intense and new sources of clients must be explored. Also adding to the increase in travelling were the large number of cities who following the Los Angeles example were regionalizing their criminal courts. Recently, San Francisco and Chicago have both established several criminal courts dispersed throughout the respective cities. The growth of crime in the suburbs and nearby small towns has also forced criminal lawyers to expand their work environment. Criminal lawyers in Denver and Miami commonly had cases spread over a six-county metropolitan area stretching out on a seventy-five-mile radius from their law offices in center city.

The explosion in criminal case law during the "due process revolution," which many believe to have originated with the *Miranda* decision (or at least in the Warren Court), has also complicated the criminal lawyer's already overburdened professional existence. As one Denver attorney mournfully related, "You must subscribe to everything and go to all the decent seminars, and collect and read all the advance sheets. It is crucial to pay attention to your clients but you must also pay attention to the intellectual side of criminal law." Time after time the senior lawyers harked back to the pleasures of the old days when one could practice criminal law out of his hat but then noted that those times were long past.

Several lawyers indicated that because their workday was so exhaustive both mentally and physically, they had vowed never to take their office problems home with them. One thoughtful Miami attorney who has been practicing six-day weeks with twelve hour days for nearly thirty years, regretfully admitted that his career had taken its toll on his home life. He believed that this kind of sacrifice makes criminal law a very selfish profession because of its monopolistic claims on the practitioner. A New Orleans lawyer was emphatic in stressing that nothing about his criminal practice was ever mentioned at home. He was willing to put in long hours and get up in the middle of the night to aid clients, but his family was to be sequestered from his professional activities. He stated that it took his wife about ten years to adjust to his brutally compartmentalized lifestyle, but both now believe it has helped to sustain a good marriage.

Of even more interest to most laymen than the difficulties of the criminal lawyer's workday, is the question of his courtroom success and the types of dispositions he is able to achieve. The question of acquittal rates, however, is of little concern to most criminal lawyers for the following reasons: (1) criminal lawyers have few clearcut victories and are lucky to obtain acquittals in more than 10 percent of the cases; (2) most criminal lawyers have therefore been forced to redefine what a victory is in such vague terminology as to turn off the layman in search of a real-life Perry Mason who consistently outwits D. A. Burger; and (3) nearly all lawyers appeared to have a conceptual problem in speaking of more than one or two cases at a time. This narrow range of conceptual vision was frustrating throughout the research project as most lawyers failed to keep records about their win-loss percentage over the past year or even month. The typical respondent had little idea how many cases he had active or handled last year, let alone their dispositions. This inadequacy may be disappointing to social scientists who desire quantifiable evidence, but it is of no concern to most lawyers.

A few of the more thoughtful lawyers in the sample did try to offer a percentage breakdown of their case dispositions. They were in fairly close agreement as to the low percentage of clear-cut victories or acquittals which were actually achieved. They generally concluded that one can only expect to win about 10 percent of the cases and that anything above that indicates a superior performance. In the remaining cases, as one Houston lawyer stated, one should "get the maximum benefit for the defendant which is usually defined as a successful plea bargain." Most lawyers talk in terms of being able to help a client rather than walking him out of the courtroom a free man. As one respected Los Angeles lawyer commented, "If he can help 75-80 percent of his clients, he is doing a decent job—and this help may be simply a good plea negotiation."

With the rarity of an outright victory, defense attorneys have had to operationally redefine what is a win or a successful performance. A famous San Francisco narcotics lawyer, who acknowledged that very few of his cases are disposed of by trials or brilliant motions, commented on this issue: "So what's winning? If I get a guy with a thousand pounds of marijuana and he ends up getting a split sentence, six months, is that losing? Is that winning? What makes a good lawyer? Ultimately it's his word. When the judge looks down at me, and sees me with my little baby on my left here, he's making a judgment; he's saying, 'Can I believe this client? Can I believe this situation?' "

In those few cases that did go all the way to trial and were ultimately decided by judge or jury, the criminal lawyer invested a great amount of energy and ego and was visibly disturbed when he was unsuccessful. A few interviewees went so far as to state their intention to leave the criminal law because they could not stand the emotional strain of losing a trial and having their client be sentenced to a lengthy prison sentence. One Chicago lawyer, however, dwelt on the more positive side of the picture, stating that he truly lived for the rescue fantasy: "Winning an acquittal, especially before a jury, is like an orgasm as the foreman announces the decision. This is all I live for."

Obtaining Clients

The criminal lawyer's most important commodity is his reputation. With so many criminal lawyers practicing by themselves or in small firms, the individual's reputation takes on even more significance. As previously noted, defendants want a specific attorney to defend them, not a general firm or association, and will refuse to be passed from one lawyer to another. The criminal lawyer's reputation is not only important within the criminal community, but also within the legal community because so many cases are referred from other attorneys. It seemed paradoxical that in a profession where nearly all of the members worked in virtual isolation, they were still able to accurately rank and list all of their fellow criminal lawyers in terms of competence and showmanship. It was amazing that in each city so many of these solo practitioners could reach identical opinions concerning their colleagues, who they so rarely observed. Whether these rankings are accurate is impossible to say, but because of their consistency and the degree to which they are believed, they remain a viable factor in a criminal lawyer's ability to achieve a successful practice. The basis for these judgments seemed derived mainly from hearsay evidence from a few lawyers who had observed the subject in action in the courtroom as well as from evaluations offered by prosecutors, judges, bailiffs, reporters, and assorted courthouse regulars who had opportunities to watch the entire bar in operation.

The development of this "rep" is most analogous to the way certain neighborhood sports heroes gain their reputation for excellence. Inner-city basketball is the best example of a sport where an athlete's "rep" as a slam dunker, unerring shooter, or magical ball handler is spread from playground to playground. Challenges are made to test the legends created, and after a summer of crosstown rivalries, the reputations of a precious few extraordinary athletes are preserved for at least one more season.

Like the playground basketball star, the criminal lawyer also fears sudden dethroning and is embittered by the temporary and shifting fancies of his colleagues. One Chicago lawyer bemoaned the fact that since the criminal practitioner has only his reputation, he will have very little to leave his children in terms of tangible business assets. If his children decide to enter the practice of law, they must begin anew to construct their own reputation for it is not a transferable commodity, even within bloodlines. The reputation is frequently made on a single case which receives a good deal of notoriety either in the news or within the grapevine of a community's criminal sub-culture. Most lawyers interviewed can point to a particular case which was a turning point in their career and formed the foundation for their reputational development.

How do criminal lawyers obtain their clients? The most common way is either through referral from other lawyers (usually civil practitioners who do not want criminal cases) or from satisfied clients sending their friends and family. Despite the large number of cases obtained through referrals, the process is not without drawbacks. In Miami, especially, we shall see that lawyers and others may extort fees for this reference service although such practices are unethical. One Chicago lawyer commented bitterly that 99 percent of the time he would like to unload his referrals. He was upset by aggravating experiences with fee collection when the money went first to the lawyer who was originally contacted. He now vowed to collect his money first and made this ground rule clear before he would accept a referral. An additional problem noted by a New Orleans attorney, but present in all cities, was that you might get stuck with some lousy cases on referral but had to take them because you might be receiving some good ones in the future from the same source.

Repeat offenders also form a sizeable source of clientele but this can be a frustrating development. A Denver defense attorney commented on this disappointment when he reviewed in his mind the low quality of recent clients and found most of them to be prior offenders. This meant to him a more difficult job with less chance not only of winning, but more importantly, of getting paid. No lawyer likes to face the prospect of his client receiving a lengthy prison sentence, and with repeat offenders, that likelihood increases geometrically following each conviction.

There are also a host of minor officials, functionaries, and assorted criminal justice actors who may refer clients. Bondsmen, policemen, and runners from the jailhouse all have been traditionally associated with sending clients to certain lawyers in return for a percentage kickback. Even though the practice has declined considerably today, it is not yet dead, and several bondsmen and professional runners in cities such as Philadelphia and San Francisco still carry on the trade in a limited fashion. One bondsman in the bay city was recently sent to jail for his abuses of this practice. An old Los Angeles criminal lawyer recalled that the booking officer may still call certain lawyers if a large group of homosexuals or prostitutes are arrested, but the police have tried to eliminate such practices.

Since so many of the younger criminal lawyers have had prior experience as prosecutors, they are frequently able to pick up cases referred to them by judges and current prosecutors who know them and respect their work, and just happen to learn of a defendant in search of a lawyer. This connection with the criminal justice system is especially useful for these beginning lawyers as they attempt to pick up an assigned case. Because the judge has almost total discretion in most cities as to whom he will assign a case, attorneys who have known him and worked in his court are in the best position to pick up these cases. Because older, established criminal lawyers are often not interested in this type of case, they are more than willing to let the younger and less successful attorneys fight among themselves for these scraps from the judicial table.

Two sources of clientele which are useful to most businesses do not seem to be available to criminal lawyers. There is virtually no trade acquired off the street. For obvious reasons, people simply do not walk into a building, peruse a list of lawyers, and randomly select their future Clarence Darrow. Secondly, there is no advertising in the newspapers, billboards, or other media, nor, for all practical purposes, in the yellow pages. Although several of the states visited (California, Colorado, and Florida) were experimenting with professional specialization and permitting limited listing as a "criminal law specialist" in the yellow pages, it did not seem to generate much of a clientele. Potential clients do not flip through the yellow pages in a random search for their attorney. Also, it was discovered that the specialization and certification programs were not working very well in any of the states. Many of the more respected criminal lawyers refused to participate, feeling the stigma of their own profession just as if they had been successfully brainwashed by the more prestigious corporate law firms. A Los Angeles attorney summarized the problem by stating that "since my certification as a specialist three years ago, the advertising hasn't brought in one dime. People simply aren't willing to go into hiring a lawyer cold. They'll go to friends and people they trust and get a name and then they'll come in."

In a few jurisdictions a real problem has developed with referrals and fee splitting. In more than one locale it has caused a great deal of tension between the criminal and civil bar. The canon of ethics for the profession[1] recommends approximately a 30 percent referral fee, but it clearly states that this is to be paid only when the referring lawyer has actually done some work in the case and is clearly not to be paid merely for the act of referring the case. Nevertheless, several civil attorneys will only send cases to lawyers who are willing to ignore this canon and give them a 30 percent share of the fee. If the lawyer refuses, the civil attorney will no longer send him cases and will soon find another criminal lawyer who is hungry enough to realize that two-thirds of a fee is better than no fee at all. The problem seems at its worst in Miami, and it is on the verge of becoming a publicized scandal according to several frustrated criminal lawyers in that city.

The strategy of obtaining clients is a constant topic among criminal lawyers and has occasionally even graced the curriculums of professional seminars, which are generally thought to examine much more esoteric subjects. Nate Cohn's irrepressible criminal law seminars in San Francisco often dealt with this topic. The following comments were offered by the famous San Francisco attorney Andrew Bodisco addressing the 1963 seminar:

Of course the best way to get criminal business, if possible, is to become an assistant district attorney or public defender because you meet all the policemen, you meet all the criminal types—when you resign, you find yourself surrounded with criminal business, especially if you are nice to them.... Another method of obtaining criminal business is to pass the work along among the bar members who do not practice criminal law—especially the insurance type lawyers, the corporation lawyers, they look down on it to some extent, this is not necessarily correct though, because sometimes a member of their family or they themselves may be involved criminally.... But you have to go to court—do not send some associate or some boy in to get a police report or to get a continuance—go yourself. I notice that every time I go down to the Hall of Justice to get a police report, in effect I pick up a case.[2]

Fee Collection and Money Matters

Obtaining clients is only half the problem confronting criminal lawyers struggling for economic survival in an increasingly competitive professional world. The second half is the collecting of the fee which allows the lawyer to continue in business. There has been a myth surrounding the fees obtained by the private criminal lawyers (a myth generated in the most part by the lawyers themselves), that they are receiving fabulous salaries. What seems to emerge from this study, however, is a bimodal curve of income with many lawyers bunched at the lower end of the scale netting between $15,000 and $25,000 and several fortunate ones at the top earning annual salaries in excess of $100,000.

Since this study did not have access to the IRS records of each of the lawyers surveyed, it was at the mercy of the respondents' veracity. It is possible that many lawyers may have exaggerated their annual salaries in the hope of impressing the interviewer. It is equally plausible to imagine that several lawyers, noting the author's relationship to the federal government and its investigative agencies, may have cautiously underestimated their income. In conclusion, it can only be stated that 90 percent of the lawyers were willing to approximate their net and gross annual incomes. It is optimistically hoped that by having a sufficiently large sample of lawyers the fallacious incomes will balance each other out and leave an overall picture of acceptable validity.

Table 4.5 shows the net income distribution for the 180 lawyers surveyed based on their estimates. Most of the sample

Table 4.5: Annual Income Distribution (net)

$10-25,000	23%
26-40,000	26
41-55,000	14
56-70,000	9
71-85,000	3
86-100,000	7
over $100,000	16

Average: $42,000
Median: $34,000

earned between $15,000 and $35,000 in annual salaries. The top criminal lawyers earned in excess of $100,000 with a select few topping the $200,000 mark. The highest salary was approximated at $300,000 and the lowest at $10,000. The figures indicate that most criminal lawyers can make an acceptable income through their practice but clearly below the level fantasized by most of the public. When viewed in light of the amount of work which they devote to their cases and the comparative salaries of other professionals, such as doctors and corporate executives, even these figures do not seem so impressive. Although comparative figures are unavailable from the civil lawyers practicing in large law firms, it was generally conceded by all lawyers interviewed that they make considerably less than their civil counterparts.

The expenses of practicing criminal law are almost entirely associated with the office. This typically includes the rent, secretarial salaries, office equipment and supplies, such as copiers, legal library maintenance, and a miscellany of general business costs. The estimates of the effect of these expenses on the gross income ranged from 40-60 percent, with the average lawyer claiming a 50 percent reduction. Thus, the typical criminal lawyer in the survey would gross between $75,000 and $80,000 a year and have a net profit before taxes of approximately $35,000-40,000.

The rising office expenses are only one of several financial problems facing the criminal lawyer. A young Chicago lawyer offered the following explanation of the range of monetary pressures facing his profession: "Most criminal lawyers are forced to run a quantity of cases but this soon clashes with judges getting rid of their backlog. Then he is forced to start turning away the cheaper cases since he can only handle a limited number of cases at a time. My current office overhead is now running about $1000 a week and most other lawyers in this city are facing the same squeeze."

The basic strategy for collecting fees was getting the money "up front." Every lawyer attempted to set a retainer, which would be collected prior to going to trial. Several lawyers even insisted on being paid half of the retainer before they would officially take the case. The retainer, which was usually about half of the final bill, was estimated by the lawyer as being the bare minimum he would accept for the case. Since so few clients pay the full amount, it was often realistic to view the retainer as the entire fee. One Houston lawyer bitterly reported that he only received about a dozen full fees in twenty-eight years of practice. Thus the only way to insure payment for service rendered was to follow the advice of the Denver attorney who believed "you had to get the fee while the tears are still flowing or you never will."

With the majority of fees going partially unpaid, the lawyers were asked if they used civil suits to recover the money from the clients. This utilization of the courts was rejected by nearly all of the sample. A few would take selected clients to court when they knew they clearly had the money and could easily afford to pay them but this again was rarely the case.

Deprived of the use of civil suits to recover lost fees, the lawyer frequently had to be resourceful beyond the basic premise of getting the money "up front" if they wished to remain solvent. Several lawyers who dealt with middle- and lower-class clients tried to set up an installment plan just as if they had sold a new color television. Since this fits into the financial lifestyle and experience of the clients, it proved fairly successful. Other lawyers tried to obtain notes and collateral from the family and friends of the defendant in order to establish alternatives and outside pressure to pay. Quite a few attorneys tried to hold the money in escrow. Chicago was unique in devising a system through its criminal courts which was of great service to the lawyer in collecting his fee. It allowed the lawyer to reach into the bond slip (which is part of the 10 percent Bail Deposit Provision used in Cook County).

Thus any defendant who used the 10 percent plan to obtain his pretrial release was permitting his lawyer to have first crack at this money if his fee was not forthcoming.

How does the lawyer determine the amount of the fee? One San Francisco lawyer speaking at Nate Cohn's criminal law seminar answered this question with the vague answer of "what is reasonable," and when pressed as to what he considered a reasonable fee, he only half jokingly replied, "It is as much as you can get."[3] This rather callous attitude was repeated by a Philadelphia defense attorney who recently wrote a book about his professional life: "Anyway the family obviously had little money, but I said if they could get $4000 together, I'd take the case. They paid me fifty dollars a week and I knew it was coming right out of their food budget. But hell, if I hadn't taken it, I wouldn't have had a food budget."[4]

Most of the lawyers interviewed did not exhibit such a blatant disregard for their clients' welfare and were very thoughtful about how to set a proper and just fee. Most complained that this was by far the lousiest aspect of their job and felt very uncomfortable during any financial deliberations. Among the criteria considered in setting a fee, the seriousness of the charge was generally thought to be the most significant. As a general rule of thumb, the degree of seriousness is proportionally related to the length of the potential prison sentence. An additional twist to this criteria was that several lawyers considered the importance of the case to the individual. Thus, the chance that a middle-class salesman might lose his driver's license might be more critical than an unemployed lower class person facing simple assault or day-time burglary charges, crimes carrying much lengthier prison terms. Another way of stating this is that many lawyers had a good sense of what kinds of fees are generally charged certain types of clients and simply insisted upon what they believed the traffic could bear. This may also be translated into meaning that they would consider the ability to pay as tempering or adjusting the general fee charged in the typical case.

The complexity of the case and the probability of it going to trial would also directly affect the amount charged. Although most lawyers refused to charge on an hourly basis, they did realize that time is money, and the longer a case will take, and the more effort they must expend in preparation, the higher the fee. There always appeared to be two fees quoted to a prospective client—one if it went to trial and a significantly lesser fee if it did not. A Washington lawyer had the most intriguing scheme for dealing with this problem of time spent and fees charged. He stated that since he knows what he should be grossing on a yearly basis, he would then divide this amount by 52 and thereby work off this more workable figure. When a case came in, he figured how much time it would take and then applied it to his scale.

Each of the lawyers weighted these criteria in their own fashion, but generally they all considered the same three basic factors, seriousness of the case, length of time it would take, and ability to pay. Translated into actual dollars and cents, it is extremely hazardous to generalize about how much the typical lawyer charges in a type of case. The following examples offer a few actual fee schedules while also illustrating the great range of fees charged:

(1) A middle-aged Miami lawyer stated he gets $750-1,000 for drunk driving cases which only require about an hour's work. A felony would go for $3-5,000, murders excluded.

(2) An experienced Denver attorney who specializes in drunk driving cases charged $400 per case and could expect to handle four-five a day when he was doing well.

(3) A young Los Angeles lawyer broke his fees down into the number of court appearances if it was a felony case. He charged $250-500 for the preliminary hearing and an additional $2,500 if the case went to trial.

(4) A hard-working beginning San Francisco defense attorney asked $1,500 for a retainer and $350-400 a day for court appearances. In addition there was a $50 per day charge for research. Felonies were a minimum of $1,500 through preliminary hearings, while homicides cost $8-10,000.

(5) A famous Philadelphia lawyer with the presence of a stand-up comedian offered his unusual and amusing "hmmmmm" style of fee setting. "You come in. You sit down. I'll ask, the charge was a serious charge?

Yeah, Mr. Peruto, it was a serious charge.

Hmmmmm, well, did they catch you in the act or did they catch you later?

> They got me right there.
> Hmmmmm, did you make a statement? Did you confess?
> Yes, I told everything to the cops.
> Hmmmmm. You take a look at their faces when they tell you the story. They're looking for some glimmer, some ray of hope, something—and you're just hmmmming. It's about $1,500 a hmmmmm."[5]

As with the issue of salary, this study is also at the mercy of the respondents with regards to their fees. With this caveat in mind, the broad national trends for fees were $500-1,000 for misdemeanors, $1,000-2,500 for nontrial felonies, and $2,000 and above for felony trials. The highest fee quoted by any respondent was $200,000 in a murder case involving a well-to-do family.

Are any types of clients identifiable as good or bad risks in terms of paying their fees? Most lawyers agreed that professional criminals, such as burglars, safe crackers, or organized crime figures were the most reliable.

Middle-class citizens arrested for the first time were often categorized as being the worst risks. Despite their initial fear of imprisonment and willingness to do anything to win their freedom, they soon became angered over their involvement in the case and cynical about the value of their legal defense. An astute San Francisco lawyer commented that "once these middle-class defendants have their case disposed of, they don't really see what the lawyer did as justifying his fee. They are unable to appreciate what he is doing. All they see is a reduced charge and maybe probation and they soon become indignant and forget the whole matter and do not pay the remainder of this fee."

Beyond these two groups most lawyers were unable to identify categories of clients who seemed to have a predilection toward nonpayment of fees. The entire topic of fees and their collection was most distasteful to most of the interviewees. The average criminal lawyer did not pride himself with money nor maintain an overconcern with financial matters, often stating if that was all he was interested in, he would have become a corporate attorney. The whole issue of fee collection was seen as an irritant to the client/lawyer relationship. Fees are, consequently, collected early not only to avoid coming up empty once the case is disposed of, but also to quickly remove a possible abrasive force between a lawyer and his client so they can get on with the more important issue of preparing the defense.

It was interesting to find in several cities where organized crime was reputed to be exerting a considerable influence, that the defense attorneys had mixed feelings about defending such clients despite the lucrative fees and certainty of payment. One reason for this reluctance was fear of being associated with the underworld and its impact on their other clients. A second and more pragmatic reason was the fear of being harassed and investigated by federal agencies due to this relationship. Every lawyer interviewed who had represented organized crime figures had his taxes audited by IRS, and one Southern attorney who defended members of a gambling syndicate chose to go to jail rather than complete his annual tax return, which would have shown his fees from this organization.

Several of the lawyers, especially the more successful ones, intimated that although they rarely volunteered for assigned cases, they would occasionally take a client who obviously could not afford their fee and either handle the case for free or set an extremely low fee so that the client could at least maintain his self-respect. Two lawyers interviewed in a large Washington firm specializing in criminal law described this latter style of pro bono work. They found that if you didn't charge anything, you usually received less cooperation. Every lawyer in their firm had an hourly rate which was applied mainly to corporations. As individuals could rarely afford this standard, the lawyers must make adjustments and simply write off the loss as part of their professional responsibility to society. Many lawyers admitted that when they considered the client's ability to pay, they were ultimately allowing the wealthier clients to help pay for the defense of the less fortunate.

If there is one final piece of advice urged by senior criminal lawyers on the issue of charging fees (in addition to the obvious strategy of receiving an early retainer), it is the importance of explaining to the client the basis for the fee and the serious consequences he may be facing. Andrew Bodisco expounded on this point before the San Francisco Criminal Law Seminar in

1963: "Tell him all of the various steps you are charging for, such as preliminary hearing, arraignment, there may be legal motions, memos may be written, briefs may be written even before trial. Tell him you are paying for all these things and tell him the consequences—tell him how, as a result of this, he may well end up in San Quentin."[6]

Besides the difficulty in collecting fees, most criminal lawyers complained that the current plethora of diversion programs (a first or youthful offender being placed on pretrial probation prior to adjudication and following a period of good behavior the record is expunged) and lenient sentences were driving away business. Their potential clients were now going to the public defender because his office could just as easily get them probation as a private attorney, and they could save a few thousand dollars in the process. The implications of these programs and sentencing practices will be discussed in further detail in the concluding chapter of this volume.

Relationship with the Client

The client poses two serious problems for his attorney. How can he be controlled during the pretrial period so that he will not further jeopardize his case by criminal behavior, and how can he be convinced to be truthful and trusting with his attorney? The issue of client veracity was a topic recognized by all lawyers as one of the most frustrating aspects of their job. The following quote from a Denver attorney epitomized the frustrations of most criminal lawyers on this issue: "You just can't believe these hoods. They will fall on you in the pinch to save their own skin. I think subconsciously that some of these guys like to go to prison because of their being a big shot behind bars compared to being a nothing on the streets."

Most lawyers were not quite this embittered and tried to develop some strategy for convincing their clients to tell them the truth. Another Denver attorney would confront his clients with sworn police statements which would contradict their original version of the facts. He hoped that this might shock the defendants into admitting the truth, but he found many clients still unable to admit to their lawyer or even themselves their guilt in the matter. A San Francisco lawyer recommended that you had to keep probing but remain careful all the while not to force the client into a corner and find yourself suborning perjury. He tried to convince his clients that he was nonjudgmental and always attempted to ask his questions as hypotheticals so that the clients could save as much face as possible. He concluded that this whole issue is the biggest drain on the criminal lawyer both physically and mentally.

Nearly every lawyer interviewed experienced these same frustrations as they tried to extract the facts from their clients. Some became tyrants and autocrats, trying to browbeat their clients into submission, some tried to be friendly and reassuring, while others simply attempted to scare the hell out of them. They often had to change roles for each client and sometimes for the same client, jumping back and forth between tyrant, friend, and aggressive prober.

A Los Angeles lawyer, long experienced in the criminal area, attacked the misconception of clients who think a lawyer will work harder for you if he believes you are innocent. Such defendants he argued, are full of half truths, white lies, and omissions, and you must spend most of your time breaking this down in order to construct a decent defense.

The best device to assist lawyers in wringing the truth from their clients is a liberal discovery procedure permitting access to police reports, witness statements, and all other pertinent data. Armed with this information the attorney can confront his client with the prosecution's uncontested arguments. Hopefully this will jog the client's memory or at least let him know that you know a great deal about his case, and that he had better disclose the rest so as to insure the best defense possible. In jurisdictions where there is limited discovery, the criminal lawyer is forced to rely on his own persuasive abilities to extract the facts of the case from the client. It results in an extra burden on the lawyer and exacerbates the already strained relationship with his client.

Concerning the second problem raised at the beginning of this section, controlling the client's pretrial behavior, nearly all lawyers were extremely pessimistic about their capabilities in this area. One San Francisco attorney was in the midst of this very problem because his client had failed to appear at his probation revocation hearing on three consecutive occasions. He was also recently arrested on a charge of assault and battery. He had been a heavy user of drugs and seemed intent, as did so many defendants, on consciously conspiring to dig his own grave. One of the few strategies offered by the lawyers was to discourage the family in certain cases where a return to criminal activity seemed imminent from raising the required bond and allow the defendant to await his trial in the county jail. A Denver lawyer offered the philosophic advice to not get overly concerned with pretrial conduct because "it all comes out in the wash eventually and they wind up either back in the system or meet some horrible end." In any event, nearly all of the criminal lawyers believed that they exerted insufficient control over their clients during the pretrial period.

Certain categories of defendants did emerge as being either relatively easy or difficult to work with. The best clients who offered the greatest amount of cooperation were professional criminals, such as drug dealers, gamblers, and burglars. One West Coast lawyer favored three groups—those who were either experienced, intelligent, or very scared. The hardest or least cooperative were first offenders, who frequently panicked, or middle-class white-collar defendants, who failed to see the criminality of their actions and were angered at being dragged into a basically lower-class institution. Most lawyers also echoed the sentiments of a Denver attorney who was continually irritated in his defense of drug users. They usually did not work to kick their habit while he was trying to get them back into programs as evidence of their sincere desire to improve themselves. When they were discovered to be still addicted, the lawyer looked like a fool, and the angry judge who sensed that the defendant was trying to deceive him, would hand out as stiff a sentence as possible.

One unexpected group which would appear to be extremely difficult to work with but who were generally viewed as being unusually cooperative are persons accused of violent offenses. These defendants, especially if they are first offenders, are very open and uncomplicated. Their criminal act, although serious, is typically related to some temporary emotional upheaval, and once completed they settle back into a relaxed and often resigned condition.

The guilty client obviously presents several unique problems to his attorney. Surprisingly, most lawyers preferred to defend a guilty man or at least did not want to know one way or the other. The reason given for the trepidation of defending an innocent client is that because so great a percentage of the clients are going to receive some type of punishment, it puts a tremendous amount of pressure on the attorney to obtain acquittal or dismissal. The failure to achieve these ends with an innocent client will have such serious consequences that most lawyers do not want the emotional strain of such a case. Many lawyers never even ask their client whether they are guilty of the specific charge and only work to obtain the facts and evidence that will strengthen their case and destroy the prosecution's.

Most laymen, however, are perplexed by the ethical issues involved in the defense of a guilty man. Criminal lawyers are continually being forced to defend their position in the adversarial struggle (although few people seem concerned with the conscience of the prosecutor who is attempting to get an innocent defendant convicted). Although bored with this issue and insulted by its underlying assumption that the lawyer must share the taint of guilt with his client, the lawyers had all contemplated the question and arrived at what they felt was a valid justification. The following are a few of the more interesting and insightful responses:

(1) A Philadelphia lawyer with a sharp sense of humor remembered his best retort on this question. He was addressing a group of first year law students at the University of Pennsylvania when the question of "How can you defend a man when you know he is guilty?" expectedly was raised from the floor. The lawyer answered quickly that he couldn't speak for other lawyers but in his entire career he had had only one client who was not innocent, but then the client's check cleared the bank, giving the lawyer a 100 percent innocence rate.

(2) A West Coast lawyer repeated the story about the famous Clarence Darrow, patron saint of all defense lawyers, who said, "If a client of mine tells me a story which is hard for me to believe, I nonetheless take the story and do the best I can with it to convince the court and jury. If after the conclusion of the trial, after the jury has heard the prosecution's story and my client's story and

finally after all twelve have agreed with my client then I am willing
to concede that I was wrong in the first place."[7]

(3) James MacInnis of San Francisco preferred the following discourse
on the subject by Boswell and Johnson:

Boswell: I asked him whether as a moralist he did not think that
the practice of the law in some degree hurt the nice feeling of
honesty.

Johnson: Why no, sir. If you act properly, you are not to
deceive your clients with false statements of opinion, you are not
to be a judge.

Boswell: But what do you think about supporting a cause which
you know to be bad?

Johnson: Sir, you do not know it to be bad until the jury
determines it. An argument which does not convince the jury, to
whom you present it, and if it does convince them, why, sir, the
jury is right and you are wrong.

Boswell: But sir, does not feigning a warmth when you have no
warmth and appearing to be of one opinion when you are in reality
of another, does not such dissimulation impair one's honesty? Is
there not some danger that a lawyer may not put on the same mask
in the common engagements with his friends?

Johnson: Why, no, sir. Everybody knows you are paid for
affecting warmth for your client. It is therefore no dissimulation.
The moment you come from the Bar, you resume your usual
behavior. Sir, a man will no more carry the artifice of the Bar into
the common intercourse of society than a man who is paid for
tumbling on his hands will continue to tumble on his hands when
he should be walking on his feet.[8]

Most lawyers defended their position on this question on less
esoteric grounds, however, and simply stated their responsibilities to provide a defense in an adversarial system. Unlike
the inquisitorial system used throughout the continent, where
obtaining the truth is the all important goal as prosecutor and
judge work together, the United States employs an adversarial
system, in which the judge and jury sit as neutral arbiters
between the prosecution and defense. In addition, our country
has established certain legal principles, such as the presumption
of innocence and the prosecutorial burden of proof as well as a
constitutional guarantee of counsel. Thus, most defense attorneys justify and defend their role on constitutional grounds,
enunciating a clear belief in the necessity for all getting a fair

trial regardless of the certainty of their guilt. It is not the lawyer's job to judge but rather to defend. It is then up to the judge and jury to decide whether or not to convict.

All lawyers appeared to be able to go to sleep at night with clear consciences. A few had had isolated experiences of being a little disturbed by their clients returning to terrorize society, but they could easily rationalize this predicament on two grounds: (1) It was actually the prosecution's fault because it allowed itself to lose the case; and (2) it is still better for the continuation of the system that an occasional guilty man go free so that the innocent may not be imprisoned. Despite the rather melodramatic overtones of these two rationales, they were nevertheless enthusiastically endorsed and repeated by nearly all of the criminal lawyers interviewed. The lawyers also seemed frustrated that the general public could not be made to grasp their function and constitutional responsibilities. They felt the taint of their clients and could not wash themselves clean of this association either before the general public or even many of their fellow lawyers.

The defendant whose conviction appears certain presents more pragmatic problems for his attorney than merely the personal and philosophical issues just raised. The two major dilemmas which their inevitable conviction creates are, first, how do you prepare the defendant for the certainty of conviction and the probability of imprisonment? and second, what can you actually do for him in this depressing situation? Examining first the issue of preparing the defendant, or "cooling him out" to use Abraham Blumberg's terminology, the lawyers all agreed that it required great tact and patience. Although Blumberg argued that this "cooling out" process is most crucial to lawyers because of its relation to fee collection, most lawyers interviewed in this study expressed concern for the defendant's mental well-being and feared that he would panic and create an even more serious problem for himself.[9] The lawyers tried to achieve this "cooling out" by keeping their clients intelligently apprised of the facts of the case and offered as realistic an appraisal as possible concerning the likelihood of conviction and imprisonment. It was generally thought to be a better policy to err on the side of a pessimistic prognosis rather than have the defendant surprised at the ultimate outcome.

One New Orleans lawyer believed that most defense attorneys were overly concerned with the psychological well-being of their clients. He felt that the defendant of today had very little remorse over his criminal activity and was entirely result-oriented. He was therefore completely disinterested in having his lawyer adopt any quasi-psychiatric role designed to help him maintain a cool psyche. Several other lawyers agreed with this and insisted that most clients, particularly if they are repeat offenders or professional criminals, regard their arrest as an occupational hazard and are only concerned with the lawyer's ability to negotiate the least severe sentence possible. Thus the second half of this problem of helping the guilty client is either being fortunate enough to achieve a dismissal if the prosecution's case has sufficient loopholes or providing a persuasive argument for mitigating factors so as to result in the minimal punishment.

As noted previously, one of the most frustrating aspects of dealing with these guilty defendants is watching them fail to do anything in their own behalf. Some lawyers sensed a subconscious drive on the part of several clients to be convicted and punished for their crimes. Most lawyers agreed with a Washington, D.C. lawyer who commented, "It was only after turning to psychology and T.A. that I finally came to realize that they are not acting rationally, and I cannot count on them to help themselves."

Criminal lawyers, probably more than any other group of attorneys, are continually having their professional behavior carefully scrutinized for unethical transgressions. The problem is compounded by the low esteem of criminal lawyers in the eyes of the corporate attorneys who dominate the bar associations' committees on professional ethics. These blue stocking lawyers would much rather focus on this disorganized and relatively low status group than engage in a critical self-examination of their own professional morality.

The major areas of ethical concern for the criminal lawyer were identified by Arthur Wood as the following: (1) confidentiality of lawyer-client relationship; (2) emotional neutrality with respect to the merits of the case and the interests of the client; and (3) participation in procedures in which a professional rather than personal relationship is maintained with other

participants (police, judge, bondsmen, etc.). Wood's study identified specific ethical violations occurring in soliciting clients,
exploiting clients, suborning clients, and certain questionable
activities with bondsmen.[10]

Monroe Freedman, Dean of Hofstra's Law School, is currently the most involved and outspoken analyst of the professional ethics of criminal lawyers. He has devoted a great deal of
time and energy dealing with what he has identified as the three
most difficult issues in the general area:

(1) Is it proper to cross-examine for the purpose of discrediting the
    reliability or credibility of an adverse witness whom you know to
    be telling the truth?
(2) Is it proper to put a witness on the stand when you know he will
    commit perjury?
(3) Is it proper to give your client legal advice when you have reason to
    believe that the knowledge you give him will tempt him to commit
    perjury?[11]

Freedman, who wishes to permit the defense attorney maximum freedom in his adversarial struggle, has answered the first
and third questions affirmatively but has hedged on the second
one. Most of the lawyers agree with Freedman on the first
question insisting that the impeachment of witnesses is often
the only chance they have. The lawyers interviewed were
sharply divided on the second and third issues. The majority of
lawyers felt that all you could do was stress that if the defendant was caught lying on the stand or had a witness lying for
them, they would not only lose any chance for an acquittal, but
probably receive the maximum sentence. The question was
always analyzed on pragmatic grounds and the client was made
to think that he had too much risk in lying before the court.
Once the defendant and his witnesses did decide to go ahead
with testimony that appeared to his attorney to be probably
false or would not likely be believed by judge or jury, the
lawyer had but two choices which were either to threaten to
resign from the case or stand by and take his chances with the
client. The majority of the criminal lawyers interviewed selected
the first option.

The entire issue of suborning perjury was on the mind of
each criminal lawyer and they readily admitted that they had to

face this ethical crisis continually, although as already noted, they approached it from the perspective of how it would affect the outcome of the case rather than from the loftier philosophical level found in law review articles and bar association committee reports. One Los Angeles criminal lawyer found the problem heightened by the failure of most of his clients to see any moral wrong in lying in court, and therefore he could only reach them by discussing perjury in terms of how dangerous it would be to their case if they were not believed.

The knowledge that ethical committees and grand juries are looking over their shoulders, has also contributed to the care with which the defense attorneys attempt to tailor the testimony of their clients and witnesses. More and more criminal lawyers are being indicted or censured for obstructing justice due to the testimony of their clients, who can often gain their own freedom by incriminating their attorney. Lawyers are now more paranoid than ever and either tape-record all conversations with witnesses and clients or bring along a third party to take notes to substantiate the exchange of information. One older San Francisco lawyer warned his younger colleagues that the quickest way to anger a client and create a situation where he might turn on his lawyer was to begin their relationship with overly optimistic promises. The defendants encourage such assurances as they are shopping around for an attorney, and the starving young lawyer may be driven to give such promises in the hope of landing the case, but when the invariable disappointment materializes, the outraged client quickly turns on his lawyer and complains to the judge and bar association.

Two additional, although less significant ethical questions are the problems of living off "bad money," i.e., the fruits of the crime, and the related problem of what to do about knowledge of other crimes committed, possibly to raise the lawyer's fee. Most criminal defense lawyers were not very interested in discussing these questions either because, as they stated, the problems occurred so infrequently as to not merit examination or because they wanted to ignore such slanderous topics. Of the handful of lawyers willing to talk about the problem, most wished to know as little as possible about the source of their fees and made a conscious effort to avoid delving into the private life of the client. The less they knew about these

questions, the better off they would be. It was a rather expected response because where would one expect a professional
criminal to raise money for legal fees except from his professional earnings. The attitude was also a by-product of a more
general posture of consciously avoiding any type of judgment
about the defendant's past or present exploits. One Denver
attorney, who was aroused by these ethical problems, con-
demned his fellow criminal lawyers for blindfolding themselves
on this issue, but was himself unable to offer any workable
remedies.

The gravest ethical issue facing nearly all private criminal
lawyers is the defendant's role as informant. Examining the
lawyer's role in the informing process, most lawyers insisted
that they had to play a central role in the negotiations. The
lawyer would attempt to clarify what information was to be
exchanged in return for some specific consideration by the
prosecution. In several cities, interviewees showed the files of
these cases where everything was carefully preserved in writing,
just as if a business transaction had been completed. Although
such documentation was beneficial to the defendant, the majority of "snitching" arrangements were much less formal and
amounted to simply trying to give the police or prosecutors as
much information as possible in exchange for some vague agreement to consider this cooperation during the sentencing. It was
obviously a buyer's market despite the fact that police departments are relying more and more on this type of data.

In cases with multiple defendants the various lawyers sometimes seemed to operate on what one established lawyer termed
the FIFO principle—the first in first out type of informing,
which usually leads to a footrace between the defendants to the
prosecutor's door. Whoever shows up first to inform on his
codefendants can usually expect the best deal. Of course, the
fear of your colleague ratting on you first is also a motivational
factor. A conscientious and realistic defense attorney placed in
this situation has little choice but to join the race and hope that
his client is not the one most highly sought after by the
authorities, for it is against the unfortunate individual that the
prosecution will direct their army of informants. Lawyers who
do have the bad luck to be stuck with this type of "old maid"

dilemma, describe themselves as being hit by a ton of bricks and then weakly throwing themselves at the mercy of the court.

The initiative to inform may come from either the defense or prosecution. Several lawyers who were not overly thrilled with the informing game would only indulge in it at the prosecution's invitation. Most lawyers, however, thought that it was strictly the defendant's decision, and if he decided to try to negotiate a deal with the prosecution, it was the obligation of the lawyer to obtain the best deal available. A few attorneys steadfastly refused to permit their clients to inform and would resign from the case if the defendant insisted upon snitching. In most cases this antisnitching attitude was premised upon realistic business considerations, such as those voiced by a leading West Coast dope lawyer, who argued that he could not have his clients turning on each other, and that utilizing the FIFO principle would probably terminate his life as well as his professional career. He found that once the prosecutors recognize his nonsnitching policy, they work well together, and he further sensed that his attitude had aided him in developing a solid reputation for trustworthiness within the district attorney's office.

The majority of lawyers had also defended clients who had been coerced into testifying (particularly at the federal level), under a grant of forced immunity. This often causes the lawyer to battle with the authorities who are pressuring the client. The lawyer may attempt to evade the questioning altogether or just try to learn the specific field of inquiry and arrange for a beneficial grant toward particular acts committed by the client. Once it becomes evident that the client has no feasible alternative but to appear before the questioning body, all the lawyers stated that the client could only choose between taking the Fifth Amendment or telling the truth. This was no time to consider even the slightest transgression from the truth.

The U.S. Attorneys in several districts have relied rather extensively on the use of forced immunity. The Chicago defense attorneys were especially critical of the U.S. Attorneys, who in this area were seemingly substituting immunity grants for diligent investigation. Since the lawyer is currently excluded from most grand juries while the defendant is testifying, the lawyer can only play a role in the early stages and is of little aid once the grand jury convenes.

Most criminal lawyers were upset over recent developments, which have markedly increased the amount of informing. The lawyers' paranoia seemed at least partially justified by the fact that the interviewees in every city recounted a horror story of a client turning on his own attorney. It was generally acknowledged that the prosecution would be most appreciative of nailing some of the local attorneys on some charge, and that if a defendant would "bag" his own lawyer, he would be able to have his case dismissed. Many times the client would not purposefully set out to snitch, but if, for example, he was caught with drugs inside the prison, he could remove his problem by merely saying that his lawyer brought it in to him during his last visit. Also, a defendant who was rearrested trying to flee the jurisdiction might try to imply that his lawyer had convinced him that this was the only way to avoid a long-term imprisonment. Taking advantage of this atmosphere, prosecution and defendant may both solve their problems by indicting the defense attorney. The fear of such unscrupulous collusion far outstrips the few isolated examples of its occurrence. Nevertheless, this is just one more irritant for the already paranoid defense attorney to consider.

As a result of all of these strains on the lawyer/client relationship, approximately 90 percent of the attorneys interviewed adamantly refused to socialize or interact with their clients outside of business hours. Since many of their clients were engaged in illegal businesses or were associated with others who operated in this "gray area" of the law, the defense attorney would be risking censure by his fellows as well as possible arrest. Also considered taboo for the same reasons was engaging in business ventures with present or even past clients. It was universally recommended to stay on the side of caution in all out of court dealing with the clientele.

The socializing issue is not of that serious concern to most lawyers anyway because the majority of their clients are from a different social class. With more and more white-collar crimes and the public defender monopolizing the lower-class or indigent defendant, this situation may be in the process of changing. It is still difficult imagining it reaching serious proportions because so many of the criminal lawyers rarely even socialize with their fellow attorneys, let alone clients.

The final topic to be discussed in this chapter is a criminal lawyers' reasons for refusing a client or for dismissing himself from the case. Each of the lawyers had a select few types of cases that they felt they would automatically refuse to handle. These usually involved sex crimes against children or, for Jewish attorneys, a general reluctance to defend members of the American Nazi party. The Wood study found that most of the sample would refuse a client because he was determined to be morally objectionable (42 percent) although refusing to pay the fee (23 percent) and failure to follow advice were also important.[12]

Since most lawyers stated how difficult it was to dump a client—either constitutionally, emotionally, or realistically, it was surprising to find out how frequently it occurred, or at least was seriously contemplated. The majority of lawyers stated as their reason an unwillingness on the part of the client to follow their advice. Ethical concerns over probable perjury also grew out of this refusal to cooperate and was cited by several lawyers. If such a dismissal was contemplated, the lawyer had to act quickly because the longer the delay, the more intractable the situation.

NOTES

1. American Bar Association, *Canons of Professional Ethics, Annotated* (American Bar Foundation, 1967).

2. Nathan Cohn, ed., *Third Criminal Law Seminar* (Central Book Company, 1963).

3. Ibid, p. 78.

4. Joel Moldovsky and Rose DeWolf, *The Best Defense* (New York: Macmillan, 1975), p. 142.

5. Tony Green, "If you did it, get Peruto," *Philadelphia Magazine,* June 1977, p. 147.

6. Cohn, op. cit., p. 78.

7. Ibid, p. 84.

8. Ibid, p. 147.

9. Abraham Blumberg, *Criminal Justice* (Chicago: Quadrangle, 1967).

10. Arthur Wood, *Criminal Lawyers* (New Haven, Conn.: Yale University Press, 1967), p. 109.

11. Monroe Freedman, "Professional responsibilities of the criminal defense lawyer: the three hardest questions," *Michigan Law Review,* Vol. 64 (1966), p. 1469.

12. Wood, op. cit., p. 100.

Chapter 5

THE WORKING ENVIRONMENT

The working environment of the private criminal lawyer is divided between two sharply divergent locales; the courthouse and the private office. The private criminal lawyer is usually at his office for an hour or two prior to his morning court appearance and will return there in the late afternoon for a few additional hours. He may also be found in his office on weekends and on those rare days when no court appearances are required. For the bulk of the day, however, the criminal lawyer will be in the courthouse. His time will be spent roaming hallways, waiting for appointments, chatting with his fellow practitioners over rancid coffee, and occasionally carrying out his professional responsibilities before a judge.

The business office and courthouse present contrasting work environments primarily because of the different types and numbers of individuals found in each locale. In the personal office, which is typically within a small law firm of less than four members, the criminal lawyer works in virtual isolation with the exception of visits from clients or an occasional interaction with another lawyer. At the courthouse it is a radically different picture. Here, the lawyer is plunged into a turbulent setting in which constant meetings, confrontations, and bull sessions are engaged in with a wide range of criminal justice actors. These may include fellow private criminal lawyers, prosecutors, law clerks, bondsmen, judges, and a host of minor functionaries. In this chapter both settings will be discussed. Let us first turn to the lawyer's personal office.

The Lawyer's Office

Just as the income levels of the criminal lawyers varied greatly so did their offices. At the meagre end of the spectrum were one-room offices in rundown buildings. There would be a noticeably absent secretary, and the office would be locked when the lawyer was in court. An answering service would be utilized to record phone calls. At the opposite end of the continuum were the opulent offices, lavishly furnished, and located in splashy new high rises on prestigious avenues such as Wilshire Boulevard in Los Angeles.

The author inquired of those criminal attorneys housed in extremely elegant offices whether such surroundings might scare off potential clients who would be fearful of being able to afford their services. Most of the lawyers answered that on the contrary, clients seemed attracted to such luxurious quarters. It offered an indirect measure of the tangible success of the lawyer if he could afford such extravagance. It was also an exciting place to visit during the trial and to reminisce about long after the case had been terminated.

The typical office had a secretary who greeted the visitor as he stepped off the elevator or entered the office. There would be a small wood-paneled waiting room with enough modern furniture to seat three or four clients. Behind the receptionist would be a typing pool of two or three secretaries. Once admitted to the inner sanctum, one would find three to four individual offices and a small law library with an even smaller supply room dominated by a coffee making device. Brown would be the predominant color in nearly every office with blue being a distant second. The lawyer's office would have an impressive desk, functionally designed. There would usually be a sofa in the background which never seemed to be used and two or three chairs for clients strategically placed around the lawyer's desk.

It was interesting to note that most lawyers took great care in how their offices were decorated and even devised certain strategies geared toward maximizing their client relationships. One New Orleans lawyer stated he made it a point not to display any academic degrees and forced his partners to do the same. His reasoning was that degrees frequently intimidated the clients and made them uneasy. By replacing these symbols of academic achievement with happy, warm paintings, he thought he could more readily break down the wall between client and lawyer. Another strategy was noted by a Philadelphian, who had the lowest chairs and tables in any of the offices visited. With soft lighting and beige and bone-colored rugs and furniture, the visitor was almost put to sleep. He thought that by relaxing and soothing the client, he would have the best chance of developing an open working relationship. The important thing to remember from these representative attempts at decorative strategies is not their success, but the great attention to detail and importance attributed to such considerations by so many lawyers. Due to the narrow scope of this study no data was collected on how civil attorneys compare in their interest in this matter, but one would be surprised if they were not equally concerned.

A puzzling decorative pattern was the great frequency of chessboards prominently displayed. No lawyer was ever observed actually playing chess, nor did boards appear to be frozen in the midst of a game soon to be resumed. Most boards were miniature works of art with surrealistic or classical chess figures several inches high. It is conjectured that besides adding to the high level of aesthetic appeal found in most offices, the chess board was of symbolic importance. It signified to the client that his lawyer had the kind of logical, cunning mind that was necessary both in the game of chess as well as in the courtroom. It is common imagery to compare the battle between defense and prosecution to a chess match, and such imagery is not wasted on the defendant.

Another recurring pattern was the presence of a Bible. This was usually carefully placed on the lawyer's desk in such a way as to connote its recent use and ready accessibility. This quasi-religious decorative motif was most prevalent in the South and rarely found in the East and West Coast cities.

A final item seen regularly in most offices was a replica of the scales of justice. This artistic reminder of the quintessence of the lawyer's professional responsibility also served as another artistic addition to the office. It offered convincing proof beyond the framed diplomas that the client was in the office of a legitimate practitioner. Because several of the lawyers interviewed were pipe smokers, their desks were also clogged with the paraphernalia essential to that habit.

Because the author, like the clients themselves, spent a great deal of time waiting to see the attorneys, a brief note concerning the reading material in these rooms is in order. Although not as bad as dentist offices (dentists seem to think that people are equally interested reading preventive dental care magazines as they are), the average reading material in these lawyers' offices is quite dismal. If the client did not bring along his own reading material, his waiting time would pass very slowly. The most common journals were the national and local bar association magazines with *Newsweek, Time,* and *U.S. News and World Report* making infrequent and outdated appearances. Only a handful of offices made a conscious attempt to offer the client a wide range of potentially interesting material. A San Francisco attorney carefully subscribed to an eclectic group of magazines embracing the entire spectrum of ideological and entertainment philosophies. *Rolling Stone,* New York *Review of Books, Business Week,* and *Ebony* were just a few of the possible choices.

With this disappointing situation occurring on such a widespread basis, it was contemplated that the lawyers may have purposefully placed such a meagre and uninteresting collection of literature in their waiting rooms. After raising the issue with several of the interviewees and receiving little or no help (other than some sarcastic comments about such an issue being irrelevant), one is forced to draw one's own conclusions. One explanation might be that the lawyers did not expect much drop-in trade and that normally all clients would have an appointment so that the waiting room would be rarely used. A more interesting hypothesis is that because most of the clients are criminals with antisocial habits, such as thievery, the lawyer could expect any decent magazines to be stolen. It would therefore make little sense to invest in subscriptions for magazines that would be so quickly liberated from the office. Thus professional journals are selected which are of little interest to the clientele and yet might appeal to a fellow lawyer who might be stopping by the office.

THE COURTHOUSE

Between 10 A.M. and 4:30 P.M., the typical criminal lawyer will be found in the courthouse rather than his office. The hallway or snackbar now serves as the primary locale for his business activities. A great deal of time is spent waiting to see people. It often means passing time in the prosecutor's office while waiting to look at some items in their case file, such as the arrest report or list of witnesses. Attorneys also have to wait to see the judge or one of his clerks if a motion has to be filed or an appearance noted.

In contrast to the introspective and pensive nature of his office behavior, the criminal lawyer is often forced to be gregarious and extroverted while passing time in the courthouse. This badinage with his fellow lawyers usually involves the exchanging of gossip and anecdotes about fellow practitioners and adversaries. Occasionally, useful information can be picked up in these seemingly jocular discussions, especially for the beginning lawyer. These sessions are also the primary vehicle through which a lawyer's reputation becomes etched upon the rest of the legal community. The heroic feats and laughable blunders of fellow attorneys forge a reputation that may significantly affect whether a criminal lawyer's career will begin to take a downward or upward spiral.

The Washington, D.C. Superior Court complex was unique among the courthouses visited because it provided a "lawyer's lounge" which offered an accessible location for the private criminal law bar to relax while waiting for their next court appearance. Although a few cities had such lounges available for lawyers, they were rarely used and none had the vibrancy of this Washington institution. Located on the third floor of Building B, this ugly room was frequently crowded with lawyers looking for a place to hang their coat and engage in lively chatter. Large (20 ft. by 40 ft.) and sparsely furnished, the room was painted the nauseating light green color found in most public buildings built several decades ago. One wall was dominated by a large coatrack able to accommodate nearly a hundred garments, if only the hangers would be picked up off the floor. The opposite wall was filled with telephones and a few tables buried under telephone books, miscellaneous legal treatises, and day-old newspapers. In one corner of the room a card table was filled with a lively game of hearts. Surrounding the players was a row of kibbitzers, whose loud guffaws filled the room. A second, larger table, near the telephones was occupied by a handful of lawyers exchanging "war stories" and extolling personal virtues. Scattered around the perimeter of the room was a collection of broken furniture commonly seen in bus stations. A few coffee tables were strewn with more newspapers, assorted pieces of clothing, trash left over from half-eaten lunches, and overflowing ashtrays.

In addition to the sounds emanating from the card game, was the bubbling conviviality among the never-ending stream of lawyers coming in and out of the lounge, presumably in need of companionship or comic relief. Several lawyers were attempting to make phone calls and had to frequently shout over the din, which only raised the noise level even higher. Lunches were quietly and quickly being consumed out of paper bags and plastic containers obviously packed at home and surreptitiously tucked away in a vacant corner of a supposedly legalistic briefcase (a subtle testimony to the unglamorous side of the private practice of criminal law).

It was a scene reminiscent of Dickens' description of London's Old Bailey. The lively anecdotes and advice-giving transformed this depressing room into a school for lawyers. Dialogues between older and younger attorneys continued throughout the day. Tips on how certain prosecutors or judges could be expected to perform were the essence of this educative process, and the patient beginner could accumulate years of legal experience based on the observations of the more senior brethren. All he needed to do was sift fact from fiction. It is disappointing to note that the city is completing construction of a new courthouse building so that within a year the lounge will only be a memory.

Most courthouses are rather dreary places. The typical urban justice establishment is housed in an impregnable fortress whose massive bulking stone structure must have an intimidating effect upon all those unfortunate souls who must enter its portals to receive judgment. Its gothic overtones are continued in the interior, enhancing the foreboding aura of the building. The Cook County Criminal Courts Building at 26th and California Streets and the Orleans Parish Criminal Courthouse at Tulane and Broad best exemplify this architectural style. Even the more modern, and less oppressive structures, such as those found in Miami and Los Angeles, are only relative improvements in degree rather than kind. As the working environment for the greater part of the criminal lawyer's professional day, these conditions present one of the most negative aspects of his practice.

Although most of the courthouses maintained a consistent depressing demeanor, there were two which were sufficiently unique to merit mention. First, in Houston the spiraling increase in crime and resulting courthouse business has necessitated the expansion of available courtrooms beyond the point of reason. Criminal lawyers must argue cases in a series of semiabandoned buildings near the city's main criminal courthouse. The rooms used by the judges are smaller than normal offices and do not seem significantly larger than a good-sized closet.

The second noteworthy courthouse condition was found in New Orleans and related not to architecture, but to the dominating presence of people from the sheriffs department. These political patronage appointees are slowly being transformed into a civil service force based on merit selection and are charged with keeping order in the various courtrooms as well as guarding the parish prison which is an appendage to the west end of the courthouse.

These men are dressed in all-black uniforms trimmed in colorful patches and insignia indicating rank, years of service, and a plethora of additional identifying and honorific symbols, which fight for space on the right side of the sheriff's shirt and sleeve. The combined effect is a uniform that might be worn by a Mardi Gras clown in mourning. The average age of these functionaries—most of whom are local ward and precinct leaders—is between forty-five to sixty. In addition to their eye-catching uniforms, their most remarkable attribute is their quantity. Gathered in groups of fours and fives outside of and inside of each courtroom, the sheriffs are an omnipresent force in the courthouse, intimidating and baffling those individuals wandering into the building for the first time.

Comparing Federal and State Environments

The working environment for criminal lawyers often exhibited greater variation within a city than between cities. The two major adjudicative institutions found within each city are the federal and state judicial systems. Because the federal system is bound by a consistent body of rules and procedures in *all* jurisdictions, the degree of difference between the two systems is primarily a function of how the state system operates. In cities such as Chicago, Houston, and Philadelphia, where there was an appreciable difference between the federal and state proceedings, most lawyers who practiced in both systems preferred the federal. The state courts in these cities lagged perceptibly behind the federal rules in terms of progressivism and reform. A Chicago lawyer offered the following explanation of why he preferred the federal practice: "I'm doing more federal work because the money is better and you get to try a better case. More professional judges and prosecutors. There is less pressure on you since you're less likely to have an irate victim as in a state case; and when you do win it is a good feeling because you have beaten a really worthy opponent. Converse is most people are not upset or simply don't expect you to win."

In states like California and Colorado, where the rules of criminal law are quite progressive and in many instances ahead of the federal rules, most of the criminal lawyers preferred the state to the federal forum. This finding was a surprise given the generally held belief that the federal system is preeminent in preserving defendants' rights and guaranteeing due process of law. Nevertheless, nearly every lawyer interviewed in San Francisco, Los Angeles, and Denver who practiced regularly in both the state and federal systems, preferred the state courts. The following quote by a Denver attorney provides a balanced evaluation of the federal courts in his district and sheds some light on why they are so disliked: "The federal judges are absolutely peremptory and inflexibly tied to their dockets. Several are absolutely tyrannical. . . . There is no elbow room. They are only an improvement over the state courts due to their superior probation department and intelligent recommendations. They are just too sterile and cold. Even the federal law enforcement officers have gotten to be a problem. They are becoming even worse than the state and local police at shading the truth."

Even in jurisdictions where the criminal lawyers found the federal practices to be preferably to those of the state, the physical and emotional ambience of the federal court system projected an aura of sterility and inflexibility. The federal courthouses are uniformly austere. The judge is perched high upon his chair at the end of a spacious courtroom. The stolid and impassive settings are a perfect backdrop to the coldly dispassionate drama that unfolds daily.

Such a setting is in marked contrast to the boisterous, seemingly chaotic atmosphere of most state courthouses. State judges were generally thought to be more approachable and reasonable in dealing with scheduling or other personal problems troubling the defense attorney. The federal judges were often thought to be of superior intellect to the state judiciary but because of the lifetime appointment and compounded by the great power accrued to their position, they were belligerent and unsympathetic. This insensitivity alienated most private criminal lawyers and was found to exist in all cities visited.

In jurisdictions within states which have even more progressive criminal rules, the defense attorneys are even more contemptuous of the federal judiciary. Thus, because the discovery procedures in California, Colorado, and Florida generally exceed the federal rules, and the defense attorney is still permitted a significantly broader role in jury selection, the lawyers interviewed in these jurisdictions were even more adamant in their dislike of the federal bench. They generally felt that the federal courts were trying to emasculate the defense effort by reducing the criminal lawyer's role in the trial and granting broader power to the federal judges in order to allow them to move proceedings as expeditiously as is constitutionally permissible.

The federal prosecutors—U.S. attorneys and a phalanx of related prosecutorial agencies—provide another justification for the increasing tension between criminal lawyers and the federal courts. Many lawyers interviewed found the federal prosecutors to be an almost unbeatable adversary. With practically unlimited funds, experienced investigators devoting countless hours to their research, an army of paid informers, and an impressive pool of legal talent from which to select their personnel, the federal prosecutor is an intimidating opponent for even the most skilled criminal lawyer. As one Denver attorney stated, "They [the U.S. attorneys] file nothing but winners." Since the private criminal lawyer is usually a keen competitor, rarity of a defense victory is another factor aggravating the tension between these adversaries. The difference is especially clear . when compared to the defense attorneys' chances of success in the state system, where their opponents are often inexperienced assistant district attorneys who are working on strained budgets and relying on haphazard police work.

Despite the obvious reasons for preferring state to federal practice, several attorneys are finding themselves forced to take increasing numbers of federal cases. The federal cases are more lucrative and are appearing in increasing numbers. While the available number of state criminal cases continues to shrink due to increasing public defender involvement, there has recently been a dramatic increase in federal criminal cases as more and more crimes have become federalized. This has occurred as a result of the prosecutors utilizing an expanding version of the concept of crossing state lines to avoid prosecution, civil rights violations, and misuse of the mails for criminal activities. Thus, despite the dislike of the federal court system, the future will probably find rising involvement in federal criminal law by the better private defense bar. It is imagined that the financial benefits can effectively counterbalance the emotional and ideological frustrations.

One final disturbing comment on the future of the federal criminal law practice was raised by a Southern lawyer as he contemplated the implications of the new federal speedy trial act: "It is really going to screw things up. The courts don't like it. Civil lawyers hate it since it pushed their cases off the docket and criminal lawyers are also in a bind because they are pushed so hard. Defendants also are handicapped in picking a lawyer since better federal lawyers can only handle a few cases since they are going to trial so fast and therefore there is less choice of an attorney. Decent ones will be filled up fast and a lot of people will be turned away and won't be able to even get their second or third choice. The court has purposefully turned loose heavy narcotic defendants to shock the public and pressure Congress to see the impact of this bill."

Interaction with Other Criminal Justice Actors

The working environment of the private criminal lawyer is more than offices, courthouses, and rules. The human element provided by his interaction with other criminal justice actors, such as judges, prosecutors, clerks, and probation officers, may often be the critical factor affecting his attitude toward his professional milieu. The final section of this chapter will briefly describe the impressions of the private defense counsel concerning the other officials with whom he must exist.

THE JUDICIARY

It was surprising to find such a large percentage of defense attorneys viewing the criminal court judge as a type of adversary, who on frequent occasions may prove to be every bit as contentious as the prosecutor. In fact, many lawyers believed that the two (prosecutor and judge) were in league against them and their clients. For a variety of reasons, most judges were not respected. The most common reason offered was the judges' lack of prior experience in the area of criminal law. As a result the judges were perceived as being unable to adequately perform their assigned tasks in a competent manner. As one Philadelphia attorney pointed out, "I really become angered when I am under a great deal of pressure from judges who are not as smart or as experienced as most private attorneys."

Other difficulties with the judiciary also stem from its lack of empathy for the plight of defense attorneys. A Los Angeles attorney offered the following analysis: "The real problem in L.A. is with judges who don't realize there are many court dates

which each lawyer has to deal with and spread all over the
county. They simply aren't considerate. They also are afraid to
rule against the police. Around here they sense the police big
shots will jump down their throat and it intimidates the hell out
of them. Judges also get pressured by the D.A.'s office and
think they will get transferred to the civil side if they rule
against the police too often."

Although the interviewees understood the necessity for stay-
ing on the right side of the judge and paying proper respect
including contributing to campaign funds and honorary dinners,
they were careful as a general rule to avoid socializing with the
judiciary. Many took this stance as a matter of propriety and
not embarrassing the judge, but in reality most of the lawyers
had rare opportunities for socialization and moved in a distinct
social strata from the bench.

As a result of the judge's control over a case and the discretionary powers vested in his position, nearly all lawyers emphasized the necessity for learning the judge's idiosyncrasies and
catering to his whims. With very little judge shopping currently
available in most jurisdictions, it is imperative for a defense
attorney to be a knowledgeable evaluator of judicial behavior. A
few lawyers pointed out, however, that with some judges who
were blatantly prosecution-oriented, there was little use for
subtle character analysis and attempted manipulation. Most
defense counsel agreed that when facing such a judge, the
lawyer had to make sure that he was getting all of the judge's
prejudicial remarks on the record and that the judge be aware of
what he was doing. The judge had to be confronted, even at he
risk of further heightening his anger and risking a possible
contempt citation.

THE PROSECUTOR

The criminal lawyers' attitude toward the prosecutor was
generally more positive than toward the judiciary. One difference was that there seemed to be consistently negative feelings
toward most of the bench as a group, whereas the attitude
toward prosecutors depended a great deal upon the particular
prosecutor under discussion. Even those defense attorneys who
disliked most prosecutors were willing to concede that a few of

their adversaries were decent human beings. One of the key factors affecting the defense/prosecution relationship was whether the prosecutor was a career type or merely in the office for a brief tenure before moving on to private practice. The career types, especially in the early stages of their service, were the most disliked and most difficult to work with. A frustrated Houston attorney summarized these sentiments: "You always have to watch our for career assholes in the D.A.'s office. They are like part-time cops. Young guys go in for a few years and get out and so there is a pretty high turnover at lower echelons. Top administrators have been there a long time. Most can get away with doing their own thing if they have balls but this rarely happens around here. Also getting to be more of a problem trusting them to keep their promises."

Another factor influencing the style of interaction between defense and prosecution was the degree of independence granted to the assistant district attorney by his superiors. A Chicago lawyer placed this problem in a historical perspective: "It used to be state's attorneys had more authority and were respected. Today it's just a big office with many tiers of supervisors. Real problem is with the decreased authority of the assistants." In cities such as Philadelphia and New Orleans where the administrators have granted so little independence to their assistants (1976), most criminal lawyers treated their opponents with disdain, realizing that no negotiation or discussion was final but must be cleared with a superior. At the other extreme, where assistants are given broad discretionary powers, such as in San Francisco and Miami, the criminal lawyers seemed prone to respect their adversaries and more willing to negotiate.

Several lawyers downplayed the existence of tension between themselves and the prosecutor by stressing the fact that both sides were trapped in the mire of the criminal justice system. They both disliked the arbitrary judiciary who could embarrass them in open court and could not be trusted by either side. A further aspect of this cooperation involves the increasingly open discovery procedures in most jurisdictions. These procedures make the defense attorney as well as the prosecutor responsible for making certain documents and information available to the other side. Since the prosecutor is in a position to control most of this important information relevant to a case, many private defense attorneys consciously court his friendship and deemphasize the contentious nature of their relationship.

Despite the necessity for cooperating with the prosecutor, several of the lawyers interviewed remained staunch competitors. They took great pride in defeating the prosecutor and gloated over public humiliations of less competent adversaries. Many of the defense attorneys did not receive great personal satisfaction from trouncing a prosecutor but viewed it as an essential element in developing a reputation as an unsparing advocate, which would not only attract clients but hopefully would intimidate future prosecutors. This could lead to shaky courtroom performances by the prosecutor, although it was more likely to produce premature and advantageous plea negotiations. A young Denver attorney candidly evaluated the significance of this intimidation: "You can make your money by scaring the hell out of the D.A.'s with your prowess. Ground 'em up and terrorize them and then live off your reputation for the next six months. You can really get some good pleas during this time since they are scared."

COURT OFFICIALS

Surrounding each judge is a group of functionaries who are underpublicized, yet indispensable members of the criminal justice system. Secretaries, clerks, and bailiffs are the grease which lubricates the entire system. Their responsibilities include scheduling cases, court appearances, private appointments, and filing of motions. They usually form a protective screen around the judge, and by their powers of selective admission, control access to the court's inner sanctum. Because of these powers, the defense attorney must carefully try to gain their favor. Once that has been obtained, the lawyer may be granted such favors as always knowing exactly when his case is about to be called. He can also expect the judge to be reasonable if he is unable to appear in court at an appointed time. Finally, he may receive tips about the judge's temperament on a particular day, which may significantly affect his courtroom strategy and behavior.

Chapter 6

PRETRIAL PERFORMANCE

Pretrial Activities

INITIAL RESPONSIBILITIES

Most of the criminal lawyers interviewed did not have their initial meeting with the defendant until after he had obtained his pretrial release. A few lawyers, who defended clients that were repeat offenders or simply wise to the ways of the court system, were sometimes contacted prior to the bail decision, allowing the lawyers some opportunity to influence the granting of personal recognizance or ensuring the setting of an attainable bail. Generally, if a defendant is financially unable to raise the required bail, he is too poor to hire private counsel and will receive assigned counsel or a representative from the public defender's office. In cases involving heinous crimes, a bail may be set so high that even a defendant who cannot raise the bail may still be able to afford private counsel. Most of the lawyers dislike having to represent a client who must remain incarcerated during this pretrial period because they will be unable to use the defendant effectively in preparing the case and securing witnesses. In addition, there is the time-consuming drive back and forth from the jail, which is usually located a great distance from most lawyers' offices, and there are other physical problems, such as finding a decent room to interview the client and the monitoring of the client's mail.

The first phone call of an experienced client will usually go to a lawyer who will be asked as his first responsibility to obtain a bondsman who will raise the required bail. The majority of clients, however, obtain their pretrial release independent of their eventual attorney, who will be contacted within a week after the arrest. In nearly all cases the defendant is able to hire his attorney by the preliminary hearing, which is scheduled seven to ten days after the arrest and initial courtroom appearance where bail is set.

Nearly all the lawyers interviewed preferred to have the initial meeting (and most subsequent ones as well) in their own offices. This initial confrontation typically allows the potential client to describe his present dilemma and offer his version of the facts of the case. The lawyer will then ask a few questions about the defendant's background and solvency and then propose a tentative fee arrangement. The lawyers were divided as to whether or not to charge for this initial conference since it was estimated that a third of the defendants were shopping around and would go on to another attorney. The most common arrangement was to charge a minimal fee and then later include it into the retainer if he was ultimately hired.

Most lawyers warned against the temptation to try and hold on to a potential client by promising him a better guaranteed disposition than another attorney. Due to the pressures of intense competition, particularly among beginning criminal lawyers, it is very easy to fall prey to this overzealous recruitment of clientele. As one elderly West Coast lawyer warned, however, "you are opening yourself to all sorts of future problems brought on by disappointed clients who are seeking revenge following the disappearance of their supposed guaranteed outcome. You are also risking the ire of your fellow attorneys who believe your fantasy enticements border on unethical behavior."

Once a lawyer is hired, he will try to obtain the police report and through discussions with the assistant district attorney and his client, attempt to piece together the facts of the case. It is also necessary at this time to use these two sources in order to construct a list of witnesses for and against his client. The lawyer usually hopes that all this can be accomplished by the preliminary hearing, especially if he is located in a jurisdiction which permits an extensive and careful examination of the prosecution's case. In situations where the lawyer enters the case after several days or where limited discovery is permitted, the defense attorney must use the preliminary hearing itself as a means of obtaining the state's version of the case as well as the list of witnesses. It also provides an opportunity in most cities to begin the filing of pretrial motions, such as discovery motions demanding additional information, or motions to suppress evidence believed to be unconstitutionally obtained.

Another important advantage of having a criminal lawyer enter a case at an early stage is his presence at any police lineups involving eyewitness identification. Judge William Neighbors of Colorado, himself a former defense counsel, offers the following list of duties of counsel at a lineup: (1) type record the identification comments of witnesses if possible; (2) if more than one identification witness appears, make sure they are segregated; (3) obtain the names of all persons participating in the lineup; (4) make suggestions as to the proper composition of the lineup; (5) suggest that the client be allowed to select his own place in the lineup; and (6) make sure that any photographs used in the identification process are preserved in order that the court can accurately determine a claim of suggestibility in the photographic identification.[1]

BAIL

Returning briefly to the issue of bail, the defense attorney has consistently been depicted as exerting the least amount of influence on this topic, relative to the judge, prosecutor, and police.[2] This is an unfortunate situation since the defendant's pretrial freedom is so important. Most lawyers perceived their function in the bail-setting decision as trying to convince the judge of his client's good character and community ties. His goal was either to convince the judge to release the defendant upon his own recognizance or reduce a previous bond set at an unreasonable level given his client's character and monetary resources. It was extremely rare to have a criminal lawyer remember an instance of lending money to a client for his bond. It was difficult enough for lawyers to collect their regular fees, and professional ethics also prohibit such a dual role.

Although the mere presence of the client's defense attorney does not guarantee a modest bail or ROR, the author conducted a study which showed that the attorney's presence did greatly improve his chances for achieving favorable results. As part of his study of bail and its reform for the Department of Justice in 1971, the author spent a week observing the preliminary arraignment court in Detroit. Here the initial bail decision was made in all felony cases. A total of 345 cases were observed. In 105 (30.4 percent) of the cases, the defendant was represented by counsel, while 340 (67.6 percent) of the defendants were unable to have counsel present. Of the 105 defendants represented by a lawyer, 50 (74.6 percent) were able to obtain ROR without having to pay any money. The remaining 55 were forced to raise the required bonds, which ranged from $500 to $2000. The 240 defendants without lawyers were not so fortunate. Only 25 percent were ROR'd with money bond being set for the remaining 75 percent, with 25 percent (45) having bond set at $5000 or above. Thus a defendant who had a lawyer had twice the chance of being released on his own recognizance. Also, if a money bond was set, he would have a much better chance of having a lower, more reasonable bond if he had a lawyer present. Since Detroit at this time (1970) had no viable public defender service, this brief study examined the performance of primarily private criminal lawyers.[3]

Probably the most important role to be played by defense counsel in the administration of bail is in his attempted appeal of the original bond requesting a reduction or recognizance release. This motion or application is not made until a week after the defendant's arrest and is usually timed for the preliminary hearing. By this time the lawyer has had an opportunity to meet with the defendant. He knows the defendant's background as well as the strength of the state's case.[4]

SCREENING PROCESS

In several of the cities visited, the prosecution's screening process is one of the most crucial segments of the criminal justice system. It is here that the prosecution reviews the police department's arrest and decides whether to file charges against the defendant or dismiss the case. Typically between 25 and 50 percent of the cases are either dismissed or reduced to lesser charges at this point. More and more district attorneys are using this screening process to select for prosecution only those cases in which a conviction is nearly certain. This permits their office to boast of an extremely high conviction rate, a figure based on the percentage of cases accepted by the prosecutor in which a conviction was obtained. Such percentages impress the general public and are beneficial for the defendants who are fortunate enough to have their cases refused for prosecution.

In cities such as New Orleans where so much attention is paid to the screening process—the prosecutor has up to ten days in which to make his decision and uses a large staff of experienced assistants who specialize in this phase—the private defense attorney can play a significant role on this client's behalf. Since the screening process often drags on for two weeks following arrest, the lawyer will have had a chance to collect some preliminary background on the case, and if it does appear to be a rather weak arrest, he can exert influence on the prosecutor to either dismiss the case or at least reduce the charges. Both adversaries usually desire to avoid going to trial if at all possible so the time is ripe for deals if the defense attorney can convince the prosecutor of the strength of the defense position and the low probability of achieving a conviction. Many defense counsel, known as "wholesalers" or plea bargainers in other cities are found devoting their energies toward the screening decision by New Orleans prosecutors. Not surprisingly, little plea bargaining occurs once a case has been accepted by the prosecutor.

One of the top New Orleans defense attorneys described the range of activities associated with his attempting to influence the screening decision: "I offer what defense I think I'll be using at the screening. I'll bring in witnesses if necessary. There is no statistical problem or publicity at this point so you can bring in all sorts of side issues such as restitution and diversion. You are just trading off certainty for unknown dangers. The prosecutors won't even bargain after this."

A Philadelphia attorney indicated his city had a pretrial conference which was the functional equivalent of the New Orleans screening conference. He described his role at this proceeding as trying to place his clients into diversion or rehabilitation programs so that a probation compromise could be achieved. Many of his clients were first offenders involved in the use and sale of narcotics so his practice was ideally suited to utilizing these programs.

PRETRIAL MOTIONS

Most criminal lawyers stressed the importance of pretrial motions. They could be used either positively, e.g., discovery motions to gather necessary information concerning the prosecution's case, or negatively, e.g., motions to suppress, which, if successful, deprive the district attorney of necessary evidence for conviction. A prominent Houston attorney offered the following list of consequences derived from an aggressive use of pretrial motions by defense counsel:

(1) It forces a partial disclosure at an early date;
(2) puts pressure on the prosecutor to consider plea bargaining; early in the proceeding;
(3) forces exposure of primary state witnesses at an inopportune time for the prosecution;
(4) raises before trial judge early in the proceedings matters the defense may want called to his attention;
(5) forces prosecutor to make decisions prior to his final case preparation and premature choice of theory;
(6) allows defendant to see immediate action by his attorney which has a salutory effect on the client-attorney relationship.[5]

Many lawyers have come to agree with one San Francisco lawyer who files motions religiously, regardless of the case, just to get them on the record. It is another manifestation of the paranoia gripping most defense attorneys as they carefully devise strategies for combating future "competence of counsel" suits by their own clients.

Criminal lawyers also use motions as part of a bluffing game. A Los Angeles attorney admitted, for example, that he used motions to suppress to see how the court would react and what each side could produce. He had been fortunate on occasions when key witnesses would fail to appear and the case be dismissed. Another Los Angeles lawyer added that he likes to use a great number of pretrial motions so as to exhaust the judge's legal rulings which might affect the case. It would also help to wear the district attorney down to the point where it would be easier for him to drop the case than to continue in a petty and time-consuming struggle to answer all of his adversary's motions.

The effective use of pretrial motions is just another example of how successful defense attorneys must combine their legal skills with that of an amateur psychologist. A West Coast lawyer gave the following example of how both skills must be blended together: "You really have to be a psychologist to win on motions to dismiss. I like to get into court early and see who is ahead of me and learn whether their motions are frivolous or serious. If my motion is serious, I want to let a number of the frivolous appeals go first and set a trend so that when mine comes along, I'll look good by comparison. If my motion is less serious, I'll want to go first so he [the judge] won't have anything to compare mine to."

PRELIMINARY HEARING

Although Chapter 3 has already examined the various usages and importance each city surveyed attached to the preliminary hearing, the present discussion will concentrate upon how the defense attorney perceived his responsibilities at this juncture and what type of strategies he is most likely to employ. The degree of importance which a city or individual judge attaches to a preliminary hearing is obviously the major factor influencing the attitude of the lawyer toward his role in this proceeding. Lawyers interviewed in Washington were disappointed by the short shrift given to preliminary hearings by their city's

judiciary, which last only about 5 minutes and could not be
used for discovery. At the other extreme is San Francisco which
permits an extensive hearing to go on for several days, if
necessary. Several lawyers sensed that it was being used in
California as an alternative to grand jury indictment. As one San
Francisco lawyer commented, "in most serious cases the preliminary hearing is a sharp dividing line between the case's
movement from municipal to superior court. . . . The lawyer at
this point should offer a series of motions directed at the
prosecution's case, either suppressing certain critical pieces of
evidence or attacking the overall weakness."

Most of the lawyers operating in jurisdictions where the
preliminary hearing is a viable attempt at discerning if probable
cause for the defendant's arrest did exist, use this proceeding
either as a discovery tool or building a record for later use. The
defense lawyers merely want to be sure there are no surprises
awaiting them at the actual trial. The preliminary hearing is
useful in building a record because it allows the attorney to
crossexamine the prosecutor and his witnesses in order to nail
them down in detail to a particular story. As one West Coast
attorney stated, "I want to develop as thick a transcript as
possible so I won't have to worry about the jury."

Oakland attorney Herman Mintz addressing the 2nd Annual
Criminal Law Seminar in San Francisco best summarized the
most important rule to follow in preparing for the preliminary
hearing: "That rule is that as you enter the courtroom with
your discovery completed, knowing all about your side of the
case, having found out as much as you can about the prosecution's side of the case, having interviewed all of your witnesses
and those witnesses of the prosecution, you are able to find. It
is important to have a distinct objective in mind at the time of
the preliminary hearing. There are two major objectives that
you can have; one is securing a dismissal on a technical ground
and the other is taking a deposition."[6]

In cities such as Washington and Philadelphia, where the
preliminary hearing is relatively unimportant, defense lawyers
face the choice of waiving the proceeding entirely. As one
Philadelphia lawyer noted, "The potential is there for discovery
but the pressure from certain judges to cut it short is excru-

ciating." Despite these pressures and the lack of tangible rewards, most lawyers interviewed were hesitant to waive the preliminary hearing because at the very least it was a chance to see the witnesses. The most common reason given for waiving is that it might be a useful conciliatory device in establishing an advantageous plea bargain with the prosecutor.

Investigations and Discovery

The private criminal lawyer attempts to learn as much about a case as possible from the client himself. Because of a variety of defects commonly present in lawyer/client relationships the defense counsel must rely upon a variety of additional sources of information in order to construct the defense. Most lawyers occasionally have to use private investigators in order to obtain the information being withheld by the defendant or simply beyond his range of knowledge.

As with the public investigators used by the prosecution, these men are usually former detectives who have left the police force for the more lucrative vocation of private investigator. Other types of backgrounds include postal inspectors, military policemen, and former FBI agents. These investigators are hired on a case-by-case basis. They are an expensive addition to the client's fee, and the defendant's financial capabilities are often the primary factor in deciding whether or not to use an investigator. Most lawyers passed the costs of the investigator directly on to the client as a separate fee, distinct from the retainer. The lawyer merely acts as a middle man in passing the fee from the client to the investigator.

Defense lawyers use investigators for a variety of tasks but their most common use is in the location and interviewing of witnesses. Several lawyers commented that this can be extremely helpful if the investigator is able to reach the witness before the police or prosecutor's office. Most of the attorneys will follow up the investigator's interviews and talk to the witnesses themselves. This allows the lawyer to make an independent evaluation of the witness as to both his veracity and to his potential performance on the witness stand. The second most frequent use of investigators is in the conducting of a technical or scientific task associated with the crime. This may range from the taking of photographs to the collection of physical evidence from the scene of the crime.

Besides saving the attorney a great deal of time and providing technical expertise in complex cases, most investigators also offer the added advantage of having established contacts with a variety of sources. This network of informants and old acquaintances is often the key to contacting community leaders, police, prison, court, probation officers, newsmen, and others who might control access to needed information. A final advantage of investigators is in cases involving racial minorities where the defense attorney believes he cannot gain access to information in the barrio or inner city ghetto. Most lawyers know at least one minority investigator who not only has a network of clients in the black or brown community but unlike most lawyers is not afraid to travel into these areas after dark.

Several criminal lawyers disdain using investigators. They cite expense and the inability of their clients to be able to absorb this added cost. A few lawyers had problems with investigators, who were prone to threatening people or misrepresenting themselves, and concluded that they were more trouble than they were worth. In Washington, D.C. where approximately 45 percent of the lawyers receive assigned cases under the Criminal Justice Act, the investigative services of the public defender's office are made available to them. This, however, has not worked out because of the time it takes to get an investigator, who under no circumstances can be used before the preliminary hearing. If lawyers attempted to hire private investigators in these assigned cases, most judges would refuse to reimburse the lawyer for the full amount of the services. Most Washington lawyers wound up doing the investigative work themselves, often employing the defendant's family.

The most important current controversy related to private investigators involves their use of recording devices while interviewing witnesses. F. Lee Bailey argues the expected defense lawyer position that "Surveillance is a technique equally available for the defense investigator as it is to the police. No investigator should rely on memory alone. You [the defense lawyer] may properly use electronic devices in certain situations. Each fact obtained by him [the investigator] should be recorded by him as soon as possible."[7] Harold Lipset, a respected San Francisco private investigator, agrees with Bailey and stresses the importance of the use of recorded interviews to accomplish the following essential goals: (1) signed statements are a desired objective but we never know if we will get one once the interview begins; (2) the attorney can better evaluate the witness if he can hear him in addition to reading the statement obtained; (3) prevents prosecution claims of tampering with or bribing witnesses; and (4) other factors may enter into the picture between the time of the interview and the trial.[8]

Private criminal lawyers must also conduct their own investigations in addition to whatever use is made of a private investigator. The complexity of the case, the financial resources of the client, and the time available are all factors affecting the quality and style of the lawyer's personal investigation. Obviously, the investigation must start with the client himself and Bailey and Rothblatt offer the following advice for this opening venture: "Even though the client may still be overwrought at the time of this interview and his memory somewhat inaccurate, you should try to obtain from him an account of what happened. An early recital, even under such circumstances, may guarantee your receiving an unvarnished tale. The longer a person remains in custody, the more likely he is to absorb ideas from fellow prisoners or guards as to how he should alter his story in order to absolve himself from or lessen the gravity of the charge placed against him. Cross examine him about inconsistencies and lapses of memory. It should be verified by comparing it with other available evidence."[9]

The purpose of these personal investigations by the defense counsel is to check on the veracity of the client's story, locate witnesses, and learn the essence of their forthcoming testimony, and on rarer occasions, attempt to discover background information on prospective jurors. These purposes are accomplished by a variety of investigative means such as surveillance, personal interviews, and collection of physical evidence as well as relevant records and documents. A Philadelphia lawyer added that as part of his investigation he always tried to keep track of the police. "I get their testimony from four or five cases and look for friends. I then start asking cops in informer cases for other cases involving the same informer and then show there was no real starting point in the establishment of reliability. Second I go over police radio car calls in order to see if messages conflict with later stories. Third I wander into police stations and look at their paperwork and pick up as many of their memos as I can. Get the same info they have. It is just part of a conscious attempt to develop the practice of getting their documents which can incriminate them later."

For the average criminal case, the defense attorney is forced to rely primarily upon pretrial discovery as his most significant investigative tool. In some jurisdictions, such as California, Colorado, and Florida, this presents no problem because the liberal discovery statutes allow the defense attorney to see nearly all the state's case. However, in places like Philadelphia, Houston, and New Orleans, the highly restricted discovery practices create a serious obstacle to adequate pretrial investigations.

In cities with restrictive discovery procedures, the lawyer must develop a series of friendly relationships with members of the district attorney's office in order to move beyond the narrow confines of the statute. The development of informal discovery techniques can often lead to strained relationships in the supposed adversarial system by investing the prosecutor with unchecked power to directly control the flow of information into his opponent's hands. A Philadelphia lawyer pointed out an additional liability of the informal system. He stated that it creates a potential source of corrupt practices. He found it necessary in his city to slip money to certain assistant prosecutors to release evidence, especially if it was damaging to the prosecution's case. Without this bribery or a long-established friendship, the prosecution would simply sit on this information.

As we noted earlier in this chapter, the defense attorney in all cities still has the option of filing discovery motions in order to obtain the required data. The success of these motions varies greatly with the lawyer's skill and the judge's attitude. A few lawyers, particularly in cities with restrictive statutes, have developed the art of discovery motions to where as one Houston attorney showed the author, a set of boiler plate tapes are prepared for every type of discovery motion imaginable. In ruling on these discovery motions, the judge pretty much exhausts his role in the defense attorney's search for evidence. The district attorney's attitude and friendship are usually the key to successful discovery practices rather than the formalistic presentment of the discovery motions to the judge.

The major problem in many cities, even with liberal discovery practices, is the emergence of multiple investigative agencies. This development, which has reached its zenith in the federal system, means that the defense attorney is confronted by a wide range of possible sources of information beyond the police or arresting agency. These various investigative institutions act in an uncoordinated fashion, frequently withholding information from each other in a constant war of petty jealousies. The defense attorney facing this phalanx of institutions is often unable to locate the needed information. Drug cases at the federal level, which may involve four or five agencies fighting over the acclaim for the arrest, are the most severe examples of this problem.

Nearly all the lawyers interviewed stressed the importance of adequate discovery practices. Without it, the lawyer is forced to rely on the questionable veracity of the defendant and must therefore expend additional time and energy either through personal or private investigation to discover the facts of the case. This not only drives up the client's fee to an uncollectible point but exerts unneeded strains on an already tenuous relationship. The few attorneys who underplayed the importance of discovery quipped that they didn't want to know the full facts of the case since it would only further prejudice them toward their client. Another practical reason given by a Miami lawyer was that discovery was a two-edged sword, and the more the prosecutor was required to give to you, the more he could demand of you in return.

Preparation and Use of Witnesses

Most lawyers interviewed agreed that the location and preparation of witnesses were the weakest areas of their defense effort. Most lawyers were content to use statements given to police and prosecutors which were obtained through discovery. Their modest goal was simply not to be surprised at the trial by witness testimony. If they were permitted, many defense attorneys would use the preliminary hearing as a prime opportunity for talking with witnesses prior to the trial.

If an attorney was willing to expend the time and effort to talk to witnesses, he usually stressed the importance of talking to them himself. Even if an investigator had been used to locate the witness and conducted an initial interview, the typical defense attorney would insist that he also have an opportunity to talk with them. A Los Angeles criminal lawyer with over forty years of experience urged the necessity of conducting these interviews if you are contemplating putting the witness on the stand. He also offered the following advice concerning the location of the interview: "I get all the witnesses together in one meeting. One can get a better composite of the action as one witness acts as a memory prod for the other. I trust my ability to examine then in this sometimes chaotic setting."

The basic goal of this phase of the lawyer's preparation is to be able to be confident of knowing what every witness on either side is going to say. As a Denver lawyer commented, he would never put a witness on the stand who did not know all the questions he would be facing, and this lawyer also wanted to know all the answers the prosecution's witnesses would be providing. F. Lee Bailey and Henry Rothblatt's cookbook style treatise on the craft of criminal law advocacy offers the following suggestion as to strategies in witness preparation:

> Prepare properly for a good interview. Be familiar with the facts of the case and know as much as possible about the witness to be interviewed. . . . Conduct the interview in layman's language. Convey the impression that you have no personal interest in the matter, that you are merely seeking information. . . . When witnesses pretend to know nothing about a crime, ask many questions, any one of which, if answered, will refute the claim that they know nothing at all. . . . Your questioning about the crime should begin with a search for such factual and incontrovertible matters as time, date, place, weather conditions, etc. . . . When the interview is underway, always allow the witness to make an initial statement in narrative form.[10]

All lawyers stressed the importance of the attorney's attitude and demeanor. "I have always," explained an experienced West Coast lawyer, "felt a need to be concerned with courtesy and appearance. You must remember that most witnesses are going to be terribly inconvenienced and may refuse to come back. Especially after there have been four or five continuances, it is very hard to hold on to your witnesses."

A second factor stressed by the defense lawyers was that each witness had to be carefully evaluated as to his credibility on the witness stand. Additionally, all witnesses in a case had to be examined as to the type of witness they would make. The three major categories to be considered were friendly, neutral, and hostile. With the friendly witness it was recommended that the lawyer obtain a written statement before the witness had an opportunity to change his mind. With the uncooperative witness it was best to first try and discover the cause of the sentiment. The hostile witness obviously presented the most serious obstacle and should be avoided or at least have a neutral party conduct the interview. Again, the lawyer should try to determine the roots of the hostility.

Police cause many problems as witnesses for the defense attorney because of their experience as professional testifiers and their ability to shade the truth in their own interest. Since judge and jury are predisposed to believe the sworn testimony of a law enforcement officer, the defense attorney's task is made even more difficult. Children are another unusual type of witness who further complicates the life of a defense attorney. It was agreed that children require a great deal of preparation. This often included trying to have the child become accustomed to the ambience of the courtroom itself.

Calling the victim as a witness was to be generally avoided. If it was necessary to interview the victim prior to trial, most defense attorneys insisted on bringing along a representative from the prosecutor's office. This would help ward off any later charges by the victim, that he had been browbeaten or harassed by the defense attorney. The only time a lawyer suggested that he needed to see a victim was to make sure that he was amenable to the plea bargain that was being negotiated and would not complain to the judge or media that he was being sold out for the sake of expediency. Even this situation rarely warranted a confrontation between victim and defense counsel.

A final category of witness is the fabled expert witness whose acumen and experience may save the day for the client. Most private criminal lawyers do not share this positive and mythical respect for the expert witness. The interviewees commonly viewed the expert as "a whore for either side depending on who paid him the most money." They explained the necessity to balance off the prosecution's experts. The most that could be derived from their use was to put a few chinks in the credibility of their adversary's armor.

As with private investigators, criminal lawyers were rarely able to utilize expert witnesses because of their prohibitive cost. If the prosecution was not going to offer damning evidence which had to be challenged by an expert, nearly all lawyers felt that it was a costly and needless frill. The three areas where expert witnesses were often used were lie detector tests, insanity questions, and complex technical issues. Many lawyers were amenable to using lie detector tests. They knew they could only be used to their benefit[11] and were therefore the most acceptable and frequent expert witnesses used by the defense. The use of psychiatrists and psychologists to decide legal sanity issues was thought by most criminal lawyers to be a waste of time and money. Most lawyers were skeptical as to the expert's knowledge and objectivity. They also saw them as easy game on the witness stand. As a young California lawyer commented, "They are the easiest witnesses to deal with and are easily manipulatable. They easily identify with the side they are on and this soon becomes obvious to the jurors who soon ignore them and simply ask themselves whether or not the *defendant looks* crazy to them."

The expert witness most feared by the defense counsel is the technical or scientific expert. His years of training in a laboratory often gives his testimony impregnable credibility. The defense can only counter the prosecution's experts by bringing in its own group to try and describe what a sloppy investigation was conducted by the police and how much physical evidence was discarded or unusable due to these second-rate investigators.

Paul Kirk, used numerous times as an expert witness as a chemist, offers the following commonsense advice to defense attorneys considering using an expert witness: "If you know exactly what you are trying to show, there are a lot of experts, the woods are full of them. You do not have to worry about getting somebody who can answer your question if you really know the type of question you want answered, and then look in that area."[12]

Plea Bargaining

Plea bargaining, to nearly all the criminal lawyers interviewed, meant only the negotiated settlement of a case prior to trial. It had none of the negative connotations commonly associated with the term as it is used by judicial reformers, politicians, and the media. It was estimated by the sample of lawyers that approximately two-thirds of their cases are disposed of through some type of plea negotiation. Arthur Wood's earlier study of criminal lawyers also showed this general acceptance of plea bargaining as 48 percent approved of it as the only avenue available, 10 percent approved of it as an economy measure, and 29 percent offered a qualified opinion restricting its usage. Only 13 percent thought it was unjustified and should be abandoned as a professional practice.[13] Our study found that only 3 to 4 percent of the lawyers interviewed evaluated plea bargaining as unjustified.

The defense lawyers, like most students of the criminal court system, find plea bargaining to be a necessary instrument in dealing with the staggering caseload facing the judges. As one California lawyer noted, "If you would change the name it would appear much less heinous." The negotiation system was generally believed to benefit *all* participants in the process. The client is well served, as long as he knows what is occurring at each stage and there is an absence of coercion, by receiving a lighter sentence than he would probably have received if his case had gone to trial. The judge and district attorney utilize it to help keep their dockets to manageable proportions. The defense attorney also uses it as an economy measure, permitting him to handle more cases by settling them at a pretrial stage

rather than after a long protracted courtroom struggle. Jackson
Battle's important article examining the cooperative practices of
prosecutors and criminal defense lawyers best summarized the
advantages derived for the defense attorney from a cooperative
venture such as plea bargaining: From the district attorney the
defense counsel would receive informal discovery, in addition to
the actual plea bargain. From the police he would be granted
unusual factfinding opportunities as well as favorable courtroom testimony. From the judge he would benefit from favorable sentencing discretion and a positive courtroom reception.[14]

The most astute critic of plea bargaining is University of
Colorado law professor Alan Alschuler. His definitive study of
the role of defense attorneys in plea negotiations discovered
some additional considerations which may also influence well-
intentioned defense attorneys to urge plea arguments not
wholly in their client's best interests:

> When an attorney lacks confidence in himself or is unsure of how
> the system operates or simply takes seriously his responsibility for a
> defendant's liberty, it must always be remembered that a decision to
> enter a plea argument can never be proven "wrong" while a decision
> to go to trial which misfires is a clear statement before the bench
> and bar of the attorney's inability and poor judgment.[15]

Despite the numerous advantages which plea bargaining
bestows upon the defense counsel, it is not without its drawbacks. Jackson Battle's article briefly explained some of these:

> What is the price of these benefits? Were they purchased with
> confidential client information; were they conditioned upon a less
> than vigorous defense, whether social relationships were cultivated,
> etc. A gauge of an attorney's adversariness would be his resolution of
> these dilemmas between service to his client and allegiance to the
> system.[16]

The essence of Alschuler's critique of plea bargaining is his
well-reasoned belief that it is "an inherently irrational method
of administering justice and necessarily destructive of a sound
attorney-client relationship."[17]

Although nearly all the criminal lawyers surveyed did not find plea bargaining distasteful, they were willing to acknowledge its numerous disadvantages. The main disadvantage to the criminal lawyer was that it degraded his professional status. A Miami lawyer said he hated to feel like a rug merchant as he haggled with the prosecutor over negotiations. A Chicago lawyer described his unhappy role in plea bargaining as a messenger boy running back and forth between his client and the district attorney's office. Many lawyers also agreed with a Washington attorney who sensed that there seemed to be a professional black mark against someone who appeared to be negotiating too frequently. A final disadvantage, and the most serious drawback thus far discussed, is the potential of plea bargaining to sacrifice one client's welfare for another. A number of lawyers noted that they knew of attorneys who would construct bargains with the prosecutor which involved negotiating several cases at a time. These "wholesalers" who depend upon a volume business would offer a beneficial deal for one client in exchange for a more harmful treatment of another.

Despite the simplicity of the plea bargaining concept as initially defined, it has recently taken on two novel twists. In Philadelphia, the lawyers spoke of the "slow plea," whereby a client selects a nonjury trial before a special panel of judges. By waiving a lengthy jury trial, the defendant is rewarded by having his case heard by a more lenient judge while still maintaining his right to appeal. The role of the defense attorney is to perform his courtroom responsibilities with acceptable vigor while not establishing any meddlesome obstacles in this slightly more than perfunctory adjudication. The second aberration was found in New Orleans and involved moving the plea negotiations forward to the screening process. The district attorney's office carefully screens all police arrests during a two week period. Once a case is accepted by the prosecutor, it will go to trial with little chance of plea bargaining. Defense counsel have therefore successfully interjected themselves into the screening process. By contributing some input into the district attorney's screening decision, it is hoped that a lesser charge will be accepted in exchange for the promise of a guilty plea.

Because of the importance of the plea negotiation, criminal lawyers have attempted to develop various strategies for optimizing their negotiation skills. The majority of the lawyers stressed that the lawyer's reputation both as a trustworthy negotiator and feared trial advocate was the basis of a successful strategy. As noted in Chapter 4, the lawyer's reputation is rapidly developed and widespread in its recognition. A San Franciscan succinctly explained this process: "Once you have the image of a trial worker you don't have to be restating the sincerity of your plea offers." Sometimes the individual lawyer profits from the reputation of his firm or associates. An East Coast lawyer working in one of the country's most prestigious criminal law firms commented that "Reputation is the all-important factor. Many in the U.S. Attorney's office are afraid of our firm and are very guarded in their relationships with us." Another lawyer from the same city also recognized this and complained (as a solo practitioner) that the court always seems more willing to settle with big firm lawyers than with the individual practitioners.

The defense attorneys are only concerned with one other court actor being influenced by their reputation. This is the assistant district attorney in charge of prosecuting the specific case. It is this adversary who must be convinced of the strength of your case as well as the weakness of his. Often it takes as much effort to convince a prosecutor of this situation as it does to prepare for a case that is inalterably going to be tried. The basic goal stated by numerous lawyers was to convince the prosecutor that if he refused the negotiation and went to trial, he would be humiliated and embarrassed in open court. The greater the reputation of a criminal lawyer as a successful advocate, the less convincing the facts of his particular case had to be. One Denver lawyer went so far as to wait for a new assistant prosecutor and then attempt to terrorize and destroy him in open court. After this humiliation, he could live off of his brutal reputation for at least the next six months. Although most lawyers were not so antagonistic nor openly aggressive toward their adversaries, this lawyer represented only a difference in degree rather than kind.

The extent to which a defense attorney can discover the strength of the opposition's case will also greatly affect the plea bargaining strategy. Once again the lawyer's reputation is critical in establishing a working rapport which is essential to formal as well as informal discovery. Many defense attorneys wanted to establish the reputation of being reasonable and honorable, rather than merely feared opponents. By convincing the prosecutor of his trustworthiness, the defense attorney can gain access to records and information denied to others. This knowledge can then allow him to make a reasonable and intelligent bargaining decision with his client. Once the prosecutor realizes that the defense attorney can be trusted in these dealings, discovery is expedited and the wheels of justice turn just a little bit faster.

Another element of plea bargaining strategy is the consideration of the proper case as well as its timing. A Philadelphia lawyer indicated that he carefully waits for the judges to be experiencing a serious backlog before he will attempt to plea bargain. Once he senses that judges and prosecutors are impatient to reduce the current logjam, he will make his move hoping to get some exceptional deals. Once the backlog is reduced or a new district attorney comes on the scene, this lawyer becomes extremely cautious about negotiations. A Denver attorney sums up this consideration: "The most important thing in plea bargaining is the type of case. For example, while middle-class marijuana cases with first offenders can be easily plea bargained, certain cases such as white-collar or cases with publicity where the district attorney wants a finding, cannot be! Biggest boon to plea bargaining has been the deferred sentencing theories where the lawyer bets the court his kid will stay clean if you give him a chance; otherwise I'll plead him guilty."

One of the most complex plea bargaining situations occurs in cases with multiple defendants. As previously noted, such cases often cause a race to the courthouse doors in order to achieve the maximum benefit from turning on coconspirators. These cases, which offer great potential for immunized cooperation, present a real dilemma for the defense attorney who believes he may have a chance to win the case but realizes the practical necessity of protecting his client from being the fall guy. These situations occur most commonly in drug cases and have caused such mental anguish to several of the attorneys interviewed that they have sworn off all future multiple defendant cases, especially if they involve narcotics.

It was generally agreed by the interviewees that it is the defense counsel rather than the prosecutor who usually initiates the plea bargaining negotiation. Most lawyers were skeptical about negotiations initiated by the prosecution and found them typically to be outlandish proposals. All agreed that the entire system could only work if the prosecutor was reasonable and experienced insofar as knowing the rules of the game. A few defense counsel started bargaining with the detective on the case rather than the district attorney but soon had to contact the prosecutor's office. A Los Angeles attorney offered the following typical pattern of interaction:

> First I see the detective and seek a lesser charge. Next I'll go to the district attorney's complaint department and ask for a lesser charge there. Then I go to the deputy district attorney handling the case in municipal court. Next I go to the deputy district attorney in Superior Court, and finally will go to his superior who is the one who will be handling the trial.

Although most lawyers would not go to so many different offices since they might be entering the case at a later time, this panorama of plea bargaining activity does indicate the parameters of a comprehensive negotiation strategy. The few defense counsel who did not enjoy plea bargaining were the only lawyers preferring to wait for the prosecutor to make the opening move.

As the earlier quote inferred, the negotiations may commence at almost any stage of the proceeding. Since the criminal justice system seems to operate like a giant sieve with the holes becoming smaller the longer the defendant remains in the system, most lawyers tried to begin negotiations as soon as possible. The longer a defendant remained enmeshed in the process and the more time and energy had been devoted to his retention, the less amenable the prosecutors were to negotiations. A few of the lawyers surveyed preferred to wait until after the case was bound over to the actual trial court because there generally seemed to be a better caliber of judges on this higher bench who might be more reasonable in plea negotiations. Again, each lawyer had his favorite time for negotiation, tempered of course, by the unique exigencies of the specific case.

It was a common occurrence for defendants who had instructed their counsel to refuse to bargain and insist on a trial to fall apart once the trial had begun. Many lawyers pinpointed this time to be the moment when the first prosecution witness took the stand. Once the collapse began, the negotiations commenced.

Every lawyer stressed that throughout the discussions of the feasibility of a negotiated plea and the actual bargaining sessions themselves, it was the client who had to make the ultimate decision. The attorney could make recommendations and evaluate the strengths and weaknesses, but the defendant still had the final word. With the flurry of federal suits involving competence of counsel growing from charges of coerced pleas by disgruntled clients, most lawyers have begun to tape record or take some type of notes, during all discussions with the client related to plea bargaining. The fear of such suits has also convinced the defense attorney to exert great care in "cooling out" his client once he has decided to plead guilty. It is much easier for a client to handle this decision, several weeks before his sentencing hearing. By this time, however, the reality of his conviction and possible prison sentence may be so upsetting that unless his attorney has not carefully prepared him for his eventual fate, he may angrily resort to punitive measures against his lawyer.

Most lawyers denied using coercion in order to force a recalcitrant client to plead guilty but were willing to speculate that several of their brethren, particularly those designated as "wholesalers" or "plea bargaining specialists," often exerted unprofessional pressure. Albert Alschuler believes that the use of this coercion is one of the major defects of the current plea bargaining system. He describes the varied styles in which the pressure may be applied:

> When a client initially denies his guilt, some lawyers use surprisingly harsh techniques to secure a confession. These lawyers emphasize

the importance of knowing the "full truth" in preparing a defense, but at the same time, a client who confesses is probably at a greater psychological disadvantage in resisting his lawyer's advice to plead guilty than one who denies his guilt. If the lawyer's own efforts are unsuccessful he may turn to the defendant's family and attempt to bend their shame and discomfort to his advantage. . . . Cop-out lawyers (wholesalers) sometimes go even beyond misadvice and emotional cajolery—on occasion they con their clients by offering them misinformation such as exaggerating their friendship with the district attorney. He may even report fictitious threats from a judge or prosecutor if a plea is not obtained.[18]

Plea bargaining is not a recent phenomenon, but, as many of the more senior private criminal lawyers indicated, it has been a permanent fixture of the urban criminal justice system ever since they began practicing. Despite its long history, however, it has only been brought under public scrutiny within the past decade. As a result of the increased publicity, staggering increases in caseload, and a variety of other, more subtle influences, there have been several recent trends affecting plea bargaining which were recognized by the interviewees.

Most defense lawyers pointed first to the increasing role of the district attorney in plea bargaining negotiations while the judiciary's role has been steadily declining.[19] A bitter West Coast attorney gave the following description of this development:

Because of having increased penalties for recidivist criminals, the district attorney now has been given undue power in plea bargaining sessions. It is the district attorney rather than the defense attorney who dominates this negotiation. This system rewards guilty defendants and penalizes innocent or not guilty defendants who are coerced to plead. The whole issue of plea bargaining is prosecutor propaganda. If they don't want it, all they have to do is stop doing it.

An additional change, noted in nearly every city, was the trend toward only charge bargaining. This means the defense attorney is only told what the recommended charge against his client will be, although the exact sentence will not be discussed. This increases the difficulty of convincing a client to plead guilty. Without the assurance of a specific disposition, the lawyer is on very shaky bargaining grounds. It is true that the defense counsel can get the prosecutor to make a sentencing recommendation and he does know the broad sentencing boundaries attached to a specific charge, but there is still a disturbingly large gray area. Most crimes allow the judge the choice between probation, suspended sentence, or a range of jail terms. Merely learning the exact charge is therefore of little utility to the defense lawyer and his client. This situation often puts extra pressure on the lawyer to attempt to predict for the client the way a particular judge will deal with his case.

A few cities such as Washington and Los Angeles have dealt with the increased exposure given to plea bargaining by formalizing the process and making it part of the standard court procedures. In Washington, for example, the defense attorney will often receive an invitation from the U.S. Attorney's office to commence negotiations and offering to accept a specific charge in exchange for a plea of guilty. If the letter is not answered within a specified time, the offer is automatically withdrawn. The offer only has to do with the charge and has no mention of possible sentence. Most lawyers appreciated the newer above-board style of negotiations but failed to see it contributing in any meaningful way to the general negotiation practices. It was generally ignored by most of the lawyers, who preferred to deal on a more personalized basis in the traditional manner.

A final recent development which has complicated the plea bargaining process and made negotiations even more difficult for the defense attorney, is the growing use of multiple billing and career criminal statutes. These statutes, which were found mainly in Houston and New Orleans, allow the courts to double or triple the length of sentence if the defendant is a "career criminal", i.e., has a record of several previous convictions. These statutes have been in force for many years but have only recently been used with any degree of regularity. Their impact upon plea bargaining is two-fold. First, it gives the prosecution added weight in the bargaining compromise, making his position even more advantageous. Secondly, the lengthy sentences have caused many defendants to disregard plea bargaining and opt for a jury trial because they have nothing to lose. The plea bargained sentence will be so severe, that whatever additional sentence they might receive as a penalty for demanding a jury trial, will be of little consequence.

NOTES

1. Criminal Law Institute, University of Denver College of Law, 1974.
2. Paul Wice, *Freedom for Sale* (Lexington, Mass.: Lexington Books, 1974).
3. Ibid, p. 49.
4. Ibid, p. 50.
5. Anthony C. Friloux, speech before the National College of Criminal Defense Lawyers, entitled "Motion Strategy–The Defense Attack," Houston, Texas, 1975.
6. Nathan Cohn, ed., *2nd Criminal Law Seminar* (Brooklyn, N.Y.: Central Book Company, 1962).
7. F. Lee Bailey and Henry E. Rothblatt, *Fundamentals of Criminal Advocacy* (Rochester, N.Y.: Lawyers Cooperative Publishing Company, 1974).
8. Nathan Cohn, ed., *1st Criminal Law Seminar* (Brooklyn, N.Y.: Central Book Company, 1961).
9. Bailey and Rothblatt, op. cit., p. 46.
10. Ibid, pp. 75-82.
11. Defense attorneys will usually not report tests with detrimental results.
12. Cohn, *1st Criminal Law Seminar,* op. cit.
13. Arthur Wood, *Criminal Lawyer* (New Haven, Conn.: University Press, 1967).
14. Jackson Battle, "In search of the adversary system," *Texas Law Review,* 50: 60, 1971.
15. Albert W. Alschuler, "The defense attorney's role in plea bargaining," *Yale Law Journal,* May 1975, p. 1179.
16. Battle, op. cit.
17. Alschuler, op. cit.
18. Ibid.
19. At the federal level the judges have been specifically prohibited from taking part in plea negotiations with regard to sentence.

Chapter 7

COURTROOM PERFORMANCE

Despite the fact that only approximately 10 percent of all the serious criminal cases will go to trial, most of the public's knowledge of and interest in the private criminal lawyer focuses upon his courtroom performance. Because of this emphasis by the public, as well as the lawyer's own concern about his litigation skills, this chapter will examine a few of the major topics inherent in his courtroom performance. Again, the topics were selected because of their interest both to the general public and the criminal lawyers themselves. A conscious attempt was made to screen out issues that were overly technical and would only interest a narrow range of readers. The major topics selected within the general issue of courtroom performance were the use and selection of juries, the range of common defense strategies, the art of cross-examination, and the private criminal lawyer's role in sentencing.

The Jury

The most basic decision to be made by a defense attorney is often whether to have his case tried before a judge or jury.

Although each option has its own assets and liabilities, nearly every lawyer interviewed stated an overwhelming preference for jury trials and would only offer one or two specific areas where he would prefer the case to be tried solely by the judge. For some lawyers it was not only a critical choice but an extremely complex one. As one Los Angeles lawyer related: "You not only have to consider which judge you are going to get but also the type of case and this doesn't mean just the subject matter, and also the complexity of the case. Finally, I am also concerned with where the case is to be tried and the resulting type of jurors I can expect."

Despite the staggering number of considerations, most lawyers were very specific as to when they would opt for a judge over a jury trial. If any general rule did emerge from their collective preferences, it was to select a judge if they were offering a technical defense and the law was on their side or the crime was especially heinous. Among the specific factors influencing their choice of judge over jury are the following:

(1) Cases involving lawyers;
(2) if your defendant has a very bad record and you do not believe you can keep evidence of this out of the record;
(3) if you wish to preserve a point a law on appeal;
(4) extremely complex cases where the defendant is guilty and the judge intelligent.

Several of the lawyers did prefer the courtroom environment of working before only a judge. It presented much less pressure and allowed the judge and lawyers to concentrate on the legal complexities of the case rather than playing to the jury. Despite this attitude, however, the defense attorneys realized that they could usually count on a jury giving their clients the best deal and being more amenable to a wider range of defenses. Also, several of the more theatrical attorneys enjoyed the showmanship involved in dealing with a jury rather than the more sterile presentation to a judge. The lawyers found that they always had a chance of convincing one juror and at least settling for a hung jury. The greater the certainty of the defendant's guilt, the stronger they felt the need to rely on the jury rather than the judge. As one cynical San Francisco lawyer put it: "I'd rather go before twelve bigots instead of just one." It was mildly surprising to find so many lawyers who found the juries to be significantly less prosecution-oriented than the typical judge. A Houston lawyer succinctly summarized jury preferences by stating: "In state court at least you have the chance to really try and pick and choose who is going to be deciding that case. Otherwise, you are stuck with whatever judge happens to be assigned to your court. I am just always amazed at what a jury will do and their instincts for a fair decision."

Nearly all of the criminal lawyers surveyed thought that the jury selection was one of the most important parts of a case, if not the most important. A small minority of lawyers felt that too much emphasis was placed upon jury selection. They were especially critical of lawyers who devoted a great amount of time and energy to "the art of jury selection." One San Francisco lawyer was very skeptical of these experts and stated that "any twelve are really okay. I rarely use up my challenges. All I look for are obvious signs and let my common sense intuition guide the way."

When questioned further about the premises underlying the importance of jury selection, the criminal lawyers admitted either directly or indirectly that many jurors do not carefully consider all of the legal arguments raised in a case. It is believed that the behavior of jurors is much more determined by such socializing influences as their ethnic and religious background, race, and socioeconomic status. Despite the overall high opinion regarding the quality of jury decision-making held by the majority of lawyers interviewed, the attorneys realized that there was normally a crucial minority of jurors who were influenced by sociological and demographic factors from their own background, rather than thoughtful evaluation of the legal arguments presented in the courtroom—and you only need one or two jurors to prevent a conviction.

The criminal lawyers have developed a strategy for jury selection based upon the above background factors. Before discussing the specific types of jurors thought to be most and least sympathetic to the defense, let us first examine a few of the general strategies utilized by criminal lawyers during the voir dire process. The voir dire process allows the lawyers for both prosecution and defense to question the jurors and determine their desirability for selection. The questioning may be done either directly to the jury panel or through the judge who interrogates the potential jurors on the basis of his own questions as well as questions supplied by the attorneys. At all time, in either method, the judge has the final say in determining whether a lawyer may ask a particular question.

Several lawyers were unable to articulate a specific set of guidelines they follow and could only describe a gut feeling of intuitive response to each juror. These lawyers often said they looked for people who appeared to be good listeners and reminded them of their friends. Thus, if there seemed to be the establishment of a rapport during the sketchy questioning period, the defense attorney would be in favor of selection, regardless of the specific answers to the questions raised. The word "rapport" was mentioned by several lawyers, often in association with the operation of their intuition and abilities as accomplished amateur psychologists. The following is a typical cross-section of some of these general strategies:

(1) A New Orleans attorney tried to exclude jurors who were not good inductive thinkers. In trying to pick a juror who would be fair, he looked to body language, rapport, and responsiveness.

(2) A Denver lawyer concentrated on the particular issue in a case. He would analyze the situation, put it into its proper legal framework, and then within that framework work out a theory of the case. Additionally, he would carefully consider the emotions that might be aroused by particular issues during the trial.

(3) A Los Angeles defense counsel went the opposite way. He would accept the first twelve jurors and then try to work with their estimated I.Q. He stated, "You have to deal with what you got. Try to determine what they are and then go after them."

(4) Juror intelligence was also critical for a Philadelphia lawyer who always tried to get as intelligent a juror as possible. He believed that the greater the intelligence, the more capable the juror would be of understanding and harboring the "reasonable doubt" concept.

For most defense attorneys, the most significant element of their voir dire strategy was their ability to discover racism and prejudice among the jurors. As Colorado lawyer Charles Traylor commented before the Denver Criminal Law Seminar, "It is

practically useless to ask the question, 'Do you have any prejudice against this defendant because of his race, color or creed?' I
have never heard a juror answer this general question in the
affirmative." The lawyer must then develop more subtle and
indirect approaches to discovering juror prejudice. Traylor
recommends some of the following types of questions in order
to come at the problem in a less direct manner:

> Are you acquainted with the activities of the (SLA) (B'nai
> B'rith), or the (John Birch Society)? Do you believe that organiza-
> tion is doing a good job? Are you familiar with Father Berrigan?
> Heard him speak? Have you ever taken part in a protest march or a
> sit-in demonstration? What is your opinion of the aims or methods
> used in protest marches or sit-in demonstrations? [The word "preju-
> dice" should be avoided, if possible; perhaps "feeling" is a better
> word.] [1]

A San Francisco lawyer recounted that Charles Garry, one of
the West Coast's most highly esteemed criminal attorneys,
would attack the problems of jury prejudice by going to a
blackboard and writing the terms "objective racist" and then
"subjective racist." He would explain each term and would
eventually have the jurors be able to admit that he was probably
a "subjective racist." By confronting the issue head-on, Garry
thought he would heighten the consciousness level of the jury
to the point that several members might even wind up overcompensating for their supposed prejudice. Unfortunately, this style
of inquiry required a great deal of lawyer-juror discussion which
is no longer tolerated in most West Coast courtrooms, where
judges are currently controlling the voir dire process.

The lawyers, despite their experience in the courtroom, are
still never sure about the possibilities of hidden racism as the
following incident reported by Philadelphia lawyer James
McDermott seems to indicate: "This guy looked like Santa
Claus. Great juror. It took a long time to pick a jury on that
trial and after a while you get tired. This was the last juror to be
chosen. The district attorney yawned and asked by habit if
there was any reason unknown to us why you couldn't be fair
in this case? Santa looked cautiously at the black defendant and
said 'Well, I don't like niggers.' "[2]

In the South where racial prejudice had for so long dominated social life, the lawyers who were interviewed found the
voir dire inadequate to the task. As a New Orleans attorney
commented, "These are generally very biased jurors. It runs in
both racial directions so it becomes a stupid game. You find
some blacks overcompensating for their race when they get on
the jury, while others are overly sympathetic." Since all cities
visited had sizeable percentages of racial minorities, the issue of
prejudice was of equal concern to defense attorneys in *all*
regions of the country.

A second general consideration in jury selection mentioned
frequently was the importance of the type of case. Lislie Gillen
of San Francisco addressed himself to this issue in a recent
seminar and offered the following advice:

> Now the type of case that you have influences the kind of jury you
> want to get. Sometimes you have a case where if you had emotional
> people on the jury, people that would be swayed alone by emotion
> and not intelligent enough to grasp refinements of legal instructions
> that they were going to receive at the end of the case, eliminate
> them for you want thinking people in such a case. On the other
> hand, there are a lot of cases where you don't want thinking people,
> you want emotional people.

This common sense approach was repeated by several lawyers
who warned against establishing hard and fast rules. They discouraged dogmatism and urged each case and defendant be
analyzed on their own merits to determine which juror would
be most advantageous. Once a profile of the ideal juror was
composed, a few lawyers thought that if the client could afford
it, investigators would be hired to research the background of
prospective jurors, especially on topics which the lawyer could
reasonably expect the judge to prohibit questioning on grounds
of relevance.

A final tactical consideration mentioned by several lawyers
was the fear of boring or antagonizing prospective jurors during
the voir dire to the extent that they would remain prejudiced
against you and your client during the actual trial. One West
Coast lawyer warned that, "You might prolong the exam to the
point where you have so tired out and worn out your prospec-

tive jurors before they are sworn in, that they become disgusted with you and turn against you. . . . I think you should change the pattern of your questioning so that it appears, at least on the surface, that you are giving it a new approach, and keeping their interest up."[3]

As the plethora of theories on jury selection indicate, the defense attorneys are perplexed and frustrated by their voir dire responsibilities. The words of a young Los Angeles attorney reflect this disillusionment: "I no longer have any idea what to look for on a jury. Sometimes you want a few crazies to get a mistrial. You can't realistically hope to get twelve good jurors so you try to pick up three or four good ones. What the hell, they never give honest answers and if either side gets a really good one, the other side will bump him off." This issue of juror veracity was noted in many of the interviews and was generally unresolved. The lawyers were especially suspicious when jurors denied hearing anything about a case which had received a great deal of pretrial publicity. The best juror was viewed as the one who admitted he had seen the article in the paper but promised to decide the case on the evidence presented in court. As a general rule, all lawyers warned against selecting any juror who appeared too interested in wanting to be selected. These zealots were almost always proprosecution.

Moving from general strategies to specific preferences, most lawyers identified certain types of people who were to be either avoided or preferred as jurors. It was interesting to note that as the lawyers attempted to select the jurors who would be most favorably disposed toward their case, they would often look for jurors who were most like themselves. One San Francisco lawyer even went so far as to prefer jurors who looked like himself. Fundamentally, however, most lawyers agreed with a Houston attorney's observation that, "We are all programmed how to think and that is why nobody wants a German Lutheran on one of their juries."

A Denver attorney composed the following list of recommended jurors:

Good for Prosecutors:
(1) Health professionals—have a stake in the community and tend to convict.

(2) Former military—identify strongly with the state and its authority.
(3) Civil servants—similar to ex-military.
(4) Senior citizens—rather intolerant of "unusual" conduct.
(5) Insurance men—stable with strong interest in community.
Good for Defense:
(1) Musicians, artists, etc.—accept unusual behavior.
(2) Social workers—contact with conditions that lead to crime.
(3) Engineers, accountants, and technical people—need almost a "mathematical certainty" before they will convict.
(4) School teachers—there are no bad children.
(5) Young—tolerant of antiestablishment behavior.[4]

The influence of ethnic and racial backgrounds generally were believed to be most important in determining juror voting predilections. Jurors from minority groups, be it ethnic, racial, or religious, were found to be the most sympathetic to the defendant. The explanation offered for this relationship is that these minorities are able to understand oppression and therefore are more sympathetic to the plight of the defendant. This usually means trying to get as many blacks and browns on the jury as possible but as Philadelphia attorney Joel Moldovsky warns, you have to watch out for the Uncle Toms. Moldovsky wants his juries to be as similar to his client as possible and, "There are blacks out there, dear to my heart, who feel that no black person should be convicted after 200 years of oppression. That's my man!"[5]

Not all racial minorities are equally desirable. The lawyers listed the blacks and then the Chicanos but urged avoidance of most orientals, with the exception of those under thirty. The lawyers explained that most orientals have a deep respect for law and authority and would blindly believe whatever the police officer testified to. Certain religious groups such as Lutherans and Baptists were also avoided because of their strict doctrines and reverence for authority. It was believed that members of these faiths would hold the defendant strictly accountable for his acts and be unwilling to consider mitigating circumstances.

Interviewees also thought that lawyers should try to get more than one minority member on a jury. Stranded in isolation, the minority juror may overcompensate and be even tougher on a defendant of similar background. In a city like San Francisco populated with a dazzling miscellany of ethnic and racial groups, criminal lawyers have a difficult time sorting out the implications of one's ethnic identity. The following categorization by one of the city's acknowledged jury selection masters indicates the complexity of the problem. "I try to exclude orientals and Italians who seem instilled with the idea of respect for police power. I also dislike Swedes and Germans, I try to get Irish, Jews, Greeks, blacks, Russian emigrés—people who are more liberal or who have suffered at the hands of the law."

Several lawyers like to stress the importance of social class and occupation, often utilizing a quasi-Marxist theory of jury selection. Generally they want people from the lower end of the bureaucratic structure who are somewhat oppressed. All advocated avoidance of lower-level managers and foreman types, who have a reputed respect for order and authority. As noted earlier nearly all defense lawyers preferred youth to the aged, citing the former's lack of blind respect for the state and their unwillingness to tolerate aberrant behavior patterns.

It was interesting to find that many defense lawyers desire particular types of jurors in particular types of cases. A West Coast defense attorney who specializes in drunk driving cases always tries to get drinkers in on these cases. He said that he looks for a red nose and bags under the eyes. A Philadelphia lawyer tries to select intelligent jurors in scientific cases, while a Denver lawyer specializing in porno and sex cases will select women because they are less shocked than men. He will also look for the best educated and well-read jurors. He avoids middle aged men who are buyers of the smut but will not admit it. Women in menopause are a final group he wishes to exclude.

Rape cases presented a sharp division of opinion as to which sex would be most sympathetic to the defendant. A very slight majority preferred women jurors, especially if the victim was young. They were thought to be more objective and knowledgeable on sexual issues while being more critical of the victim's behavior. A sizable minority of attorneys, however, believed that men would be most tolerant since they could empathize more easily with the defendant's sex drives and frustrations.

Even after the voir dire, the relationship between the defense attorney and the jury may significantly affect the outcome of the trial. As one San Francisco attorney pointed out, "It is absolutely critical that it be recognized that there is a psychodrama occurring in the jury box. Jurors are doing different play acting with each other and this can seriously affect the outcome of the case. Some are trying to emerge as leaders while others are flirting and even making sexual advances."

Realization of the internal machinations of juries is just one of the considerations defense attorneys must keep in mind as they attempt to communicate effectively with its members. The difficult task of winning the friendship of the jury is probably the lawyer's most challenging task. A West Coast lawyer found the situation analogous to a comedian who specializes in improvisation appearing before a new audience:

> You have to try and alert yourself to their inclination and their reactions. If they are people who are apparently good natured, are ready to smile, a little moderate humor injected may be all right, but don't overdo it because it appears that you are being callous to the tragic plight of the client you are representing. On the other hand, if you look at the panel and they all have the expressions on their faces that was worn continuously by the late Calvin Coolidge, stick right to business.[6]

Continuing the analogy with the comedian, a highly successful (and flamboyant) Philadelphia lawyer added that he never saw a laughing jury convict anyone. After observing this attorney, and several others perform in the courtroom and the barroom, the author is confident that if they ever gave up the practice of law, they could always become successful professional stand-up comedians.

Most interviewees were careful not to appear to be talking down to or pandering to the jury. A conscious effort was made to develop a low-key style which would be nonthreatening to jury members. A Florida lawyer went so far as to admit that his facility for language allows him to alter his dialogue and speech pattern so as to be congruent with whatever part of the state he is in. A Texas lawyer, who sensed that he did the same thing, agreed that it was done almost subconsciously, although he believed it was vital to establishing an agreeable relationship with the jury. Most lawyers felt that there was a dislike of outside attorneys. It was very difficult to overcome this initial hostility without some peace offering or evidence that one was not as "foreign" as first suspected. Several lawyers would also attempt to belittle themselves and flatter the prosecutor in an attempt to win the jury's friendship and sympathy.

Most lawyers also recommended that defense counsel should try to have it appear that the jury had reached the desired judgment independently. This was especially true in a long, protracted trial where it is difficult not to appear to be leading the jury around by the nose. This is an uncomfortable feeling, and juries will often punish defendants whose lawyers have placed them in this condescending position.

Coming before the courtroom with your good reputation preceding your appearance, was usually thought to have more negative than positive ramifications. A few criminal lawyers believed that prosecutors would try harder; judges would lean over backwards to "even things out"; and the jury would sit back and wait for miracles or at least a few magical tricks. If something dazzling was not forthcoming, the jury might take out its disappointment on the defendant.

A small minority of lawyers did not find their relationship to the jury to be of such critical import. They believed that it is often imperative during the course of the trial to ignore the jury in order to concentrate on what the witness is saying and doing. These lawyers believed that since the jurors are probably reacting in the same way you are reacting to the various witnesses, you can simply use yourself as a model of what turns them on or off. Consistent with this attitude was a generally low opinion of the ability of jurors to concentrate for very long periods of time or grasp a very wide range of isues of moderate complexity.

In several jurisdictions visited—San Francisco, Los Angeles, Washington, and Houston—there was a continuing trend to decrease the role of the lawyer during the voir dire. Viewed by most judges and court administrators as one of the most abused privileges of the defense attorney, this power to question prospective jurors was being turned over to the judge, who would ask his own questions as well as a few acceptable questions from each lawyer. Nearly all criminal lawyers objected to this lessening of their role and lack of control over who might be selected as a juror. Nevertheless, the trend seems inexorable and is just another manifestation of the court's attempt to streamline the judicial process in order to reduce the mounting backlog of cases. Another feared curtailment of the defense lawyer's control over juries is the establishment of the nonunanimous jury, which can prevent mistrials and further facilitate the decision-making process. Thus far, it has only been operating for a brief period in a handful of jurisdictions. The reduction of jury size is a far more probable development, but does not seem to have any significant consequences for the criminal lawyer. In Florida, where reduced juries are currently being used on a rathter selective basis, most lawyers did not find it to be of much import in affecting their success rate or courtroom style.

An interesting recent trend, for those who can afford it, is to have psychologists and other experts advise the defense counsel as to the best type of juror in a particular case. The successful lawyers in the recent Maurice Stans trial argued that their experts aided them in selecting a juror that was sure to acquit. One lawyer interviewed went so far as to have an expert in "body language" advise him as to what importance could be assigned to the various physical movements of prospective jurors while they were being questioned. It must be remembered that the use of these experts and investigators in jury selection is found in only a select number of cases, usually at the federal level. The costs are prohibitive for all but the most affluent defendants.

In concluding this section on juries, it was noteworthy that so many criminal lawyers found the jury system to be very acceptable. They did not offer this opinion based merely because they thought that juries would reach favorable dispositions but rather because jurors were able to reach intelligent and just decisions.

Defense Strategies

This section will discuss the variety of defenses most commonly used by criminal lawyers. We shall also examine how these defenses are presented and some problems from unique types of cases. Since entire textbooks are devoted to the topics examined in this brief subsection, it will of necessity be an extremely cursory review which will serve as a general introduction to the subject of defense strategies with a limited analysis of lawyer preferences.

One of the pervasive myths of defense strategies is that the astute lawyer can maneuver the case before a sympathetic or lenient judge, thereby guaranteeing a favorable disposition. It is true that "judge shopping" was a critical task of criminal lawyers in past years, but our survey indicated that it is rarely practiced in the nine cities visited. Today, in most cities, the defendant's case is randomly assigned to a particular courtroom and there is little room for adjustment although one switch is permitted if a serious personality conflict appears inevitable. Many lawyers hesitate to even use this solitary opportunity for fear of alienating the judge, who they may have to face again in the near future in another case.

Philadelphia had a unique plan for assignment of judges which was tactically tied into their "slow plea" process of negotiation. It was common knowledge that the calendar court judge had established two groups of judges—a group of lenient judges, who would try only nonjury trials, and a group of hard-nosed judges, who would try jury trials. Thus defendants who opted for a jury trial would be systematically penalized for taking this more protracted alternative and could expect to receive harsher sentences. Beyond this choice between jury and nonjury there was very little maneuvering permitted.

The defense attorneys were indifferent to the loss of an opportunity to judge-shop. As the number of criminal court judges has greatly increased in nearly every jurisdiction, the lawyers felt content to simply go with the luck of the draw. Many lawyers were appreciative of the change stating that it was one less problem they had to consider. Several also noted that it had a positive effect in reducing corruption and payoffs to certain unscrupulous judges.

This discussion of the range of defenses commonly used by criminal lawyers has been divided into two basic categories: (1) the defenses that are negative in their thrust, i.e., are attacking the prosecution's case and pointing out its numerous weaknesses; and (2) the defenses that are positive in nature offering alternative theories or mitigating circumstances. Turning first to the negative group, most lawyers viewed their major goal to be the creation of a reasonable doubt in the minds of the judge or jury. Since the burden of proof is placed upon the prosecutor to prove the defendant's guilt *beyond* a reasonable doubt, all a defense attorney has to show is that his adversary has failed to satisfy this obligation. Thus, a defendant's freedom is often tied to the strength of the prosecutor's case rather than that of his own. Several defense attorneys warned that you usually need at least a hint of something beyond the negative approach to satisfy an inquisitive jury, but once you have offered this modicum of an alternative, you can return your energies entirely to destroying the prosecutor's case. One Houston lawyer referred to this style of defense as his "slip and slide" approach, where he would hold the prosecution on predicates and challenge it on everything. Frequently it is difficult for laymen to realize that the defense attorney has only to show that the state has been unable to prove its case, rather than being able to convince the court of the defendant's innocence, but these are the rules of the game, and it is the most common perspective from which a criminal lawyer plans his defense.

Merely raising reasonable doubt as to the defendant's guilt is a very vague objective which is usually broken down into more specific strategies, such as suppressing evidence, attacking the credibility of witnesses, challenging the acceptability of the identification process and a wide range of other constitutional and miscellaneous errors or deficiencies.

By challenging the prosecution's evidence through suppression motions based upon illegal search and seizure or related due process violations the defense attorney can establish a successful defense. If the court dismisses crucial evidence because it has been illegally obtained, the prosecution may be forced to dismiss the case. As a New Orleans lawyer, who relied heavily on such motions, stated, "The purpose of a trial is to keep out what hurts your client and put in what will help. If the state is able to get everything into the case that they want, then it is inevitable you will lose the case. My job is mainly to confuse witnesses and jurors so as to raise probable doubt."

An equally important negative defense in creating this probable doubt is the lawyer's ability to challenge or impeach the credibility of witnesses. Given the large number of cases dependent upon the informant's testimony or a state's witness (such as a coconspirator who won the race to the prosecutor's doorstep), it is critical that the credibility of such testimony be destroyed. In these types of cases this is often the *only* defense available.[7] Although a few defense attorneys are so adept at cross-examination as to show the jury that the witness has lied, it is more common to cast doubts as to the character of the informer and his personal stake in seeing the defendant convicted. A Los Angeles lawyer who frequently finds his clients the victim of such informer testimony stated that he tries to emphasize the relationship between the informant and the government. He always makes a motion for the disclosure of the informant and has won several cases where the government thought it was more important to maintain the anonymity of the informant than to prosecute the defendant. He also added that there are elements of bluff here, and that the prosecution may back down because it realizes that the informant's credibility is not thoroughly verified according to constitutional standards.

A third area where astute defense attorneys can challenge the prosecution's case is the identification of the defendant. Most witnesses are not professional testifiers (such as the police) and they can easily be challenged by the defense attorney as to the certainty of their identification. Especially in cases which are drawn out over several months and years and where the lawyer appears especially aggressive, the identifying witness often has a difficult time convincing the jury of the accuracy of the identification. Many lawyers tried to have the judge speak to the jury concerning the foibles of the identification. Most lawyers said they preferred this defense and used it most frequently in robbery cases where they tried to infer that most victims are so hysterical during the actual holdup as to be incapable of making a certain identification.

A final negative defense noted by several criminal lawyers was that of entrapment. This defense argues that the defendant was induced by the state into committing the act and would not have done so but for this encouragement. This defense is used most often in narcotics and gambling cases although it is becoming fairly common with prostitution and other victimless crimes. The primary job of the lawyer who utilizes this defense is to first establish the relationship between the informant and the state agency and to then prove that they initially planted the idea for the criminal act.

The defense is also anxious to offer its own positive arguments or alternative theories, in addition to attacking the prosecution's case and raising reasonable doubt. The large majority of lawyers stated that their most commonly used positive defense was to show that the defendant lacked the required statutory intent. This defense is usually termed "diminished capacity" and is often used in conjunction with such negative defenses as entrapment. Many lawyers were skeptical about the saleability of the diminished capacity defense to a jury that was unmoved by subtle semantic nuances. It was a defense either to be used before a jury in combination with other more convincing strategies or reserved for a bench trial. In crimes such as murder and burglary, most lawyers agreed with a San Francisco attorney who almost always used it in these serious crimes and tried to stress that there are different degrees of intent. He also believed this is a relevant time to bring in the emotional stability and drunkenness of his client.

A second defense strategy is the broad tactic of raising a narrow or technical issue. A Miami lawyer explained this style of defense in the following way: "Play the rules to your benefit—technicalities, failures to comply with the rules. I have no sympathy for the prosecutor in these kinds of errors. Even half of the cases can be dismissed due to the clerk's failure to file properly. Just simple negligence on their part and you are a fool not to take advantage of it." A few lawyers have successfully relied on this type of defense. They typically specialize in drug cases or drunk driving. They have a ready crew of expert witnesses who can come on to attack the government's credibility. The sloppiness of the police laboratories was recently documented by a Justice Department survey.[8] Even though a technical error may be only a small hole in the prosecution's otherwise airtight case, it is up to the defense attorney to enlarge it to the point where it casts doubts on the credibility of the entire charge.

In cities where the criminal court docket was badly overcrowded, many lawyers tried to stall their case as long as possible. If the case was not very serious, the prosecutor might be convinced to drop the charges or drastically reduce them. As one Washington, D.C. attorney commented, "If you can make your client be enough of a logistical hassle for the prosecutor, his case can often be allowed to fall between the cracks." A few lawyers, such as Cecil Moore of Philadelphia, have developed the tactic of stalling to a fine art, as described by Joel Moldovsky, another Philadelphia defense attorney:

> If Cecil Moore is on the case, the district attorney can throw out all his plans for cutting costs and reducing the backlog. Cecil can find more ways to get a trial postponed than a confirmed bachelor for avoiding his wedding day. Either Moore is already involved in another case when the district attorney would like to schedule a trial or he has a defense witness who is missing, or he objects that one of the district attorney's prosecution witnesses is missing or any one of a thousand other reasons. . . . And while the case is dragging on, Moore's clients fondly hope that the prosecution witnesses will grow old and die or get hit by a truck or get discouraged at always showing up in court and being sent home again, or forget whatever it was they planned to say.[9]

Many lawyers agreed with Moldovsky and found that the longer they could delay, the better the chance for a beneficial plea bargain. The cardinal rule stated by a Denver lawyer and repeated in city after city was, "They never beat me as long as I keep out of the courtroom."

Defense lawyers also try to introduce as many mitigating factors as possible into their presentation. Even if they do not lead to an acquittal, they may influence the jury's sentence recommendation. This defense emphasizes the positive aspects of the defendant's character and attempts to portray the current charge as an irrational act in an otherwise law-abiding life. A wide range of personality attributes may also be introduced as alternatives to the sociopathic personality the prosecution is attempting to describe.

The two most common defense strategies seen on television shows—self-defense and alibi—are rarely used by private criminal lawyers. Several lawyers said that they were such trite and overused strategies that juries were strongly disposed toward not taking them very seriously. This can be very frustrating to the defendant who does have a legitimate claim to either defense but is prevented from doing so by its previous overuse.

Alibi witnesses are rarely believed because most are friends or relatives of the defendant and because their credibility can be easily destroyed by even the most inexperienced prosecutor. Once the jury senses that the defendant is considering perjuring himself or his friends to save his own neck, they often feel the necessity for punishing him.

A few lawyers have used the ultimate in mitigating causes which is an insanity plea. Many lawyers were hesitant to offer such a defense because of its cumbersome nature as well as the horrible conditions existing in most mental institutions. As one Denver attorney complained, "It may be easy to get them in but it's very very difficult to get them out of these institutions, and when they do come out they are often worse off." Many of the lawyers also complained that their most serious mental cases are in bizarre misdemeanors which really places them on the horns of a dilemma. Do they make a big deal out of helping the crazy client or do they simply dispose of the case easily with a guaranteed light sentence? It is a messy problem, particularly when the family becomes involved, with no one ever satisfied with the outcome.

Most lawyers found that the insanity defense rarely worked. Juries were believed to be too unsophisticated to deal with the complexity of psychiatric issues. The psychiatrists who appear as expert witnesses for either side are rarely persuasive. A Washington defense lawyer found that the jurors rarely paid close attention to the psychiatrist and simply scrutinized the defendant during the trial, making their independent judgement as to whether he "looked" crazy. Defense attorneys realize this and often instruct their client to display nervous tics or other unusual mannerisms that might appear convincing to the jury.

A Denver attorney who has earned a national reputation for his expertise in the use of the insanity plea offers the following recommendations regarding its use:

(1) Take a complete biographical history;
(2) an immediate massing of experts and lay witnesses (psychiatrists, psychologists, toxicologists, neurosurgeons, etc.);
(3) be ready to document and prove bizarre behavior by witnesses (suicide attempts, deviant sexual practices);
(4) usually best not to put defendant on the witness stand;

(5) plea of competency for trial;

(6) credibility of experts enhanced or lessened by the quality of examinations and time spent with defendant;

(7) utilize presumption of sanity to go forth first with evidence of insanity—hit first and impress the jury.[10]

After selecting his strategy, the defense counsel must decide how to work it most effectively into the course of the trial. Among the major opportunities he has for presenting his defense are the opening statement, direct examination of witnesses, cross-examination, redirect examination, and finally the summation. One additional tactical decision of extreme importance is whether or not to allow the defendant to testify in his own behalf.

Most lawyers were concerned over the style and composition of the opening statement but did not attach great significance to its capacity to influence the judge's or jury's ultimate decision. It was an opportunity to lay the groundwork for the defense and direct the jury to the flaws in the prosecution's case. Many lawyers also stressed it was an opportunity to educate the jury as to the concept of reasonable doubt and the prosecution's burden of proof.

Morris Shenker, nationally respected defense counsel, summarizes the purpose of the opening statement in the following way: (1) It serves as a guideline for the jury to follow the defense; (2) it is a vehicle to create a favorable attitude in the jury's mind toward the case, the accused, and the lawyer; (3) it creates an interest by the jury in the defense of the case; (4) it establishes in the minds of the jury that the prosecution is presenting only one side of the case; and (5) it should be waived only in the rarest of cases.[11]

As the examination of witnesses will be discussed in the next section of this chapter, let us move on to the opposite end of the trial and see what use is made of the final summation. Again, let us return to Morris Shenker of St. Louis: "In terms of the lawyer's direct participation and responsibility in the outcome of the trial, final argument is the single most important aspect of the case. . . . Every conceivable matter that has transpired since the inception of the case is culminated in the brief time span of the closing argument."[12]

The interviewees varied as to their evaluation of the relative importance of the closing argument, although the majority thought it to be the most important stage of the trial and none were willing to discount it entirely. One Philadelphia lawyer strongly believed that juries are much more strongly affected by evidence than speeches but most lawyers were not willing to take the chance of underplaying this final opportunity. Jim MacInnes of San Francisco, acknowledged to be one of the city's leading criminal lawyers, offered the following simple rule for constructing an effective final argument: "The all-engrossing rule is the rule of work. . . . Because no wonderful presentation, barring accident, ever came easily. You get out of an argument pretty much precisely what you put into it."[13]

Most lawyers would prefer not to have to put their client on the witness stand. It is only when they have no choice such as in an extortion or bribery case where the defendant must tell his side of the story that a defendant will be permitted to take the stand. The reason for this reluctance is that there is a strong feeling that the defendant rarely helps himself. Most of the lawyers could recount recent cases which had been lost when the defense counsel attempted to institute a positive defense with the defendant's testimony being a key factor. The majority of lawyers were confident that the jury would understand if it was carefully explained during the opening statement as to why his client would not have to take the stand.

Most of the lawyers interviewed looked forward to going to trial with great anticipation. A Philadelphia lawyer described his feelings as being so intense that he would almost throw up on the morning of the trial. It was reminiscent of the way athletes describe their high emotional state just prior to the championship game. Many of the lawyers sequestered themselves from all distractions, such as family and friends, once the courtroom drama began. They realized that it is actually they who are on trial and not so much their clients. The spotlight falls on the defense attorney as he aggressively battles the prosecutor, interrogates witnesses, and spars with the judge. It is often on the basis of his performance even more than the defendant's actual guilt or innocence that the case may be ultimately disposed.

The two key words that were linked to courtroom success in interview after interview were preparation and aggressiveness. A respected San Francisco lawyer explained the importance of preparation: "Basically the way to win is to prepare. Investigate all the witnesses, look at the law to find all possible defenses, and prepare your client to be acceptable to the jury."

A Philadelphia lawyer discussed the intellectual preparation as a type of orchestrated chess match. Several lawyers linked preparation with the way a theater production is planned and then executed. The jury, of course, is analogous to the audience which the performers must control and manipulate.

The other element of defense—the art of controlled aggressiveness—was best described by William Ferdon of San Francisco, who reminded lawyers that they must remain basically contentious: "If you are not criticizing what the other side has said, if you are not pulling it apart, then you are not trying to make things in the defense image after the prosecution has offered theirs. If you are not going to be as destructive as you possibly can be, you are not arguing, you are giving a nice speech."[14]

A younger defense counsel from the same city, echoed Ferdon's comments but with a semantic style bred in the 1970s: "Good trial lawyers must have an intuitive feel for the dynamics of aggressive behavior. You must be able to anticipate and assume a positively aggressive stance which will earn their respect."

Not all lawyers were so enthralled with the courtroom drama. Several had become bored and found a certain recognizable pattern developing in cases involving the same offense. Their preparation was eased by the repetitious nature of their work which had begun to take on a monotonous tone. Many younger criminal lawyers with three-five years experience were most frequently disappointed in their practice and suffered from this ennui. Since most of the lawyers comprising this group were unable to defend the more interesting federal cases or the heinous state crimes, they were forced to compete for the few remaining cases not going to the public defender, and it did seem that these cases fell into a repetitive pattern and were rarely intellectually challenging. Drunk driving, shoplifting, and narcotics were the most common categories of cases handled by this group.

Cross-Examination

If litigation is the most essential element of the craft of lawyering, then cross-examination is generally conceded to be the quintessential art of the litigator. Jim MacInnes of San Francisco compares cross-examination with an "unequal struggle that ensues when a prize fighter holds a man with one hand and hits him with another."[15] Its basic objectives are noted by Bailey and Rothblatt as either discrediting the direct examination and testimony of witnesses against your client or bringing out something which is in favor of the defendant. Their treatise, entitled *Fundamentals of Criminal Advocacy,* offers the following strategies for accomplishing these objectives: (1) Show that the witness is incompetent as to the events he claims to have observed; (2) show that the passing of time and suggestions of others (i.e., police and prosecutors) have colored or exaggerated his recollection of the facts; (3) indicate contradictions in his testimony; (4) induce the witness to admit his uncertainty as to statements made directly; (5) expose his bias or prejudice; and (6) impeach his character.[16]

The lawyers interviewed in this study generally agreed upon three or four cross-examination strategies or rules which were necessary if any of the previously noted objectives were to be reached. They all stressed the importance of preparation and the necessity of knowing all of the answers from both sides. The worst thing that could happen to a defense attorney was to be surprised by a witness's response while the stupidest thing he could do was to ask a question that he did not know the answer to. It was also frowned upon to ask the type of question which was so open-ended as to permit the witness to slide by the intended answer. The successful cross-examiner had to maintain careful control over the questioning process, being sure to plug all possible escape routes. Jake Ehrlich, the Dean of West Coast criminal lawyers, offered the following advice on this issue of client control: "There is no point in giving a witness an opportunity to add facts which further probing may recall to him. The lawyer is not always smarter than the witness and the

witness who is honest and is obviously trying to tell the truth as
he understands it, has the jury on his side. Personally, I never
cross-examine unless it is absolutely necessary."[17]

All defense counsel agreed with Ehrlich that if the cross-
examination was not handled carefully, it could have a deadly
effect upon the jury. Most lawyers had to ask themselves
whether the cross-examination should be done at all, which
items should be included, and—the most important issue—when
the questioning should be terminated. Ehrlich's common-sen-
sical and well-respected advice on these topics is well worth
repeating:

> No matter how long the witness has taken on direct, if his testimony
> has not harmed you, then do not cross-examine even if you think
> you can confront him with certain misstatements.... It is not
> necessary to cross-examine on every single matter which the witness
> has testified. It is wise to pick out one or two salient points which
> you think you can discredit him on completely rather than review
> everything in detail. If you succeed on these points, let it go at that
> and argue to the jury that if he erred in part, he erred in whole.[18]

As Ehrlich's cautious advice indicates, there are practical
limits to what cross-examination can accomplish. Also, if a
defense counsel forces his cross-examination beyond this point,
the law of diminishing returns quickly envelops his case and
jeopardizes his success. The general public are snowed by the
dazzling results accomplished by television and theatrical lawyers, whose withering and brilliant cross-examination breaks
down the most hardened prevaricator. The lawyers interviewed
admitted that the reality of cross-examinations almost never
corresponds to these fictitious accounts. Criminal lawyers realize that they can hope for their cross-examination to accomplish little more than erode the credibility of prosecution witnesses and possibly present the defendant in a slightly better
light. A San Francisco lawyer realistically observed that "the
purpose of cross-examination is impeachment. If a witness is
lying, unless you have direct evidence, you must have a lot to
talk about before exposing him to the jury. Even impeachment
material must be subtly constructed so as to allow the witness
to get in as deep as possible, clearly showing the jury the extent
of his antagonism toward your client."

Beyond the knowledge of what type of strategy to employ during cross-examination and following clear and reasonable objectives, the criminal defense lawyer is most concerned with the development of a cross-examination style. This style relates to the personality and emotionality that the lawyer believes are best suited for obtaining maximum results. For most defense attorneys it was a question of determining the degree of aggressiveness best suited to their own personalities. The advice of nearly all the experienced defense lawyers was to tailor the cross-examination to one's own natural demeanor, and let loose with the type of theatrical aggressiveness and emotionalism so commonly depicted on television or in the movies only after one had a hostile witness on the ropes. There was also the repeated warning from many older lawyers not to waste anger prematurely but to save it for the opportune moment when it could have its optimal effect. Many lawyers felt that by careful planning, one could conduct a devastating cross-examination while still appearing to be a pleasant person. A Miami lawyer warned that not only can you use up the impact of your emotions by their overuse, but by being overly abrasive in your aggressiveness you can force the jury to sympathize with the witness and become antagonistic toward you and your client.

Two additional considerations in developing a cross-examination style are first, the ability to come at the witness in such an unexpected fashion as to surprise him and secondly, the significance of the witness's hostility. Turning to the development of the oblique style of questioning, most lawyers described this maneuver as "coming in sideways." This approach has the lawyer forcing the witness to commit himself to a basic line of assumptions, and if he refused to maintain his consistency, the lawyer can question his credibility. The master tactician, Jake Ehrlich, is relied upon again for his advice on this topic:

Bait the trap well before you spring it. To be effective you must draw your witness out before you confront him. If the witness appears strong or firm or vigorous it is best to attack indirectly. Suppose a witness testifies to a particular conversation and there is no indication that the witness did not have a distinct recollection of the conversation. Then do not question him concerning it at the start. Instead, ask when he was first informed that he would be a witness, what subject matter were reviewed. . . . Maintain a serene appearance during cross-examination. Do not evidence satisfaction or dissatisfaction.[19]

A fellow San Francisco lawyer, younger but equally eloquent, offered the best imagery of his style when he described cross-examination as being like a loose thread and once you find it and begin pulling on it, the whole case falls apart.

The type of witness also has an important effect upon the style of cross-examination. The degree of hostility toward the defendant will raise the level of aggressiveness. Most lawyers clearly differentiate between the damaging witness who is purposely hiding the truth as opposed to the neutral witness who has simply made an error. The police are a group which are most difficult to deal with since they are frequently hostile and adept at shading the truth in such a way as to critically undermine the defense. There is also a fear of appearing before the jury to be bullying these officers who generally have the respect and sympathy of most citizens. A rather unique cross-examination problem is presented by the informer. A highly respected Wisconsin lawyer offered the following advice on this treacherous topic:

In order to cross-examine an informer successfully, the first and foremost facility a defense lawyer must have is luck. Sometimes it is the kind which is thrust upon him in spite of his efforts and other times he may earn it. Secondly, the defense lawyer must consider his case as a whole. The lawyer must determine before he walks into the courtroom to try the case just what his defense is going to be. Cross-examination therefore is to be keyed to a specific goal that is tied into the defense.[20]

Role in Sentencing

Whether a case is disposed of without a trial by a plea of guilty or following a courtroom decision finding the defendant guilty, the defense counsel has one final responsibility towards his client. That is his role in the sentencing decision. Since the overwhelming majority of cases are disposed of without contention through a guilty plea, this may be the lawyer's most important task.

Most lawyers agreed with a young Denver attorney who defined his sentencing role as making it as hard as possible on the judge's conscience to send his client away to prison. This was described as presenting him as a human being with all the mitigating circumstances possible. In addition to emphasizing the defendant's personal attributes, many lawyers have also stressed their role in offering the judge as many alternative forms of disposition as possible. The recent development of diversion programs, community release centers, and a broad variety of other rehabilitative organizations are all attractive alternative to incarceration. It is therefore the added responsibility of defense counsel to be aware of these programs and to be able to effectively package his client as being well suited for them.

Since the sentencing process continues to be part of the adversarial system, the criminal lawyer must also be cognizant of his obligation to balance off the recommendations of the probation department, prosecutor, and sometimes even the judge. Although the sentencing decision is less charged than the most combative courtroom confrontations between prosecution and defense, the criminal lawyer must always remember he is still charged with presenting the defendant's side and articulating his best interests.

The defense attorney can fulfill many important obligations vis-a-vis the judge related to the sentencing decision. Several of the lawyers interviewed devoted a great deal of time to preparing their own presentence reports. This report usually gives the judge a detailed background check on the client replete with character references and personality sketches. The lawyer also tries to present several recommended dispositions, all of which are usually alternatives to incarceration. These reports are used either to counterbalance the more critical, prosecution-oriented reports typically emanating from the local probation department or to fill a need in jurisdictions where no other report is prepared.

In most cities a judge would hold a presentence hearing in which the defense counsel would be given an opportunity to defend his client's character, emphasize any mitigating factors, and offer suggested forms of punishment (which would be of maximum benefit to both the defendant and society). The lawyers were generally disappointed in these pro forma hearings and thought that the judge had already made up his mind, after being influenced by the probation department's report and the recommendation of the prosecutor. Although the attorneys feared putting undue pressure on the judge, they still felt that the only way to equalize the influence of the prosecutor and probation officer was to visit the judge's chambers prior to the presentence hearing. The defense lawyers emphasized the continued adversarial nature of the sentencing hearing and stressed the importance of checking the accuracy of the information reaching the judge from the probation department and prosecutor. These reports could be highly biased, and occasionally contained erroneous information which had to be corrected. The judges in the surveyed cities varied greatly as to their accessibility during this postconviction period. It was the job of the defense counsel to know which judges were approachable and in what manner.

Most defense attorneys try to maintain friendly relations with the probation department, especially if they are in a jurisdiction where the department's report is respected by the judge. In addition to extending professional courtesies to the probation officer in charge, the defense counsel also tries to view copies of the officer's report prior to its being sent to the judge and contribute some of his own information concerning the defendant's background. The wide variety of abilities between the probation departments surveyed in this study is documented and analyzed in Chapter 3. At this point, it need only be pointed out that the professionalism of the department does directly influence its relationship with the defense bar. It appeared that the higher the degree of professionalism, the greater the cooperation between defense counsel and probation officer.

Whether he is talking to the judge, prosecutor, or probation officer, the defense counsel is trying to present his client in the best possible light to these officers of the court. This typically means stressing the defendant's good character, introducing mitigating factors which must be considered, and finally, emphasizing that the current charges stem from an aberrant form of behavior which is shockingly out of character with the generally sensible and law-abiding manner in which the client has conducted the greater part of his life.

It was noted that the lawyers who were most effective and spent the most time dealing with the sentencing issue, usually were able to place their clients in rehabilitative programs well before the presentence hearing. As a Philadelphia lawyer observed, this offers the judge tangible and convincing proof that the defendant is sincerely committed to improving himself and can be trusted in third-party custodial programs.

Several lawyers noted that their input into the presentencing decision might not only influence the judge's final ruling but also the parole board's later evaluation of the defendant. A few lawyers commented that in cases where it is obvious that their client will have to be sentenced to a lengthy prison term, their presentence work is actually aimed at effecting this later parole decision. Parole board members have told criminal lawyers that they appreciate this added input and do consider it in their decision-making process.

NOTES

1. Denver Criminal Law Institute, University of Denver College of Law, 1974.

2. Tony Green and Jean Donahue, "Take twelve," *Philadelphia Magazine*, November 1975, p. 86.

3. Denver Criminal Law Institute, op. cit.

4. Ibid.

5. Green and Donahue, op. cit., p. 88.

6. Denver Criminal Law Institute, op. cit.

7. A Chicago lawyer commented on this point by stating that "my last five cases were involving bribery of public officials and the *only* defense you have is to call the other side a fucking liar."

8. "Laboratory proficiency testing program," The Forensic Sciences Foundation, 1977.

9. Joel Moldovsky and Rose DeWolf, *The Best Defense* (New York: Macmillan, 1975), pp. 124-125.

10. Denver Criminal Law Institute, op. cit.

11. Morris Shenker, speech before the National College of Criminal Defense Lawyers, Houston, Texas, 1974.

12. Denver Criminal Law Institute, op. cit.

13. Nathan Cohn, ed., *2nd Criminal Law Seminar* (Brooklyn, N.Y.: Central Book Company, 1962), p. 135.

14. Nathan Cohn, ed., *1st Criminal Law Seminar* (Brooklyn, N.Y.: Central Book Company, 1961).

15. Ibid.

16. F. Lee Bailey and Henry E. Rothblatt, *Fundamentals of Criminal Advocacy* (Rochester, N.Y.: Lawyers Cooperative Publishing Company, 1974), p. 305.

17. Nathan Cohn, ed., *3rd Criminal Law Seminar* (Brooklyn, N.Y.: Central Book Company, 1973), p. 39.

18. Ibid., p. 41.

19. Ibid., p. 42.

20. Al Kreeger, speech before the National College of Criminal Defense Lawyers, entitled "Tiptoeing through the tulips," in Houston, Texas, 1975.

Chapter 8

ALTERNATIVE SYSTEMS AND CONCLUSIONS

This final chapter has a twofold purpose. It will first discuss the major alternatives to the private criminal lawyer, i.e., public defenders and assigned counsel. Both alternatives will be examined primarily from the perspective of the private defense attorney. The second half of the chapter will offer a concluding analysis of the private criminal lawyer reiterating the major themes of the study. Emphasis will be placed upon the declining position of the private criminal lawyer and his future role within the criminal justice system.

The Public Defender

As a result of recent Supreme Court decisions,[1] the government has been forced to provide a legal defense for any defendant arrested for a crime which might result in his incarceration. Since nearly two-thirds of all defendants have been found to be indigents and therefore unable to afford a lawyer, the local, state and federal governments have had to devise some system for providing a defense. In most cities, a public defender program with a full-time staff of lawyers has been developed. Although public defender programs have been in existence in a variety of forms for many years, their expansion has been meteoric in recent years, following the Supreme Court mandate. Los Angeles, for example, which has had a public defender program since 1914, has expanded its legal staff 600 percent since 1966.[2]

The typical public defender program offers a style of defense in marked contrast to the personalized lawyer/client relationship established by the private criminal lawyer. Due to the crush of numbers, the public defender program is typically institutionalized and impersonal. It usually finds itself closely wedded to an assembly line process which passes defendants from one lawyer to another as they proceed through the successive stages of each city's criminal justice system. This often results in a defendant having a battery of lawyers; one at the preliminary hearing, another at the arraignment, and still another if the case goes to trial. In addition to this fragmented defense, the defendant is forced to deal with a bureaucracy, rather than an individual. In the cities visited, the public defender programs had anywhere from 25 to 200 lawyers and an assisting staff of nearly equal size. As a result of this impersonal, fragmented, and bureaucratized style of defense, the indigent defendant has developed an attitude best exemplified in a defendant's answer to Professor Jonathan Casper's question whether or not he had a lawyer when he went to court: "No, I had a public defender."[3]

In the nine cities, only Houston, which relies entirely on an assigned counsel system, and Washington, D.C., which uses a mixed system dividing the work between public defenders and assigned counsel, did not rely entirely upon a public defender program to provide for the criminal defense of indigents. It was estimated that in these seven cities approximately 75 percent of all defendants were indigents and would be given a public defender. This left only 25 percent of the cases to be handled by private attorneys.

It was surprising to find that generally there was very little animosity between the public and private criminal defense bar. In several cities, most notably Denver and Washington, D.C., the public defender office went out of its way to help the private bar whenever it could. This usually took the form of conducting seminars on recent decisions as well as mailing out newsletters keeping interested lawyers apprised of recent developments in criminal law. Several offices also opened their law libraries to any private practitioner wishing to utilize their facilities.

The major irritant between the groups was competition over certain defendants who were adjudged to qualify for the public defender, but appeared by reasonable standards to have been able to afford their own defense. The blame for this problem was placed upon the judge, who usually tried to give as many cases as possible to the public defender's office, failing to make any meaningful inquiry into a defendant's financial ability to hire his own attorney. It was thought by most attorneys that the judges believed that they could best get through the mounting backlog of cases by having them placed within an institution more directly under their own control than among a loose assortment of individual private attorneys who might prove difficult to manage. Regardless of whose fault it was, the private defense bar was still angered over losing potential paying clientele to the public defender office.

It was thought by most defense counsel that the public defenders were generally as competent as the average private criminal lawyer. They went on to add, however, that legal expertise is only part of the equation for a successful lawyer, the remainder falling under the rubric of personal relations. It was in this second area where the public defenders were found to be inadequate. The lack of personal relationships with public defender clientele was caused more by the crushing caseloads and bureaucratic structure of the office rather than a planned policy, but the results were identical just the same.

It appeared that although the middle 50 percent of public defenders and private attorneys were operating at similar levels of ability and achieving nearly identical results, there were marked differences at the extremes. Thus, it was generally agreed by the criminal lawyers that the top 25 percent of private attorneys were clearly superior to the best public defenders, while the bottom 25 percent of public defenders were believed to be significantly better than the bottom group of private attorneys. The bottom line to all this is that if you can afford to pay for one of the better private criminal lawyers, you will be getting your money's worth, but for the remaining 75 percent, going to a private practitioner would not make much difference and might even be detrimental. Most private lawyers candidly admitted that a defendant would be much better off taking a public defender over a lawyer with minimal criminal law experience.

Many lawyers agreed with a Los Angeles defense attorney that the only reason the private attorney is able to survive is the distrust and hatred of the public defender's office. The competence of the public defender's office is adequate but is not rationally evaluated by the typical client. He is annoyed by the absence of "hand holding," which many believe is essential to their defense. This inattention to psychological needs has alienated most public defender clientele and affected their consideration of their lawyer's efforts. It is equally plausible to imagine that indigent defendants who are forced to utilize the public defender's services are highly frustrated by their inability to hire their own "Perry Mason."

A minority of the private criminal lawyers interviewed believed that as a rule the public defender would not get as good results as a private attorney. A Philadelphia criminal lawyer explained the reasons for this:

> First is the problem of client control and veracity. The public defender is often viewed by his client as simply being another part of the system oppressing him and will barely cooperate. On top of this is the public defender's inability to coddle their clients. They just can't handhold like a private attorney. A second important thing is that the public defenders are in court too often and therefore the judge can't throw any bones your way since he'll be seeing you four-five times a day. The private attorney with his infrequent appearances is in a much better position to give and receive judicial favors.

Researchers have recently attempted to gather empirical evidence on the question of whether the type of counsel—private, public, or assigned—makes any significant difference in the disposition of the case. With a few minor exceptions, the results of these studies have generally concluded that the type of counsel, whether public or private, does not seem to make a significant difference. These studies typically compared case

dispositions of private and public attorneys and found almost
no statistical variation. The findings from the following studies
conducted in Washington, D.C., San Diego, and Denver are
representative of these research efforts. All reached similar
conclusions:

(1) A study by Jean Taylor and others of the San Diego Superior
    Court for the *Denver Law Journal* found that 76 percent of the
    defendants with retained counsel were convicted while 77 percent
    of the public defender clients were similarly convicted. They also
    found that if one controls for offense, any difference between the
    categories of counsel disappears even further. The only hint of
    differential treatment was in the area of sentencing, where a larger
    portion of convicted defendants with retained counsel were re-
    ceiving suspended sentences. This probably is more closely related
    to the background characteristics and socioeconomic status of the
    wealthier clients who could afford private counsel than in the
    lawyering abilities of either category.[4]

(2) Also appearing in the *Denver Law Journal* a year later was a
    thorough analysis of the significance of counsel in Denver and the
    report concluded that only slight variations in performance were
    found between the city's retained counsel and public defenders.
    Sixty-five percent of the retained counsel clients were convicted
    while 67.7 percent of the public defender's reached a similar fate.
    Again, the sentencing variation favored the retained counsel but as
    noted earlier, he is blessed with clients who are more likely to
    appear to be better prospects for probation.[5]

(3) In April of 1975 the Joint Committee of the Judicial Conference
    of the D.C. Circuit Court and the D.C. Bar (Unified) issued a report
    on criminal defense services in Washington. In their chapter on
    quality of representation the following comparative statistics were
    presented which clearly indicate the similarity of performance
    between public and private attorney.

Disposition	Public defender	Private attorney
Dismissed at preliminary hearing	5%	5%
Dismissed after preliminary hearing	36%	38%
Pleaded guilty	29%	29%
Trial—acquitted	6%	5%
Trial—convicted	6%	8%[6]

Although we have thus far lumped all public defender programs together, there are considerable differences between them. One factor that did not vary a great deal was the percentage of cases handled by each program. The percentages ranged from 65 to 75 percent in the seven cities utilizing public defender programs. (Washington, D.C., with its mixed system, handled only 15 percent of all the possible cases, while Houston was without any program at all.) Among the intervening variables that did seem to affect the image and style of a public defender program were its degree of professionalism, degree of politicization, degree of independence from the judiciary, and degree of personalized treatment of the client (contrasting assembly line procedures with solitary defender). A public defender program was perceived on these various issues by the general public, the defense bar, and the clientele themselves.

The reputation of a public defender program was based primarily on the competence of the legal staff. It was generally believed that the more professional, and less political, a public defender program, the higher its reputation. For example, the private attorneys in Los Angeles applauded the efforts of the local public defender program which had been in operation for over 60 years. It was believed to be isolated from political and judicial influence. Its long history had allowed it to become a highly professional organization, taking great pride in its high quality defense. The general public and clientele joined in this positive view of the program's image. At the opposite extreme is the situation in San Francisco, where the public defender's offices were generally perceived by the interviewees to be a political operation, rewarding party loyalists. Its low reputation based on its past political linkages, is slowly receding, but most of the lawyers interviewed still had a low opinion of the office. The defendants would do almost anything to raise enough money for a private attorney and avoid public defender representation.

It is probably to a defense lawyer's benefit to be located in a city whose public defender program has the lowest reputation. In Philadelphia, Los Angeles, and Denver, where the local public defender programs enjoy modest success and good reputations, the private criminal lawyers are having a very tough time surviving. In cities such as San Francisco and Chicago, where the public defenders have not gained much respect, the private criminal law bar seems to have a slightly better chance in the battle to avoid extinction.

Despite the fact that most criminal lawyers do regard public defenders as competent attorneys, they share many criticisms of the institution as a whole. The most frequent complaint was leveled against the judges who failed to adequately screen the defendants in determining their indigency. The second most frequently voiced criticism was that the public defenders had lost their independent stance and had become too cozy with the judge and prosecutor. Eventually such collusion could destroy the essence of the defenders' adversarial function. This problem was especially apparent in jurisdictions where the prosecutor and public defender were caught up in an assembly line style of justice, which dictated assigning permanent representatives to a specific courtroom or judge for a set period of time. After a short while, the three officials begin to act as one, placing institutional imperatives above professional responsibilities. Jackson Battle's study of Denver confirms this observation: "Public defenders more than retained counsel seemed to rely upon cooperation with the district attorneys in small routine matters that otherwise consume much of their day."[7]

Several lawyers criticized the public defender program for becoming overly bureaucratized and failing to maintain any kind of meaningful lawyer/client relationship. The problem was also heightened by rapid personnel turnover and inexperienced defenders who were not prepared to offer competent counsel. This loss of the "human element" was blamed more upon the caseload and resulting organizational requirements rather than an inherent disregard for their clientele. Nevertheless, the client suffered and the defense process weakened.

Most lawyers were much more positive about their local public defender programs and perceived a wide range of advantages for the private criminal law bar. Many lawyers echoed the sentiments of a Denver attorney who was thankful that public defenders were taking the lousier cases off his hands. Several lawyers were appreciative of the willingness of most public defender agencies to permit private attorneys to use their investigative and research facilities. A few noted that if new blood was to continue coming into the private sector, the public defender's office provided an excellent apprenticeship for beginning lawyers.

In the courtroom, the public defender was also acknowledged to have a few advantages over the private criminal lawyer. Through his total immersion in the criminal justice system, the public defender quickly develops an expertise and familiarity with its procedures and personalities. With this experience he is in an excellent position to negotiate and dispose of cases in an expeditious manner. A Los Angeles criminal lawyer thought that the public defender possessed a great deal of potential power to pressure judges. He could eliminate a judge in his city by a coordinated effort to avoid his court or impose some other kind of obstacle. He quickly acknowledged, however, that the public defenders have chosen not to exercise such power and have been overly timid in exerting the leverage of their sizeable caseload.

In summary, the public defender has had a devastating effect upon the private practice of criminal law. In most cities these agencies defend three-quarters of all defendants charged with crimes. Given their generally competent treatment of cases, the defendant is becoming more and more willing to forsake the expensive personalized attention offered by the private bar. The result has been the continued eradication of the private criminal lawyer in the state courts.

Assigned Counsel and Its Variations

As an alternative to the public defender system, many communities use an assigned counsel system for the defense of indigents. Although most of our country's urban areas rely primarily upon public defender programs, smaller and mid-sized communities most commonly use the assigned counsel system. A recent survey indicated that it was used in 2900 of the nation's 3100 countries.[8] In the nine cities studied in this project, the assigned counsel format was found in three distinct adaptations. First, in the seven cities with large public defender programs, cases were assigned only where there were multiple defendants and a conflict of interest would arise if the public defender had to defend several of the codefendants. Second, in Washington, D.C., we find a unique mixed system where the public defender has limited himself to only about one-fourth of the indigent cases and the remainder are dispersed through an assigned counsel program (administered by representatives of the public defender office). The third variation was Houston, Texas, which possesses no public defender program. The municipal and county court judges have responsibility for assigning counsel in all cases where a defendant is declared indigent.

Turning first to the most common form of assigned counsel, we find that the average percentage of multiple defendant (conflict of interest) cases handled by a public defender to be approximately 10-15 percent of their total caseload. When such a conflict arises, the judge is notified and he usually resorts either to a list of private counsel who have volunteered for assigned cases or he simply picks a lawyer of his own choosing who he thinks will be interested in handling the particular case.

In most jurisdictions the criminal lawyers must volunteer to be considered for an assigned case. The list of volunteers may be kept by the Calendar Court Judge and serve as a central directory for the entire judiciary or a series of lists, each maintained by a judge for his specific courtroom. Either list may be carefully rotated or simply a guide to be used at the discretion of the individual judge. The abuses of the latter system will be discussed later in this section, but it should not be surprising that nearly every city had numerous private attorneys making charges concerning the favoritism and cronyism rampant in their assignment process. A secondary problem is trying to select a competent lawyer to a difficult case. Any attempt at classifying lawyers on the basis of their competence seemed doomed to failure and left a trail of bruised egos.

Washington, D.C. provided the most unusual form of assigned counsel as part of its "mixed system." It was thought to be an advance over other forms of indigent defense because it offered the poor defendant a wider cross-section of lawyers to choose from. It also eliminates the zone coverage—assembly line form of defense found in most public defender systems. In addition, recent studies have indicated it is not any more expensive than other programs.

The appointment process, as explained by one of the city's criminal lawyers, appeared to work in three ways: (1) if on a given day the lawyer decides to try for one of these cases, he calls down to the assignment office coordinator and volunteers by 8:00 A.M.; (2) the felony judge is responsible for reviewing the assignment list, which matches all volunteers with the indigents arrested the previous day. He may have a case before him where a defendant is without an attorney and call immediately to the coordinator's office; (3) the judge, while sitting in the courtroom, may find a lawyer there and has the option of assigning the case to him right there.

The system was developed out of the Criminal Justice Act in which Congress envisioned getting a large number of lawyers involved in the defense of indigents. In fact, however, only about 40-50 regulars dominate the system and make their living off their appointments. The fee is $20 an hour out of court and $30 an hour in court. Although the judge does have discretionary power to veto the coordinator's assignment, this was done in less than 10 percent of the cases and 90 percent of these go to the courthouse regulars.

Two interesting innovations in the Districts' assignment process deserve mentioning. First, Washington was the only city visited that was trying to establish a system for the middle-class defendant who did not qualify as an indigent but could not afford the price of a decent lawyer. He is allowed to contribute a partial payment of the legal expenses based on the judge's inquiry into his financial capabilities. Since the court has not proved helpful in aiding the private lawyer wrest his partial payment from the defendant, most criminal lawyers dislike the system. The second innovation, which is only in the initial implementation stage, is a pilot project with three lawyers, who will handle all indigents during their initial appearance and preliminary hearing, after which time the clients will be assigned to other lawyers. It is hoped this reform will speed up the system, although most lawyers interviewed were highly skeptical.

The failings of Washington's assigned counsel system as it operates under the Criminal Justice Act emanate from the great power given to the judges. Several judges have abused their broad grant of discretionary powers, which gives them final say in the selection process as well as total control over how much of a defense attorney's expense voucher they are willing to pay. Criminal lawyers in the city understand this judicial control and even sense that if their courtroom performance proves offensive to the judge, they will find their expense vouchers severely reduced and can forecast few opportunities for selection in future cases. A young Washington attorney summarized his frustrations from having to deal with this system as follows:

> Because of ceilings and backlogs, until you get your money, you are really at the mercy of the judges, and they know it, and some abuse it. Judges seem to have a contemptuous attitude toward the private bar who handle CJA (Criminal Justice Act) cases. For those in a CJA practice they spend most of their time in record keeping so their voucher will be accurate. Another problem is waiting time, and administrative delay where the judges are most likely to cut vouchers even though this is a legitimate expense and the judges themselves are most responsible for this delay.

These complaints against the judicial management of the CJA are not the ravings of a solitary lawyer. These and related abuses were noted in the recent report of the D.C. Bar and the Joint Committee of the Judicial Conference of the D.C. Circuit. The report stated the following observations and conclusions concerning the city's assigned counsel system:

(1) The report found that voucher cutting tended to encourage ineffective representation and to discourage the infusion of new talent.

(2) The Court has adopted no overall policies or guidelines to inform judges and practitioners alike of applicable standards for reviewing, cutting, and approving vouchers.

(3) The procedure for dealing with nontrial vouchers (more than 85 percent of all vouchers) is close to unworkable.

(4) Attorneys are rarely, if ever, told what has been cut and why.

(5) There is no grievance procedure available to attorneys who feel their vouchers have been cut unjustly. The individual judge is the court of last resort on such questions and is naturally reluctant to reverse an earlier decision.

(6) Delays in getting payment—at least during 1974—have at times been extraordinarily long. Some attorneys have waited as long as six months to be reimbursed for outlays of time and expenses.[9]

One of the most serious long-term consequences of the city's C.J.A. program is the breeding of distrust and creation of tension between the bench and bar. One young lawyer stated that he was seriously considering abandoning his criminal law practice (which was predominantly assigned cases) because of the way he and others had been treated by the courts. They had been made to feel like beggars, groveling at the footsteps of the judges, grateful for whatever crumbs were thrown their way. What seemed to make the situation even more intolerable was the blindness of the more successful criminal lawyers who did not have to rely upon C.J.A. cases and were blissfully ignorant of the problem, frequently siding with the judiciary.

The third form of assigned counsel programs found in the nine cities visited was the Houston system. Houston, being the only city in the sample without a public defender program, relies entirely upon a dual assigned counsel system with both the municipal and county criminal court judges exercising overlapping assignment responsibilities. The current system is rather confusing with the indigent defendant being the consistent loser in the battle between the city and county judges. Currently, an indigent can have three different attorneys assigned to his case. First, there is a two to three man legal staff operation available at the initial court appearance (referred to in Houston as the probable cause hearing), where bail is set and charges are read. A lawyer can stand with the defendant at this time, offering advice and serving mainly as a calming influence. The second group of lawyers are appointed by the justices of the peace who run the municipal courts. Each justice of the peace has total discretion in the selection process, although most try to use a list of volunteers, which is rotated. In misdemeanor cases this will be the final defense attorney but in felony cases bound over to the county district court, these judges may replace the justice of the peace's selection with a lawyer of their own choosing. Again, they have nearly total discretion over whom they will choose.

The system is rife with problems and, in fact, the federal district court has warned both court systems to clean up the program or suffer serious consequences. The major failings are related to inadequate compensation, abuse of the discretionary privilege, and favoritism in the selection process. Fearing the establishment of a public defender program to correct these evils, the county's organized private defense bar has tried to propose an innovative reform plan for appointment of counsel. The leading proposal, offered by the Harris County Criminal Lawyers Association, would place the administrative control over the assignment of counsel with the association, who would also supervise the staff attorneys and their supporting personnel. The association was careful to add that the judges would always have the ultimate say in the assignment process but that the association would do the initial selection. All lawyers in the county would be eligible for joining the selection pool, but a special category of lawyers would be created for capital crimes or particularly serious cases. The proposal is under deliberated by both the justices of the peace and the county district court judges.

The advocates of the assigned counsel system believe that it has two important advantages over the public defender program. First, it will help to involve a larger section of the legal community. This will introduce more lawyers to the problems of the criminal courts while also breaking up the monopoly of a few court regulars of questionable competence. Secondly, this system permits the infusion of much-needed new blood into the defense system by offering numerous opportunities for the beginning practitioner.

Despite these benefits, most of the private criminal lawyers interviewed were very upset over the operation of the assigned counsel program in their respective communities. The major complaints were divided among the inadequacy of the pay, the favoritism of the judges, and the low level of competence of those lawyers monopolizing the assigned counsel business. The lawyers realized that the defense counsel who were least aggressive and most easily controlled by the judiciary, would be rewarded by continual selection. The lawyers who were strong advocates of their defendants' rights would rarely be asked to handle future cases. The meagre pay and the unwillingness of the system to support investigative services, also contributed to the inadequate preparation and frustration of assigned counsel work.

A final problem associated with the assigned counsel system was that of classifying lawyers according to competence. Judges and lawyers alike agreed that some categorization was needed to distinguish beginning lawyers from those who would be competent to handle the most serious cases. Several cities tried to establish objective formulas for tabulating an attorney's experience in the criminal law, but even these seemingly objective systems were upsetting to several members of the legal community. San Diego and Los Angeles have been most successful in this categorization issue, but even here several good lawyers declined to volunteer because they refused to have their competence judged by their fellow lawyers.

Conclusions and Prognostications

One of the purposes of this book has been to strip away the many myths which distort the realities of the private practice of criminal law. The portrait of the profession which remains at the conclusion of this examination is highly complex. The private criminal lawyer is operating within a profession which appears to be continually pulling him apart and making his job increasingly difficult. The following are four such strains which, when combined in effect, are responsible for creating excessive professional tension.

First is the necessity of being an extrovert in the courtroom, while being able to exercise extremely cerebral skills in preparation for such a performance. Most people are unable to combine such frequently contradictory skills of public and private competence. The contrasting working environments of the office and the courthouse, contribute to this dichotomy. In the solitude of his office, the lawyer is a pensive strategist. Within a short time, however, he must return to the backslapping banality of the courthouse and prepare to exhibit a winning personality before the judge, jury, and fellow practitioners.

Second is the necessity for the successful criminal lawyer to be both an adroit negotiator with the prosecution while also appearing to be a viable and, hopefully, feared adversary. Many prosecutors, experienced in such criminal justice paradoxes, are not troubled by the inconsistency of a defense counsel trying to wheedle an acceptable plea bargain one moment and then trying to destroy the prosecutor in open court the next. In fact, several of the lawyers interviewed did not find any difficulty in combining such talents, and went so far as to believe that one facilitated the other. They thought that the feared adversary was more likely to be an effective plea bargainer in subsequent cases. The converse was also believed to be true. Lawyers who gained reputations as only able to plea bargain were rarely feared in the courtroom, and ultimately found their negotiating effectiveness diminished. Despite the obvious linkages between these two talents, they nevertheless require divergent abilities, rarely found in most individuals.

A third difficulty had to do with renumeration. Several of the criminal lawyers interviewed stated that the very clients whose fees were most lucrative such as white collar and organized crime figures were often the least desirable. The upper middle class and corporate criminals were often the least cooperative, most belligerent, and stingiest in terms of fee payment. The organized crime defendants could be counted on to pay but the taint of associating with such a person usually meant Internal Revenue Service audits, grand jury appearances, and a host of difficulties with civil clients. Not all defense counsel sensed these tensions and would vigorously defend anyone who could afford the fee.

The final professional difficulty of the private criminal lawyer is the complex problem of maintaining a lofty reputation while continuing to practice in virtual isolation. As was noted in Chapter 4, the criminal lawyer's reputation is his most significant commodity and yet it is generally the product of hearsay, gossip, and only an occasional bit of empirical evidence. It is, consequently, no wonder that so many defense counsel become somewhat paranoid concerning what is said about them. The problem as we have previously noted is exacerbated by the fact that so much of what the lawyer does—plea bargaining with the prosecutor, meeting with the judge in his chambers, and dealing with his client—occurs beyond the public purview. Rarely will a judge, prosecutor, or client comment about what really happened during these encounters. Nevertheless, within a short time a reputation mystically evolves which may mark the attorney for the rest of his professional life.

Since the publication of Arthur Wood's *Criminal Lawyers* a decade ago, the professional lives of the private defense lawyer have experienced considerable turbulence and change. Most of the lawyers interviewed marked the mid-sixties as the radical turning point for their profession, pointing specifically to the Miranda and Gideon Supreme Court decisions. In *Miranda v. Arizona,* we have what has been acknowledged to be the beginning of the due process revolution affecting criminal cases in both federal and state courts. Following this 1965 decision, we find the Supreme Court devoting more and more of its time to criminal law topics, especially in the areas of lawful confessions, presence of counsel, and search and seizure.

Several of the older criminal lawyers who had practiced most of their law prior to the 1965 decision, felt overburdened by the steadily increasing case law which they were required to know. Criminal law was now becoming as complex as other fields of law. Many were sympathetic to the words of an older San Francisco criminal lawyer, who has since given up his practice due to these developments. He yearned for the old days, "when you could read the transcript on the way down to court in a streetcar. After a while, doing it every day, you could try a case without preparation. The trials were quick with very few motions complicating the procedures. Justice was speedy and efficient." Today he found the lawyers and the entire criminal justice system hamstrung by all the new law and procedural guarantees which, in turn, had led to "a lot of goddamn motions and other wasteful bullshit." He felt that rather than help the defendant it had actually had the opposite effect of preventing substantial justice.

The second case most frequently cited as initiating this critical turning point for the criminal lawyer was *Gideon v. Wainwright.* This 1963 decision, which forced the states to provide legal assistance for all indigent felony defendants, marked the beginning of the nation's public defender system. With the impact of the decision being expanded to cover misdemeanants as well as felons, in the 1972 *Argersinger* case, nearly every city in the country has had to develop public defender programs. Since nearly two-thirds of all defendants are indigents, we are finding the majority of cases in our larger cities being handled by these public institutions. It is this development, more than any other, which has sounded the death knell for the private practice of criminal law.

Many other changes have occurred in the past decade which have also affected the criminal lawyer. Most had their origin long before the sixties, but it was during this period that they seemed to gather speed in a type of snowballing effect, which still is causing most criminal lawyers to be reeling from the combined impact. Not all of the changes have necessarily been bad. Among the positive developments occurring during the past ten to twenty years has been a lessening of corruption and a liberalization of discovery procedures.

The decline in corruption was generally agreed upon to be a good thing. Most lawyers were happy to see the payoff system on the wane. The elimination of bondsmen and other middle men was a welcome relief. No longer did lawyers have to be concerned with referral fees, payoffs, and bribes—dangerous ploys that threatened the lawyer's professional and personal life. There were still isolated incidents, reminiscent of the old days, especially in Chicago or Philadelphia, but overall, nearly every city was adjudged to be "clean" by its criminal lawyers.

The rules of discovery have been greatly broadened in nearly every jurisdiction visited. This book has already noted how this development had aided the lawyer in dealing both with the prosecutor and his client. A few defense lawyers did comment, however, that the liberalized discovery rules were not entirely beneficial. They pointed out that these rules compel the defense attorney as well as the prosecutor to open up their files. Thus, the days of the private criminal lawyer surprising the prosecutor, à la Perry Mason, on the day of the trial, are over and so is a little of the glamour of the profession.

Although the rising crime rate would seem to be a positive indicator for the criminal lawyer of continued business, in fact most of these cases are going to the public defender. One area of the criminal law, however, which has greatly accelerated in the past five years and has provided many new clients for the private criminal lawyers is the increase in white-collar prosecutions. This has been steadily on the rise in state courts, but has been exhibiting meteoric increases at the federal level.

Most of the lawyers, when reviewed the changes occurring in the past decade, emphasized the negative developments which appeared to be undermining their profession. They sensed that as the preliminary hearing and the voir dire were shortened, the role of the criminal lawyer was being continually reduced. Particularly at the voir dire, where many states are allowing only the judges to question potential jurors, the defense counsel clearly see the court's attempt to expedite proceedings by decreasing their responsibilities as an extremely frustrating turn of events. Nearly all of the lawyers interviewed agreed that the criminal justice system had become so large and bureaucratized that it could no longer tolerate the courtroom antics of a lawyer frantically trying to do everything in his power for his client. The institutional goals of system maintenance, expedience, and efficiency had become more important than permitting the defendant to have his day in court.

At first glance one would suspect that most criminal lawyers would be pleased by the recent growth in diversion and rehabilitation programs, which would allow the defendant to avoid long-term incarceration. Yet, because these reform programs are offered as inducements for guilty pleas and can be obtained by any defendant regardless of the type or competence of counsel, the private attorneys view these reforms as deleterious to their professional existence. As one Philadelphia lawyer explained, most defendants are streetwise enough to realize that they can get into these programs just as easily if they are defended by a public defender as a private attorney. So why spend all the money for a private attorney when you can obtain the same results for free? Several criminal lawyers candidly admitted that they were definitely harmed by this continuing trend in sentencing leniency, and wished for a return to tougher sentences which would scare the defendants back into their offices.

One final disturbing trend which was upsetting to most lawyers, and especially those practicing in the federal courts, was the use of the immunity statute. This allows the government to have one defendant testify against his codefendant. The testifying defendant may be offered freedom from prosecution on the specific charges involved as a reward for his cooperation. This has resulted in lawyers involved in multiple defendant cases and conspiracies being coerced into literal races to the courthouse doors in order to be the first in line to turn on codefendants. It is virtually impossible for a defense counsel to plan a winning defense when he is surrounded by codefendants working with the prosecution.

Because of the changes just outlined and additional professional pressures to be discussed in the next section, it must be concluded that the private criminal lawyer is, indeed, an endangered species. Although a few will survive by specializing in federal work, middle-class crimes, or the most serious of cases, the large majority of criminal lawyers will become extinct in the near future. Most of the lawyers estimated their professional life expectancy in the criminal field at ten years. This was the opinion of lawyers from nearly every city visited. The sole exception was Miami, which is experiencing a crime explosion, particularly in the lucrative federal area of narcotics and fraud.

In the cities visited, the number of criminal lawyers was estimated at being one-half to one-third the figure of twenty-five years ago, despite the continued rise in crime. An elderly Philadelphia lawyer reminisced about the old days when two hundred lawyers were courthouse regulars. Today the number has dwindled to between forty and sixty. In Chicago, the figures were almost exactly the same, and the experienced lawyers talked of the good old days and brought forth numerous scrapbooks offering visual proof of what a glorious life the criminal lawyer seemed to enjoy in the thirties and forties.

The problem is compounded by the lack of new blood coming into the profession as well as by the early exit of older lawyers into either premature retirement or other areas of the law. As the statistics presented in Chapter 3 indicated, nearly the entire sample of private criminal lawyers were between thirty and fifty-five. Only one was under thirty, and a mere handful over sixty. What else but extinction can be the fate of a profession which does not replenish its supply of youth and has its middle aged members rushing into premature retirement? A few are making decent livings and experiencing worthwhile careers, but they are a small and declining minority, whose professional success has little import for the rest of their beleaguered colleagues.

Nearly every private criminal lawyer placed primary blame for the demise of their profession upon the growth of their city's public defender program. In all the seven cities surveyed who utilized a full-time public defender system, this program provided the defense for approximately three-quarters of all defendants. The extreme growth of the public defender operation which began in the mid-1960s has probably reached its zenith. This still only offers 25 percent of the arrested defendants as likely candidates for the private bar. Beyond these harsh economic realities, however, are a wide range of other problems which are hastening the decline of the profession.

Most criminal lawyers are still upset over the low status accorded their profession. Several lawyers optimistically thought the profession had significantly improved its social position in both the public and the general bar's opinion, but this represented a minority viewpoint. The majority of lawyers interviewed believed that they were still identified with their clients and were considered unscrupulous in their clients' defense, ignoring the welfare of society.

It was also felt by most of the interviewees that the profession was no longer lucrative. They thought that they could make much more money with much less effort in areas of the civil law, such as personal injury, real estate, divorce, and family. Why stay in a profession fostering such intense competition for survival that one might be forced to do things that were considered personally repugnant? The resulting moral and emotional hazards were too high a price to pay, especially when the monetary gain became so questionable. This book has already chronicled the broad range of physical and mental problems, which occur so frequently as to be viewed as occupational hazards. A San Francisco lawyer alluded to the inevitable neuroses by commenting that, "You have to be paranoid to be a good criminal lawyer. Your only friends are people in trouble. They are frequently charming and you're easily exposed. If you have a weakness they will exploit it and you to the fullest."

Among the other aggravations and grievances, several were directed at the government. These complaints ranged from a conscious effort to destroy the defense attorney's role in criminal trials for the sake of expediency to the harassing investigations of private criminal lawyers conducted by varying governmental agencies, particularly the Internal Revenue Service. Criminal lawyers were angered by what they thought was prejudicial treatment by the government's tax collectors as they found themselves continually audited and questioned. Their association with "the criminal element" also makes private defense counsel prime candidates for grand jury investigations, and with the increased use of the federal immunity statute by the U.S. attorneys' office, there appears little room for evasion.

Many of the criminal lawyers not only disliked their clients, who were generally categorized as either a necessary evil or simply a "pain in the ass," but were also contemptuous of their colleagues. Lawyer after lawyer complained of the incompetence of most of his fellow criminal lawyers. Most thought that only a handful of decent criminal lawyers existed in their jurisdiction and that the large majority were either ineffective or immoral. By adopting this type of we/they mentality, the majority of criminal lawyers appear to have established a distance between themselves and their profession. If one combines this state of affairs with the already existing cleavage between the successful and unsuccessful criminal lawyers as well as the general tension between civil and criminal lawyers, one should not wonder that all attempts at organizing the profession have ended in dismal failure.

As this study draws to a close, we seem to have been describing a rather dispirited group of professionals whose noble goals have fallen prey to economic hardships and social ostracism. The future as envisioned by the majority of private criminal lawyers, is rather grim. It is expected that the decline will continue and that within the next ten years of the profession will be depleted all but its most hardy members. These survivors, legal dinosaurs, will be either defending a narrow range of lucrative clients or stubbornly clinging to a profession which can no longer offer much beyond mere subsistence.

Not all lawyers interviewed would agree with the dismal prognosis just offered. They still believe that there is hope for the profession but changes are imperative. Several lawyers argued for the adoption of a voucher system according to which a defendant could select his own lawyer, whereafter the state would repay the attorney at a fixed rate. This would eliminate many of the problems of the current public defender system, which has failed to gain the confidence of most of its clientele.

It would also be a needed bit of sustenance to the private criminal lawyers, especially those just beginning. It is argued that making the defense services more competitive would necessarily force an increase in the competence of counsel.

A related reform would be to try to implement the Washington, D.C. plan of contribution orders on a nationwide basis. These orders are used to allow the middle class to receive the same opportunity for a qualified legal defense as the poor and the rich. The judge reviews the defendant's financial abilities and then decides what percentage of the lawyer's fee he is able to afford. The remaining amount will be paid by the government. The program is off to a rather shaky start in Washington. The city's lawyers believe that its main drawback is the judiciary's unwillingness to help them collect their part of the fee. A threatened boycott of the program is contemplated unless the courts take a more active role in guaranteeing that the lawyer's fee will be paid.

A few lawyers in each city believed that the pessimistic prognosis for the profession was badly overstated and that a competent lawyer who is willing to work hard can still earn a decent living practicing criminal law. They argued that there are still enough cases around, and although you probably will not become rich, you will at least be comfortable. A young successful Denver attorney captured this optimistic spirit in the following statement: "If you work hard and gut it out and develop a reputation for honesty, you can make it. There are still many defendants getting into trouble for the first time and most standard lawyers will refer cases to these competent and honest defense attorneys. There really seems to be no slack in the demand for good criminal lawyers."

Most lawyers interviewed do not share this optimism. They stay in the profession because it is in their blood. They talk about it as being habit-forming. Once you start in it, it is very hard to leave. They imagine the other areas of the law are too dull. They sincerely believe that they must remain as one of the last bastions against state oppression of the individual. The public defender as a paid agent of the state cannot claim the untainted independence of the private criminal lawyer. As a Philadelphia criminal lawyer eloquently phrased it, "You get a psychic income here. You're tracing your mark on the sands of time."

This book will close with an important comment by Ephraim Margolin, one of the nation's preeminent criminal lawyers, who portrays the difficult task facing his fellow defense counsel in the years to come:

> The Perry Mason image is merely a harmless illusion in the American dream of always aiming at superhuman accomplishment, but the image of a Charlie Chaplin working his assembly line is a much more dangerous example of what could befall our profession. Dedication and excellence in the field of criminal defense can never be subordinated to expeditiousness and unreasonable budgetary constraints.[10]

Thus he offers a challenge not only to his profession, but to the politicians and court officials who are responsible for insuring that the criminal justice system does not sacrifice its lofty goals for bureaucratic expedience.

NOTES

1. *Gideon v. Wainwright,* 372 U.S. 335 (1963); and *Argersinger v. Hamlin,* 407 U.S. 25 (1972).

2. Paul Wice and Peter Suwak, "Current realities of public defender programs: a national survey," *Criminal Law Bulletin,* March 1974, p. 163.

3. Jonathan Casper, "Did you have a lawyer when you went to court? no, I had a public defender," *Yale Review of Law and Social Action,* Spring 1971, pp. 4-9.

4. Jean Taylor et al., "An analysis of defense counsel in the processing of felony defendants in San Diego," *Denver Law Journal,* 1972, p. 233.

5. "An analysis of defense counsel in the processing of felony defendants in Denver, Colorado," *Denver Law Journal,* 1973, p. 9.

6. Joint Committee of the Judicial Conference of the D.C. Circuit and the D.C. Bar (Unified), "Report on criminal defense services in the District of Columbia," April 1975 (mimeographed), p. 111.

7. Jackson Battle, "Comparison of public defenders and private attorneys' relationships with the prosecution in the City of Denver, *Denver Law Journal,* 1973, p. 101.

8. Lee Silverstein, *Defense of the Poor* (Washington, D.C.: American Bar Foundation, 1965).

9. Joint Committee of the Judicial Conference of the D.C. Circuit, op. cit., pp. 46-47.

10. Ephraim Margolin, Chairman, *14th Annual—Defendant Criminal Cases* (Practicing Law Institute, 1976).

APPENDIX:
LIST OF RESPONDENTS

Chicago

George Crowley
Richard Manning
William Barnett
Terry McCarthy
Jim Coughlin
Ed Genson
William Cain
Jim Alfini
Herb Barsy
Warren Wolfson (Judge)
Harry Busch
Gerald Werksman
Sam Banks
Tom Decker
Bill Nellis
Pat Tuite
Harvey Bass

Denver

Lawrence Deckman
Charles Vigil
Arthur Schwartz
Rollie Rogers
Stan Marks
Walter Gerash
Tod Baker

Tom May
Jim Marrato
Martin Zerobnick
Al Zinn
Al Dill
Brian Morgan
Ed Sherman
Rich Schaeffer
Barry Mahoney
Joe St. Veltrie
Ted Rubin

Houston

Joe Moss
Sam Robertson
Tony Friloux
Lee Ducoff
Jack Rowitscher
Andrew Jefferson
John Gilleland
George Ellis
Gabe Nahas
Clyde Woody
John Herrara
Paul Jensen
Jim Tatum
David Bires
Marvin Teague

Neal Cannon
Gerald Applewhite
Richard Powell
Dean John Ackerman
David Gibson
Woody Monica
Ken Ventucci

Los Angeles

Jim Cooney
Max Soloman
William Drake
William Cain
Mel Albaum
Richard Hirsch
John Minor
Paul Posner
Mel Smolen
Arthur Lewis
Alan Ross
Al Garber
Ned Nelson
George Vaughn
Richard Walton
Harry Weiss
Roger Rosen
Steve Bromberg
Charles Hamel

Miami

Dave Peterson
Tom Weed
Jeffrey Cohen
Barry Garber
Nick Buoniconti
Phil Carlton
Marco Laffredo
Sam Sheres
Bernie Yedlin

Max Kagan
Dan Pearson
H. T. Smith
George Nicholas
Neal Sonnett

New Orleans

James A. McPherson
Tom Ford
Numa Bertel
Irwin Dymond
Ed Baldwin
Steve Murray
Lyall Shiell
Ross Sciacca
Jerome Winsberg
Frank Larré
David Neubauer
Jack Nelson
Milt Bremer
Robert Glass
Phil Stein
Dennis Waldron
Wilfret McKee
Milt Masinter

Philadelphia

Donald Goldberg
John Anderson
Joel Rome
Herb Hardin
William Harris
Richard Atkins
Ray Bradley
Donald Marino
Ronald Brockington
Dennis Eisman
Joel Moldovsky
Stanford Shmukler

John Rogers Carroll
Jack M. Myers
Denny Cogan
Salvatore Cucinotta
Milton Leidner
Louis Natale
Charles Peruto
Max Bockol
Benjamin Lerner
Peter Hoffman
Robert Simone
Sarah Duffy

San Francisco

Ephraim Margolin
Joseph Williams
Nathan Cohn
Jerrold Ladar
John Golden
Alvin Goldstein
Richard Carpeniti
John Keker
Jack Berman
Michael Traynor
Roger Ruffin
Carlos LaRoche
Don May

Marcus Topel
Sal Ballestrere
Tony Serra
Mike Stepanian
Herb Yanowitz

Washington, D.C.

Herbert Miller
Albert Cole
William McDonald
Tom Guidobono
James Mundy
Ken Mundy
Theophilus Jones
Joe Rubin
Joel Finkelstein
Richard Cys
Tom Farquhar
Geoffry Alprin
John Perazech
Stefan Graae
David Schmitt
Al Preston
Bob Tucker
Robert Watkins
David Povich
Robert Clem
Jim O'Dea

BIBLIOGRAPHY

ALSCHULER, W. A. "The defense attorney's role in plea bargaining." *Yale Law Journal* 84, 6 (May 1975): 1179-1314.

American Bar Association Project on Standards for Criminal Justice Standards Relating to the Prosecution Function and the Defense Function. New York: Institute of Judicial Administration, 1970.

"An analysis of defense counsel in the processing of felony defendants in Denver, Colorado." *Denver Law Journal* 50, 1 (1973): 9-44.

AUERBACH, S. "Lawyers paid to help D.C. poor held incompetent." *Washington Post* (July 7, 1977): B1.

AUSTIN, S. L. "What's a nice girl like you doing in a field like this." *Criminal Defense* 3 (May 1976): 27-31.

BAILEY, F. L. *The Defense Never Rests.* New York: Stein and Day, 1971.

––– and ROTHBLATT, H. B. *Fundamentals of Criminal Advocacy.* Rochester, N.Y.: Lawyers Cooperative Publishing Company, 1974.

BATTLE, J. D. "Comparison of public defenders' and private attorneys' relationships with the prosecution in the city of Denver." *Denver Law Journal* 50, 1 (1973): 101-136.

–––. "In search of the adversary system: the cooperative practices of private criminal defense lawyers." *Texas Law Review* 50, 1 (December 1971): 60-118.

BAZELON, D. "Defective assistance of counsel." *Cincinnati Law Review* 42, 1 (1973): 1-46.

BELLI, M. *My Life on Trial.* New York: Morrow, 1976.

BLAUSTEIN, A. for PORTER, C. *The American Lawyer.* Chicago: University of Chicago Press, 1965.

BLOCK, M. "How the B & B boys won law fame: being honest." *Chicago American* (August 18, 1959): 3.

BLUMBERG, A. *Criminal Justice.* Chicago: Quadrangle, 1967.

BOCKOL, R. M. "The criminal law as a prophylactic." *Camack Review* 12 (July 1965): 70-91.

BOHANNON, P. *Law and Warfare.* Austin, Texas: University of Texas Press, 1976.

BRENNAN, W. "The criminal prosecution: sporting event or quest for the truth." *Washington University Law Quarterly* 1963, 3 (June 1963): 279-95.

BROWN, E. *Lawyers and the Promotion of Justice.* New York: Russell Sage Foundation, 1938.

CAPLOW, T. *The Sociology of Work.* New York: McGraw-Hill, 1964.

CARLIN, J. *Lawyers' Ethics.* New York: Russell Sage Foundation, 1966.

―――. *Lawyers on Their Own.* New Brunswick, N.J.: Rutgers University Press, 1962.

CASPER, J. D. *American Criminal Justice: The Defendant's Perspective.* Englewood Cliffs, N.J.: Spectrum, 1972.

CHAMBLISS, W. *Crime and the Legal Process.* New York: McGraw-Hill, 1969.

COHN, N. (ed.). *Criminal Law Seminar.* New York: Central Book Company, 1961.

――― (ed.). *2nd Criminal Law Seminar.* New York: Central Book Company, 1962.

――― (ed.). *3rd Criminal Law Seminar.* New York: Central Book Company, 1963.

COLE, A. Y. "Time for a change: multiple representation should be stopped." *National Journal of Criminal Defense* 2, 2 (Fall 1976): 149-156.

COLE, G. F. *The American System of Criminal Justice.* North Scituate, Mass.: Duxbury Press, 1975.

Colorado State Public Defender Annual Report. July 1, 1975-June 30, 1976. Denver, Colorado (mimeographed).

Criminal Law Institute. University of Denver College of Law, Denver, Colorado, 1974.

"Criminal law practitioners dilemma—what should the lawyer do when his client intends to testify." *Journal of Criminal Law, Criminology, and Police Science* 61, (March 1970): 1-10.

DAHLIN, D. C. "Towards a theory of the public defender's place in the legal system." *South Dakota Law Review,* 19 (Winter 1974): 87-120.

"Defendant and his attorney." *Mississippi Law Journal* 35, 5 (October 1964): 484-494.

EHRLICH, J. W. *A Life in My Hands.* New York: Putnam and Sons, 1965.

EISENSTEIN, J. and JACOB, H. *Felony Justice.* Boston: Little, Brown, 1977.

FEIT, M. A. "Before sentence is pronounced: a guide to defense counsel in the exercise of his postconviction responsibilities." *Criminal Law Bulletin* 9 (March 1973): 140-157.

FINER, J. J. "Ineffective assistance of counsel." *Cornell Law Review* 58, 6 (July 1973): 1077-1120.

FREEDMAN, M. H. *Lawyers' Ethics in an Adversary System.* Indianapolis: Bobbs-Merrill, 1975.

―――. "Professional responsibility of the criminal defense lawyer: the 3 hardest questions." *Michigan Law Review* 64, 8 (June 1966): 1469-1498.

FREUND, P. A. "The legal profession." *Daedalus* 92 (Fall 1963), 689-700.

FRILOUX, C. A. "The criminal defense practice: an introduction." *National Journal of Criminal Defense* 1, 1 (Spring 1975): 1-2.

GEORGE, B. J. "A new approach to criminal law." *Harpers* 228 (April 1964): 183-186.

GILBOY, J. M. "Perspectives and practices of defense lawyers in criminal cases." Unpublished Ph.D. dissertation Northwestern University, June, 1976.

GOODMAN, E. "Shortage of defenders of those accused of crime." *Detroit Lawyer* 27, 9 (September 1959): 117-118.

GRAHAM, K. and LETWIN, L. "The preliminary hearing in Los Angeles." *UCLA Law Review* 18, 4 (March 1971): 635-757.

GREEN, M. and NADER, R. *Verdicts on Lawyers.* New York: Thomas Y. Crowell, 1976.

GREEN, T. and DONAHUE, J. "Take twelve." *Philadelphia Magazine* November, 1975.

HANDLER, J. *The Lawyer and His Community.* Madison: University of Wisconsin Press, 1967.

Harris County Criminal Lawyers Association. "Harris county plan for appointment of counsel." (Mimeographed), 1977.

HEIDEMAN, R. D. "Pre-trial motions: an alternative approach to plea bargaining." *Criminal Defense* 3, 2 (March 1976): 7-11.

HELLER, L. B. *Do You Solemnly Swear?* New York: Curtis, 1968.

HOFFMAN, P. *What the Hell is Justice: The Life and Trials of a Criminal Lawyer.* Chicago: Playboy Press, 1974.

Institute of Criminal Law and Procedure, Georgetown Law Center. "Plea bargaining in the United States: phase I report." (Mimeographed), Washington, D.C. 1977.

ISRAEL, J. and LaFAVE, W. R. *Criminal Procedure in a Nutshell.* Minneapolis: West Publishing, 1971.

JOHNSTON, Q. and HOPSON, D. *Lawyers and Their Work.* Indianapolis: Bobbs-Merrill, 1967.

Joint Committee of the Judicial Conference of the D.C. Circuit and the D.C. Bar (Unified). "Report on criminal defense services in the District of Columbia." (Mimeographed), April 1975.

KAMISAR, Y., LaFAVE, W., and ISRAEL, J. H. *Modern Criminal Procedure.* Minneapolis: West Publishing, 1974.

KENT, S. "The female lawyer." *Criminal Defense* 3, 3 (May 1976): 4-10.

KINSLEY, M. and PETERS, C. "Now you're thinking like a lawyer." *Washington Monthly* 7, 9 (November 1975): 40-49.

KIERNON, L. A. "Losing baggy pants image." *Washington Post* (June 21, 1977): C1.

KRANTZ, S. et al. *Right to Counsel in Criminal Cases: The Mandate of Argersinger vs. Hamlin.* Cambridge, Mass.: Ballinger, 1976.

KRAUSE, E. A. *The Sociology of Occupations.* Boston: Little, Brown, 1971.

KREIGER, A. "Tiptoeing through the tulips or cross-examining an informer." Address, June 1975, before the National College of Criminal Defense Lawyers and Public Defenders in Houston, Texas.

"The lawyers: a special issue." *Texas Observer* February 25, 1977.

"Lawyers images of yesteryear are crumbling." *Washington Star* (September 13, 1976): A1.

LEVY, N. "Dilemma of the criminal lawyer." *Criminal Law Review* 7 (1961): 28-34.

LEWIS, M. R. "The expert witness in criminal cases." *Criminal Defense* 3, 1 (January 1976): 4-14.

LUMBARD, J. E. "The adequacy of lawyers now in criminal practice." *Judicature* 47, 8 (January 1964): 176-181.

MARGOLIN, E., Chairman *14th Annual: Defending Criminal Cases.* New York: Practicing Law Institute, 1976.

MARU, O. *Research on the Legal Profession.* Chicago, American Bar Foundation, 1972.

MAYER, M. *The Lawyers.* New York: Harper and Row, 1966.

MATHEY, M. D. "Role of the court appointed attorney." *Texas Bar Journal* 36, 8 (September 1973): 789-796.

MILLS, J. "I have nothing to do with justice." *Life Magazine* 70, 9 (March 12, 1971): 55-68.

MILLER, F. W. *Prosecution.* Boston: Little, Brown, 1969.

MOLDOVSKY, J. and DeWOLF, R. *The Best Defense.* New York: Macmillan, 1975.

MOORE, W. E. *The Professions: Roles and Rules.* New York: Russell Sage Foundation, 1970.

MORRIS, E. F. "Lawyers role in the war on crime." *Los Angeles Bar Bulletin* 43, 5 (March 1968): 205-210.

NADER, L. (ed.). "The ethnography of law—special publication." *American Anthropologist* 67, 2, 6 (December 1965).

———. *Law in Culture and Society.* Chicago: Aldine, 1969.

NAGEL, S. S. "Effects of alternative counsel." *Indiana Law Journal* 48, 3 (Spring 1973): 404-426.

National Advisory Commission on Criminal Justice Goals and Standards. *Courts.* Washington, D.C.: G.P.O., 1973.

NEUBAUER, D. W. *Criminal Justice in Middle America.* Morristown, N.J.: General Learning Press, 1974.

NEWMAN, D. J. *Conviction.* Boston: Little, Brown, 1966.

OAKS, D. and LEHMAN, W. *A Criminal Justice System and the Indigent.* Chicago: University of Chicago Press, 1968.

O'GORMAN, H. J. *Lawyers and Matrimonial Cases.* New York: Free Press, 1963.

OWEN, I. *Defending Criminal Cases Before Juries: A Common Sense Approach.* Englewood Cliffs, N.J.: Prentice-Hall, 1973.

PAULSEN, M. G. and KADISH, S. *Criminal Law and Its Procedures: Cases and Materials.* Boston: Little, Brown, 1962.

President's Commission on Law Enforcement and Administration of Justice. *Task Force Report: The Courts.* Washington, D.C.: G.P.O., 1967.

"Rebel with a cause: the movement lawyer in the criminal courts." *American Journal of Criminal Law* 2, 2 (Summer 1973): 146-186.

REISMAN, D. "Toward an anthropological science of law and the legal profession." *American Journal of Sociology* 57 (1952): 121-137.

RICE, C. *Defender of the Damned: Gladys Towles Root.* New York: Citadel Press, 1964.

ROBERTSON, J. A. *Rough Justice: Perspectives on Lower Criminal Courts.* Boston: Little, Brown, 1974.

ROBINSON, E. S. *Law and Lawyers.* New York: Macmillan, 1935.

ROBINSON, L. O. "The ABA standards for criminal justice: what they mean to the criminal defense lawyer." *National Journal of Criminal Defense* 1, 1 (Spring 1975): 3-20.

ROSENTHAL, G. S. "The criminal defense lawyer." Address given to the National College of Criminal Defense Lawyers and Public Defenders in June, 1975, Houston, Texas.

ROTTENBERG, D. "The superlawyers." *Philadelphia Magazine* (April 1974): 100.

SEVILLA, C. M. "Between Scylla and Charybdis: the ethical perils of the criminal defense lawyer." *National Journal of Criminal Defense* 2, 2 (Fall 1976): 237-286.

SHELLOW, J. M. "Charge to the jury." *Criminal Defense* 3, 2 (March 1976): 12-19.

SILVERSTEIN, L. *Defense of the Poor.* Chicago: American Bar Foundation, 1965.

SKOLNICK, J. "Social control in the adversary system." *American Bar Foundation.* Chicago, 1967.

SMIGEL, E. O. *The Wall Street Lawyer.* Bloomington: Indiana University Press, 1973.

SMITH, A. B. and NEIDERHOFFER, A. "Psychology of power: hubris vs. chutzpa in the criminal court." *Crime and Delinquency* 19, 3 (July 1973): 406-413.

SMITH, G. W. "Comparative examination of the public defender and private attorneys in a major California county." Unpublished dissertation, University of California, Berkeley, 1968.

STEPANIAN, M. *Pot Shots.* New York: Delta, 1972.

STRICK, A. *Injustice for All.* New York: G. P. Putnam, 1977.

TAYLOR, J. G. et al. "An analysis of defense of counsel in the processing of felony defendants in Denver, Colorado." *Denver Law Journal* 50, 1 (1973): 9-44.

WALLER, W. L. "The fundamentals of criminal practice." *Mississippi Law Journal* 37, 4 (1966): 562-568.

WARREN, E. "Advocate and the administration of justice in an urban society."
Texas Law Review 47, 4 (March 1969): 615-622.
WELLMAN, F. *The Art of Cross-Examination.* London: Collier, 1976.
WICE, P. B. *Freedom for Sale.* Lexington, Mass.: Lexington Books, 1974.
WOOD, A. *Criminal Lawyers.* New Haven, Conn.: Yale University Press, 1967.

ABOUT THE AUTHOR

PAUL B. WICE is an assistant professor in the Department of Political Science, Drew University, Madison, New Jersey. He received his Ph.D. in political science from the University of Illinois in 1972. He has been the Research Director of a project for the U.S. Department of Justice entitled Criminal Justice and the Elderly and a Visiting Fellow at the Department's National Institute of Law Enforcement and Criminal Justice. He is a consultant to both the Institute for Law and Social Research and the Bureau of Social Science Research in Washington, D.C. Dr. Wice is the author of several articles and monographs dealing with the criminal justice system. His previous books are *Freedom for Sale* (D.C. Heath, 1974) and *Criminal Justice Behavior* (West Publishing, forthcoming 1978) with Stuart Miller and Clemens Bartollas.